IN HIS HANDS

ROSE KAUSER

Text Copyright ©2023 Rose Kauser
The moral rights of the author have been asserted

(Paperback) ISBN 978 10 687054 4 1

All rights reserved. No part of this publication may be reproduced, stored in a retrieval system, or transmitted, in any form or by any means, electric, mechanical, photocopying, recording, or otherwise, without the prior permission of the copyright owner.

*This story is neither the beginning nor the end.
Enjoy.*

Chapter 1
Kassian
16/12/2016 (Friday)

Today could not have come any sooner. If it wasn't the want to feed curiosity, it was the need to get away.

Though this area has gone through some changes, it is still some place my brothers wouldn't be caught in. A joke really, as like this place, they too are rough around the edges—if not all the way through.

The journey to my seat is short. I say it's my seat, my spot, but really, it's just a public bench that faces the other side of River Lea where another bench is placed to view mine.

I read the time, in precisely one minute my entertainment will arrive.

She does not.

Sitting up from my casual lean position, I look over to see if she's making her way down the secluded area to the bench that mirrored mine.

She is not.

"Who are you? And why the hell have you been waiting and watching me for the past two weeks?"

Ah the curiosity has arrived.

One hand of hers is held up to keep some distance between us just in case I were to get up and approach her. Her other hand held a phone up to her ear whilst also showing me that she had '*999*' already dialled in.

I try not to let my lips curl up too much.

I could walk away, not say anything. There would be no harm in that, I would be in no trouble if she does decide to file some sort of complaint. This is a park, a public area and just like her I could (do) have a schedule to come and enjoy the view (her). There's no crime in mine and her schedules lining up at some point.

In the time I realise that she is waiting for me to do something, to make a move so that she could make hers, I discern that I do not actually want to walk away. Walking away would mean not seeing her again, well, not being out in the open to see her. So, I get comfortable on the bench with my arms resting on either side of me. Theory is, if I stay seated, giving her the power to look over me whilst I look approachable, she would calm down and we could actually communicate. I have no desire to convince her that she is wrong.

She is not.

And I wasn't going to start our relationship on a lie—ignoring the accent I will put on—she would see through it, at least I think she would. She seems to be a smart one.

"The truth is, I came out here for a breather. It's quiet down here and away from everyone." I think about how to word the next bit, then decide that I don't actually care how it comes across. "Then I saw you completely demolish a meal as if it were nothing." I watch to see any changes in her expression, there was, but I have to continue before she comes to the wrong conclusion, like me being perverted. "Watching you scoff down food as if you were being timed, had temporarily gotten my mind off whatever had forced me to come to this polished shithole of an area in the first place." The sight of her at the time was slightly disturbing, but the shock and growing amusement of a small woman eating in that way *did* get my mind away from what I thought had been cemented into my brain.

Nothing is said on her end, minus the expression that gave away her waiting for the punchline of a joke.

I have scrambled her mind, it could not be made any clearer.

"You've been watching me for two weeks because of the way I ate?" She lowers the arm meant to separate us, but continues to hold up her phone.

"Yes, and no. The way you ate was what initially got me. After that, I admit, curiosity took over. I found myself wanting to know your story whilst also doing some guess work here and there."

Her mouth slowly parts as if her words are at the tip of her tongue, but with a little shake of her head she outwardly goes against speaking.

Letting out a scoff, not being able to believe what has been going on, what *is* going on, she turns on her heel to walk away.

"I'm Koda by the way!" I call out, momentarily halting her. "And you are?"

Turning to face me with her mouth open, she continues to show how hard it is for her to believe this is real.

I smile. I can't help it, but it makes her expression change to one questioning my audacity.

Raising my brows, signalling that I'm still waiting for her to say her name, she responds with a face that says I'm asking for too much, and in a way, I get it.

"A fake name then?"

Her eyes move to the floor as she contemplates, a few seconds after, and she is ready with an answer to my request. "Iris."

"*Iris*, lovely. Take a seat."

'Iris' was well chosen and ready to use, almost like she'd been waiting to give someone another name.

"No thanks."

Realising I couldn't coax her into sitting a seat or two next to me, I get up.

Iris instantly takes a step back as her body jumps. Stupidly, I forgot about the point I made to myself earlier about my height, that, and the fact that I was still a strange-male-stranger.

"Sorry, sorry." I hold out a hand as I take steps away from the bench. "I was just getting up for you to take a seat." I now hold both hands in front of me as if I were surrendering.

Showing her I hold nothing in my hands to ease her mind as if my hands aren't weapons themselves is a joke, but necessary.

Despite the fact that I am up and away, Iris still refuses to sit. Stubborn little one, but I guess I have to understand the situation. She doesn't actually know me, but still, our bodies standing, lingering around each other at a distance must've painted a strange picture.

Iris clearly has boundaries I must learn to respect if I want to continue these interactions. She's not like the workers, she has the freedom to do what she wants and I have less power over her. If I were Kade, it would be another story. He would've had her in his studio last week if he had willed it, or even in his container. But me? I would like to do this the proper way.

I want to make a friend like normal people do.

"You're very jittery, aren't you? I could see it from this side of the river. Anything you would like to talk about?" I cock my head to one side, already aware that she was nowhere near ready to talk about her life. "You know, sometimes it's best to talk to a stranger."

Now she looks as if she were debating the possible discussion.

"Strangers have no tie to your life, and what are the chances there ever would be?" I continue to persuade.

Iris lets out a nervous dry laugh. "I guess you haven't heard the phrase '*It's a small world.*'"

I click my tongue. "Nah."

"If we—If I tell you things, you have to tell me things too." Iris gives in quicker than expected. "On the condition that we don't actually give too much away, like real names. That way none of us can somehow track the other one down. Agreed?"

'*Track the other one down*,' cute. I could've tracked her down the first time I saw her, had I not wanted to keep my life separated from this 'new-normal' one.

"Agreed."

She nods to herself several times before aggressively shaking her head as if she disagreed with one of her own thoughts. "Wait! How old are you?"

"I recently turned eighteen. You?"

"I recently turned sixteen."

Oh thank you God.

"When did you turn eighteen?"

"August 24th"

"When did you turn sixteen?"

"September 18th"

"So what's your story then?" I steer us away from our ages, her phobia of real names and tracking each other down. I almost want to laugh at how I should be the one worried about her discovering things about me.

"It's not that long or interesting. First daughter and an

older sister to four kids. Some builders ran off with a chunk of my dad's money. I'm working at the food court to help out, but I don't make nearly as enough as I need to, to fill the gap they left us with. Before you assume, this job isn't something that my parents forced me to get, it's something that I wanted to do. I have the need to help. On top of that, I want to be a doctor, so I need to keep on top of school work and get the best grades. But with everything going on around me, I don't really have time to revise or get the work experience that I need to put me in league with kids who have advantages. So, to conclude, nice things have not been written for me, at least not yet anyways." She continues to fidget and look over her shoulder as if someone is after her.

The want to smile is strong, but she wouldn't understand. I know that offering things to her may be overstepping boundaries, but it's nice to know I have the means to make her life better. As long as I remember that this is a journey and not the final destination, this will end well. We're not friends yet and I cannot come across as a creep or someone with all the solutions. Not only would that waste all the time and energy I have put into this, but it would quickly put her on the same level as a worker. Her purpose for talking to me and wanting to be friends would not be for me, but for the doors I can open.

"And there's no one for you to talk to? To express yourself to?" I say instead of stupidly grinning and prematurely offering the world.

"I do have someone. She's the type of person to get a job, despite the fact that she doesn't like interviews and needs money herself, to help me help my dad. But I can't ask her to do that, I won't let her do that. And besides, she helps me in other ways. This is just something that I need to do myself."

"How long are you planning on working here for?" I would like to know how long I have to make her class me as a friend. Then we could see each other outside of this area and perhaps stand or sit closer to one another. Right now, she is about the length of two benches away. The only reason we can hear each other is because of how quiet this area currently is.

"Till school starts, or maybe till the end of term. I don't know." She looks around again as if she is exposed to some sort of danger.

Now seems like the right time to pivot.

"I assumed you were an only child, or had at least one older sister. And I knew that you must've had a job somewhere around here, it was the only thing that made sense for you to be in an area like th—"

"Oh my God. I need to go." She looks up from her watch, then turns around, almost running away.

"Wait! What days do you work?"

Currently, I only saw her once a week, but if I play my cards right, I could escape more often and see her for more days. And it's what she would want too, why else was she so quick to talk to me?

She needs me.

We both provide a form of escapism.

Chapter 2
Kassian
19/12/2016 (Monday)

Tapping my foot on the ground, trying to suppress how anxious I feel, I turn to see an out of breath Iris.

I almost drop to my knees at the sight of her. Her working today was guesswork, one that I could barely afford. But my weekend had been taken up by the excitement of seeing her again and Friday was just years too far. She's the first person I spoke to outside of work, outside of the family, which meant that she was talking to me because she genuinely wanted to talk to me and not because of who I am, or who I am related to.

"What are you doing here? You're only allowed to see me once a week." She threw back a part of her head covering as she strut to her designated spot: the length of two benches away from me.

I almost ask when that became an agreed rule, but decide against it. "But this works out. Think about it, you get a break from me over the weekend and then again during the week, as the next time I show up would be Friday." The bullshit rolls out my mouth as smooth as Kade's does. I was planning on seeing her as many days as I could, but since her display of bother, I quickly feed her an argument as it popped in my head.

She turns to leave, which sets my body on auto as I follow more than a few steps behind like some sort of lost dog.

"Okay, *fine*!" I'm desperate.

Iris doesn't stop walking despite the fact that I am agreeing with her conditions.

"I'll only come once a week!" I raise my voice slightly higher so she definitely hears.

Iris stops walking and turns the top half of her body. "Good."

Despite it being her lunch period, she is still choosing to leave and I cannot help but beam. She could have easily let this day slide and stayed here with me, but she wants to teach me a lesson. I'm just grateful it's not one from Maverick's handbook.

"Friday's your turn to share!" Iris doesn't even bother to turn this time, but I know that she's addressing me.

"But that means I only get to see you two more times before you quit for school!"

She doesn't respond but I know for a fact she heard me. Am I a little frustrated from not being used to someone not doing what I want? Yes. But is my smile growing at the thought of this budding friendship and the fact that she's not doing what I want out of fear or for a favour? Yes, yes, it is.

Chapter 3
Kassian
23/12/2016 (Friday)

I arrive at the park a little earlier today. I need a breather on top of the breather (Iris). I don't know how deep friendship talk goes, so I cannot tell her about what's bothered me today, or any other day really. And on top of those topics, I'm also worried about what I should say instead. On Monday, she'd said that she wanted me to share, but I don't know what to say. What if I go too far and she leaves? What if I say too little and she gets bored or worse, she sees me as someone who doesn't know real struggle?

One thing I am certain of, she will not know about Kade or Maverick, or anything about the River family, at least not yet. If I do feel the need to talk about them, I will switch it up a little. Make brothers be friends in my stories and so on and so forth.

I make my way down the stairs that lead to the bench and see that Iris is already here. She's standing next to the barrier that separates us from the slight drop to the rivers current.

"You're here early." I grab her attention, making her take a few steps away from the barrier as if I would chuck her over. Luckily for her, I'm not the brother with those tendencies.

"I'm just curious about your..." She drags out the word, her hands circling each other. "Story. It's been on my mind and it's annoying me."

Iris thinks about me.

I try not to look smug.

"My life is also demanding, so I come here to clear my head." I give her the truth, but in a way that she would understand.

"Demanding in what way?"

"Let's just say that I should've read the contract before agreeing to do my job." Not that I had a choice, or a contract, but she does not need to know that.

"What do you do?"

Curious this one.

"I help people, sometimes at the discomfort of others."

"Oh, so like a lawyer?"

I was not expecting another question so quickly.

"In a way, but also no." I recognise confusion from her expression and before she could ask another question (one which I may not know how to avoid telling the whole truth on) I continue, "I also manage inventory."

"What kind of inventory?"

Another question. But for some reason I'm more amused than repulsed, even when I know that her innocent curiosity, Iris in general, is quickly growing to be my kryptonite. If Maverick find's her, he would be sure to use her, if not completely dispose of her.

"Family heirlooms." Heirlooms being weaponry, art, estates, jewellery, equestrian—

"That's a lot of heirlooms. You know? 'Cos you're managing a whole inventory. My 'heirloom' wouldn't actually be mine until I'm married."

"Married?" How did we get here? I didn't even think of someone else being in the picture.

"Yeah. My mum has gold jewellery to pass down to me, but she also wants me to wear them on my wedding day. And the guy I marry—if he's South Asian, might even have some sort of family jewellery for me to wear as well."

I do have South Asian genes running through me, granted it's somewhat distant, but who's keeping track anyway? I'm not exactly head of the family either, so I'm not being pushed into marriage just yet, nor have I been filled in on what countries are options. Besides, since I can't remember where exactly those specific South Asian genes come in, Iris should be okay to be my wife.

Ugh, what am I saying? 'My wife?' No, I couldn't do that to someone. I couldn't tie my name with hers, couldn't put that burden or target on her back.

"Is everything okay?"

"Yeah." I breathe the word out as I feel relief from Iris snapping me out of my pointless thoughts (something else that proves our connection).

I almost laugh out loud, '*my wife.*' Why am I worrying about that right now? I'm eighteen.

"Don't you have any friends you can talk to? Instead of escaping to here out of all places." Her question is made with no mean to offend, she's genuinely curious.

"I have a friend." My brother. "He rarely allows himself to have fun or to enjoy the little things, and he thinks I don't notice but I do, and to make things worse, I know he's like that because of me."

She pulls a face. "What do you mean?"

I think things over and try to explain in a way she may understand.

"We were brought up together, like brothers. And though we have experienced the same environment, I am not as strong as him, nor am I as clever." Well, not clever in the way's he is, but she doesn't need to know that. I've seen from experience girls warm up to hurt males. I just can't be too hurt, she might run away, and I'm in no mood to hunt.

Iris listens intently, nothing about her indicates she is bored or wants to cut in.

"He was pushed to be my protector. I guess me being younger than him plays a part as well." An hour to be exact. "He's already done a lot for me, and though he is someone I can talk to, this is just something I need to figure out by myself."

"Is there anything I can do?" She asks, triggering alarm bells from within.

She wants to help me? Why does she want to help me? Does she want something in return? Does she know who I am?

"No, your company seems to be helping just fine." I politely smile while pushing any new suspicions of her away.

"Not to be a bitch—"

Never.

"—but I have to go now. I need to see a friend before I go back to work, and she's come a little early." Iris stands as she pushes the longer part of her head covering over her shoulder. And all I can think about is how I'm going to make sure her friend is just that.

A friend.

"What is that called? I know that you guys have a name for it, but it's not coming to mind." I pretty much ignore the fact that she has to leave because... why would I think about that?

"It's called a hijab... well a headscarf." Just as she's about to say more, she shakes her head. "I haven't got time for this, I'll explain it to you next time, or just, I don't know? Look it up?" She rushes through her words then leaves.

Finally, I have something to do that's not fighting the urge to find out every little thing about her. I pull out my phone to do a simple google search, but I'm interrupted by a call from the devil himself.

Chapter 4
Kassian
30/12/2016 (Friday)

Iris abuses the bench some more as she works her way through a laughing fit. "No you don't understand." She dramatically gasps for air. "It felt like something out of a movie."

Her experiences (with her friend) are like something you would see in Looney Tunes, whereas mine are like sad documentaries or some sort of messy thriller. So, it's safe to say, no, I do not understand. Our euphoria's have been different.

"How could we run into a room to hide, not knowing that it was his room, only to find out when we decided to log into the computer. And then—" She gasps for more air as she still has not stopped laughing.

"—and then someone walked in and you girls thought it was the teacher you were hiding from, but it was actually another student who snuck in to put their homework in a pile."

"Yeah!" She claps her hand at the memory. "And all our faces dropped because we thought that we got caught, then we died together after explaining ourselves."

'*Died.*' Her way of saying that they laughed extremely hard.

"Was this your first 'movie' experience?"

"No me and…" She thought of the name to give her friend. "Wifey, have lived through so many moments like that."

"Wifey? Why did you name her that?" I couldn't help but have a '*that's a funny interesting fake name*' expression, smiling through the pain. I didn't even consider her liking females, no hints arose when I saw her with her little friend either.

"When we're together, it's hard for people to not notice us and not be jealous. And for some reason they can't wrap their minds around the fact that friends can be like us, so they all assume that we're lesbians—the teachers included. So, after being fed up, we kind of just call each other 'Wifey' to take the piss, but to also accept the fact that we are in a lifelong-after death type of relationship."

Oh thank you God. They're just really good friends.

"I like it. It's..." I want to say odd, thought provoking, or even misleading. "Cute."

"I'm telling you. If you met her, you would love her. It's hard not to. She's so funny and stupid, but smart and daring, and sweet—"

I refuse to acknowledge any negative thoughts about the words she's listing.

"—and she's most definitely not a bitch, although she can definitely be that bitch."

I'm not sure I know what that fully means.

"Really?" There's no chance I could be swayed into thinking about someone else. I'm already close to being tightly wrapped around Iris's finger.

"I swear to God. She's peng as well."

Peng?

Iris pulls out her phone, determined to make me see what she does. She doesn't even realise that she is exposing more parts of her life.

Her paranoia's slipping, good.

"Look." She slides her phone on the bench so that it's closer to me. Since I can see the picture clearly, I don't really feel the need to pick it up.

'*Wifey*' is cute, but she's no match for Iris. I'm certain she is the friend that often visits, but for some reason I haven't been introduced to her. Her eyes are brown, not a brown that needs light being shun on them for someone to see the colour, but still, just brown. And she still has a baby face, her structure is there but it's not as prominent as her partners. Iris has large hazel green eyes and a natural contoured face paired with light freckles that look as if they had been specifically placed to enhance her beauty. She may keep her distance, but luckily for me, it allows me to get more of a good look at her.

I realise I'm not actually looking at her phone. I'm too fixated on Iris, who's too busy doting on her average, too good to be true friend. Before she snaps out of whatever spell is on her, I quickly turn my attention to her phone, trying so hard not to point out the obvious differences between them. I may not have real friend experiences, but I do know that no one wants to hear someone put down a person they love (a mistake many have made in the past).

Sliding the phone back to her, I rub my hands together, getting ready to say goodbye as this would be the last time I see her unless we happen to bump into each other one day (obviously planned on my end).

Before I even get to say my faux goodbye, Iris cuts in as though she knew what I was going to say. "I've decided to continue to let you see me."

I chuckle at her choice of words.

"Because believe it or not. You actually help get my mind off things too."

"Looks like your wife's doing a shit job." The words escape before I check them.

"Er, no." She almost snaps at me. "She's doing a great

job *actually*. I just have a habit of worrying myself when I'm away. Also she has her own troubles, what kind of friend would I be to ignore hers and add my own onto her plate."

"She shouldn't make you feel like you're burdening her." At least that's what I would want from a proper friend anyway. Family on the other hand, that's different. Whether you like it or not, you're a burden when you share the same blood. It's like a rule.

"She doesn't, I just know that I shouldn't take her for granted." Her annoyance grows and becomes hard to ignore. Anymore comments from me and she'll change her mind about continuing to see me.

"You're right, I'm sorry. I didn't think of it like that." It's still difficult for me to grasp the concept of caring for someone—the way Iris does—who is not blood or someone you fancy.

She sighs. "Mondays and Thursdays and maybe Fridays. That's when you can see me."

Chapter 5
Kade
01/01/2017 (Sunday)

Kassian is getting better with his throws, but there is something distracting him and I'd rather not be a part of practice when his mind's not 100% on trying not to impale me.

I've noticed him walk around with a spring in his step, not that it's a problem but it's been a while and I'm growing impatient. I keep thinking he would reveal what it is that's been helping him, partly because I want to know if it can help me, but also because this is the first time I've seen him feel better without my help.

He throws a knife too close to my neck, a millimetre or two away from nicking it, but he doesn't seem phased.

That's not like him.

Why is he not panicking? Why is he not apologising and asking to stop?

Cocking my head to the side away from the knife, I walk away from the wooden backdrop, indicating the start of our break.

I lean on the table near Kassian, who continued to throw knives despite not having something to miss.

"Who is she?" I try to show I'm amused to go with the jokey tone. If I'm too intense, too cheerless, he could put his walls up.

Kassian's face drains of all blood, which means I'm right.

There is a girl.

My face, no doubt, displayed my sense of accomplishment.

"Is she a girl from work? The one we caught you screw—"

"She's not from work." He says in Spanish which automatically makes this more serious. "You know I wouldn't do that now. It's our rule. You have been following it haven't you?"

If it were anyone else, I would say that they are trying to spin this conversation to get it away from themselves, but as it's Kassian, I know that he's genuinely worried I've been breaking the rule we—mostly him—came up with.

"Of course I've been following it. I'm not a monster." A white lie. "So, when did this happen? This girl? And don't try to change the topic, we are past that." I carry the previous conversation on in Turkish. It's something we've developed to do, not only does it keep us safe (majority of the time) but it also helped us quickly learn the languages of our parents.

Kassian's eyes search the room as though he doesn't already know we are alone. His pupils grow exponentially, transforming his human eyes into ones that replicate a pair off a fascinated feline. Whilst he lets his emotions build up until he's ready to burst and drown me with his situation, I'm stuck with the mundane task of waiting. I never wait, even Kassian knows better than to make me do that, though he is given that leniency.

"Her name's Iris. She wears a headscarf. She's funny, always in a rush—is constantly paranoid and she can eat. I saw her by chance, then actually spoke to her and now she has agreed to see me twice a week. Mondays and Thursdays. Oh and sometimes maybe Friday."

Damn, I should've stuck with not knowing.

The amusement on my face attempts to dissipate as I quickly realise this is serious.

I uphold the interested look for Kassian's sake.

"How long had you been watching her?" I know my brother. If this girl has taken over his mind, it was at first with his own fantasies and then their reality. He doesn't have a selfish bone big enough to approach and befriend her, not when it would wrap her up in our complicated life. He would've been admiring her from a distance, itching to know more, to confirm the assumptions he's made. Which means, she approached him. Further meaning, he was sloppy.

Kassian opens his mouth to tell me he hadn't been watching her, but then lowers his head as he owns up to his actions. "One month."

"*One month?*" I raise my voice.

Kassian shushes me. "Maverick might hear. Or his minions." He picks up a knife and throws it across the room, letting some of his annoyance fly with it.

There were many things that aggravated us, rightly so too, but at this particular time Kassian is peeved by the fact that he knew taking his anger out on said 'minions' would be more unjustified than right. In his words, '*they have no choice*,' so we shouldn't be too harsh with them. And I agree, to an extent. Having your life be controlled and in danger if a mistake is made, is unfortunate, but that doesn't make it right for them to not have a backbone when it comes to making the right decision. Like not telling Maverick about what me and Kassian get up to, especially when it's something he disagrees with and would most definitely punish us for.

"Speaking of which, aren't you afraid of him finding out?"

"Oh, deathly. But that's part of the reason why I'm telling you. I need you to make sure he never finds out."

"*Oh*. Here I thought I was told because of our amazing

brotherly bond." I 'fake' offence.

"I like to think that we would have this bond regardless of our blood." He attempts to win me over with his innocent belief.

"Yeah, and I think that we only have a bond because you stole my looks, and now you're trying to steal my time."

"*Please* Kade. I rarely, if ever, ask for something to be done. Please just make it safe for her to see me, if this goes right, I'll have a friend. I'll have a—"

"A friend?" I can't believe what I'm hearing. "You're going to put us through this for you to make a friend?"

"So you'll do it?" His eyes are filled with hope. I've seen a similar look a stupid number of times, but this one was different and I can't figure out why.

'Because it's attached to your brother and not a worker.'

"I'll consider it."

Kassian pulls me forward to latch onto me.

His words of gratitude are slightly muted as now my senses and concentration are on where our bodies touch. More specifically, the pressure he's adding to my new wounds.

I hug him back, it's the key to release.

"It was cruel to talk of our bond and then to say you want to make another." I say what I feel in a way he will not overthink. I don't want him to regret asking for my help.

"Oh come on! I know that I'm great but don't you want to make a friend too?"

I haven't really put much thought into it. Correction, I haven't really had the luxury to think about it. If my time wasn't wasted on Maverick's needs and wants, it would be on getting my head straight, and protecting Kassian, who was basically a spitting image of me, so in a weird way it felt like I was helping myself through helping him.

"She has a friend you know? Maybe you could be friends with her?"

"What's her name? Pupil?" I sarcastically let out a bad joke knowing that it was enough to humour him.

Kassian holds a laugh behind his smile as his shoulders lower themselves. "She's your type. Or at least what I think you need."

"And what's that?"

"Someone who's too good to be true." He hits the top of my head with the flat part of the knifes blade, then tries to walk away.

I grab the back of his neck before he gets too far. "I'm the one that has a new task. You stay here and hone your new skills because when I come back, I won't go easy on you."

"What's he making you do now?" He was just unbelievably high on emotion that it seemed almost impossible to bring him back down, yet there's slight concern in his voice.

"Something about someone's son, so I don't need to take it too far." I say as an upside then turn to walk away.

"Be gentle." Kassian's words are firm but quiet.

I grin.

"This is why I was given the task."

Chapter 6
Kade
02/01/2017 (Monday)

I may have taken things too far with the kid.

I say kid but really, he's a year or two older than me, which should've been intimidating but I felt nothing. Why would I be intimidated when Maverick's already thrown me in with men double, sometimes triple my age?

He put up a decent fight when I was toying with him, but somehow, something he'd said, maybe even something he'd done, triggered me into taking one too many steps too far. Now my skin, my clothes are decorated with his blood and I expect Maverick to find his way to me soon. With tasks like this, usually I would report straight back to him, but since this was one of those times I had to be peeled away from the boys limp body, I was, and continue to be in no mood to merrily skip back to report my failing.

I mix some colours then bring my brush to the canvas, filling in the shadows of the cloth that barely covered the worker in front of me.

Turning to art, to creating new things, was one of the ways that got my mind off the life I live. But today, as the sun rises, all I could think about is what new punishment Maverick would think of. Would he take it out on me? Or would he take it out on Kassian?

I shake my head as though it would get rid of the thoughts.

My attention is forced towards the individual lines and texture the brush creates as I continue to fill in her figure. Her body is more posed then natural looking and I can't stand it. If she's going to be that posed, I have a better idea. My subject would be better if it were strung up. She needs a rope. I need a rope. I need to guide it up her legs, around her arms and allow it to follow her form. Allow her to wear the design. The rope would have twists and knots, and be tighter in some areas than others, creating beautiful pinks, reds and purples, all showing her skin aching to be released. Her wrists brought together by force and her hair is the only free looking thing. Her face holds drops of blood as though she herself had made something bleed to that deathly extent then allowed its blood to rain on her. Her eyes are now wide and teary, mixing with the drops of blood below. And the rope, being its own entity, restrains her, not realising it inflicts pain.

"Is everything okay? Would you like me to try a different pose?" Her questions snap me out of vivid thoughts.

I look down at my new painting and see the new violent strokes and texture as I *slightly* deterred from what is directly in front of me.

My eyes move to the girl on the stage, her questions replay in my head as her fragility consumes my mind. Abruptly dropping my paint palette, I watch how she jumps then quickly recovers as I approach.

"Do you mind if I touch you? Give you another pose?" I transform my voice into something much softer, much more polite and low as if the setting is not intimate enough.

She nods, holding onto the mesh fabric that barely hides her figure.

"What's your name?" I ask as I gently remove the fabric.

"Nina." She's timid, it does not match her strong features.

"*Nina.*" I smile as I repeat like some sort of charmer.

The stiffness in her body, the one that pulled her shoulders, elbows and hands in until her own body looked as though it were suffocating her, drops. I take it as a sign that she's beginning to warm up to me, so I tug at her. Not too aggressively to harm her, but enough to quickly get her to the edge of the stage so that her legs are able to dangle off.

She hasn't done anything to indicate that she's uncomfortable, so I keep my eyes on hers just in case they communicate what she's too afraid to say.

But there's nothing but eagerness.

Starting from the top, I stroke her thighs until I get to her knees, quickly parting them to stand in between. Her wrists are separated from one another as I hold and guide them behind her. As our bodies follow her wrists, I continue to search her eyes for disapproval until her hands are exactly where I want them to be.

As I am about to bring myself to a stand, Nina latches herself onto me. Her lips eagerly sucking on mine, her tongue pushing through and I allow it until I remember Kassian recently bringing up our rule.

Nina is a worker and a worker would do anything to end their contract, or even shorten it. Which makes them desperate enough to pull stunts like this, making us abuse our powers over them. But hey, if they could get one of us to develop a crush, some pity, or even fall in love, then it'll be worth it, *if* they somehow survive what Maverick does to them when he finds out.

My arms hold her away from me as I become irritated. Not just because she thought that she could use me, but also because I need another distraction and this honestly may be it. Whilst I still have my morals in check, flashbacks of the last time I were in this state with a worker decide to make an appearance.

Let's just say that I did not wait till I had gotten to the plastic covered container.

"Have some respect for yourself. I'm not Maverick, this won't work on me." Truth be told, it worked on me in the past, someone playing with my pity strings. Worked on Kassian too, but Maverick quickly put an end to those weak ideas.

"Sit on your knees."

I don't have to say it twice. She does as she's told and waits for more instructions. I pick up the material I had carelessly thrown to the side and tie her forearms together, placing them folded over her chest so that her breasts are covered.

Two knocks happen at the open studio door.

"Are you sure that you're an artist?" Maverick walks in with no hint of anger. Once his eyes are done momentarily ogling Nina, he looks to me. "I do hope that you're done. You're needed."

Not bothering to look at Nina as it could inspire something new in Maverick, I decide against helping her. She should be able to get out of her restraints by herself, if not, I'll just deal with her when I get back.

I follow Maverick out the door.

"Hendricks is getting out of hand. He wants more than what we had agreed on and is threatening to expose your antics—"

My antics being doing whatever Maverick wants me to do. But since it's Hendricks we're talking about, he would specifically be threatening to expose my *other* distraction.

"—Do not worry. My reason for bringing this up is for you to expose his daughter. Not to the world, although that's the real threat, but to Hendricks. He may be a twit but he's not that big of an idiot to not know the stain that would cause, especially for a woman with his name."

I'm unable to properly process anything he's said due to the lack of attention towards me taking things too far yesterday, well today, before dawn. I also happen to be confused with what girl he was talking about. Several privileged Sheila's have been under me, if not bent over their own dressers.

"She had bleached large sections of hair that framed her face. Don't tell me you forgot about her." He sneers and it's almost close to his classic sinister look.

After that little added detail, I remember exactly who he was talking about. I was required to get her to do something crazy. '*Shit that would force her to stay indoors for the rest of her life if it were to be exposed.*' And it wasn't that hard, I didn't need to prompt anything, she was the one who had the drugs and drinks ready, she was the one who took multiple partners at once. I just made sure that it was all documented in one way shape or form.

We were both freshly fifteen at the time, but I doubt the world would care for how young she was. If anything her age would make it even more of a scandal. With the clear videos and pictures, there would be no mistake on telling if it was actually her or not.

I'm going to see this 'request' through, I have no choice. It would destroy her life, yes, but from what I could remember, she was perfectly okay with doing the same to others when she slipped drugs into drinks.

I won't feel remorse, she deserves this, her actions were willingly done in front of a camera, she had to have known that it would come out one day. Besides, I've finally seen Kassian be happy outside of everything, I'm not about to risk him getting caught up in my consequences again.

Chapter 7
Kassian
04/01/2017 (Wednesday)

His studio is empty. I thought for certain he would be here to let off whatever steam he had now, but I'm wrong. I admit, I am here to talk about my new stories with Iris, but also because I haven't seen my brother since Sunday.

Reflections aren't always enough.

The studio is filled with many of his pieces, both the completed and pending. I've seen art, I've seen and witnessed it's many forms, but when it comes to the forms Kade takes part in, no one can hold a candle to him. His paintings alone are truly the kind to pull you in and take you to a place where you are forced to feel and imagine. Kade has talent in anything art related—in anything really—and it's draining to think that he could've made a name for himself if he wasn't stuck in Maverick's claws.

Just as I were about to move onto his sculptures, Kade stumbles in, eating an apple.

"To what do I owe the pleasure?" He holds his arms out in the air as if he were about to hug a fat giant, he couldn't have made his drunkenness more obvious. "Is Iros too busy? Has your mind found something else to occupy itself with?"

"*Iris*." I correct him. "And Nene's coming today, so you can't be in this state and you most certainly can't have company."

Kade lets out a raspberry laugh, obviously remembering the last time our grandparents came round and now, so am I.

Maverick was away, '*taking care of business*' as per usual, so I was the one who welcomed them. We had dinner together, but Kade did not join us, so I had the bright idea to take them to his studio as he was probably busy trying to finish a painting. Nene, bless her heart, was so excited to see him in action (he doesn't let people watch him, doesn't like it), that she stood beside me when I opened the double doors. Kade, the devil, was indeed in action, but not with painting. He was too busy holding a girl down and eating her out for him to notice us in shock at the door. '*Guess he wasn't in the mood for roast,*' they'd said.

I gave him shit for it later because she was a worker, one that Maverick had favoured.

"Pull yourself together, we need to temporarily transfer the breakable workers."

"When does she leave?"

"Sunday."

"*Aww* Sunday. Does that mean Kasey-Wasey can't see Iris?" He puts on a baby voice and attempts to squeeze my cheek.

"No, I will. You owe me, so you'll be spending the day with her and if Maverick questions my whereabouts, you'll tell him that I went to get her a present or something."

I notice a canvas snapped in half on the side so I walk towards it.

"<u>I have to distract her *and* keep Maverick away from your business?</u> Seriously?"

I put the painting together. Underneath thick layers of paint was parts of a woman looking off into the distance. The aggressive layer of paint on top, was a girl with a thick tight rope around her. If it were a movie, by the end of it she would've been engulfed by its bonds. She faced up—

not by choice—her face decorated with sweat, dirt and drops of blood mixed with drying tears, all of it beautifully drawn to detail. The emotions in her eyes were one's that mirrored Kade's.

He had one of his episodes again and I could only thank it was taken out on a painting and not another person.

"When did you do this?"

Kade scrunches his face as he scratches his forehead as if it would help him remember. "T-two day ago? Yeah. Two days ago."

"Why are you drunk?" It wasn't because of the episode, it's something else. Maybe because I'm not spending much time with him?

"D'you remember that girl with a bleached blonde fringe?"

It was more than her fringe, but yes. I do remember her. There's only one girl with that kind of hair that we've encountered.

"I had to expose her to her dad, and instead of it making him back away from whatever he was doing, he made her join Baronial. Said that if she was happy to be doing that for free, she should be ecstatic doing it for some money."

The girl was young, attractive and the daughter of someone high up in the food chain, '*some money*,' would be millions, especially since it would be kept low and offered to those desperate and in need of more of a power trip.

"He would be taking a chunk of his daughters money." Kade bites into his apple, then speaks with a tone too cheerful for the subject. "Can you believe it? There are actually people out there who almost touch Maverick's level of cruel."

Chapter 8
Kassian
30/01/2017 (Monday)

Sometimes we spend half an hour together, sometimes we spend an hour and a half, other times she's willing to see me after work as well. But it didn't matter how long it actually was because it felt less and less each time.

Iris has come a long way from being paranoid.

I know a lot about her whilst simultaneously not knowing much, which to be fair could be said about me from her point of view.

She's in the middle of telling me another funny story about her and her friend, it must be funny anyway, she's assaulting the bench again.

"And then she got sent out of class instead of me!" She slaps her own thigh as she bends over to laugh. "But on her way out she hit the back of my head so hard." She uses her own hands to demonstrate how her Wifey slapped her. "And to make things worse for her, I held in my laugh and acted hurt, pointing out as if the whole class didn't see. '*Sir! Did you see that? Sir she just slapped me!*' Obviously I couldn't hold my laugh in as well as I wanted to, but it still got the reactions I wanted. Medisa was so pissed but she was laughing her arse off too because for once she was getting told off instead of me, and I was dragging it, 'cause God knows when that would happen again."

Throughout her story, she'd been laughing, but now her face drops. I know why of course, but I did not care about what she'd exposed, I was more concentrated on how happy she looked. I *could* ignore her slip up, but where's the fun in that?

"So, her name's Medisa huh? Now I have a *real* name to go with the face you showed." I rub it in despite my uninterest.

Blood drains from her face as she brings up a hand to cover her gaping mouth. I realise that she's not about to say anything and looks as if she's about to run for it, so I chuckle, as I really see no harm in me knowing.

I'm not my brothers.

"Would you relax? I don't actually care about your friend. I just wanted to tease you. I don't even remember what she looks like." A white lie.

Her hand still covers the lower part of her face and her eyes look numb with a hint of fear.

"Iris, it's okay. Seriously, you should know by now that I'm not a threat." Correction, I'm choosing not to be a threat (she doesn't need to know that). Being a male is already more than enough of a threat and on top of that, I have to work hard in trying to convince her otherwise.

"No, I know. I just can't believe I let her name slip like that."

She must subconsciously trust me.

"Okay, how about I tell you something I've never told anyone? Would that make you feel any better?"

Her eyes finally start to move as she slowly lowers her hand.

"Depends on what you tell me." She's got a cheeky look to her now, but I could still see remnants of shock from what has been revealed.

I pull my sleeves up so that my forearms are exposed,

then put them on display for Iris. Showing the back of my hands and then the front, in turn, showing all of the parts of my arm no longer hidden.

We still keep a distance between us, so it takes a few seconds for her to process, but I've never done this before, never shown someone else these marks, so I grow a little impatient.

"They're scars, not tattoos. My guardian liked to draw… on skin."

Her face is one that shows every emotion she feels, every judgement she makes and I see them on her now. Iris hesitates to take a step closer. A battle within herself, I suppose.

"Yeah." I breathe out the word as the air gets thicker and embarrassment seeps into me. "You're the first person to see them outside of my household. I don't really like the look of them or the memories they come with, so I keep them covered."

"Don't cover them." Iris says with a bit of a punch. "The guy obviously goes on some sort of power trip when he hurts you, and you covering them up would definitely give him some sort of satisfaction. He probably reads it as you—no offence—being a little bitch."

I never saw it like that, but it makes sense. Truth be told, as the days go by, I find myself wanting more and more and I don't want to be seen as Maverick's bitch anymore.

"You're right. I shouldn't hide them."

"Yeah, you shouldn't. You should own them, show them off, highlight them even. Just don't hide them. Rub them in his face, as much as you can."

She sounds like Kade, but for some reason I feel like I can do what it is that they want, when she says it.

"I don't mean to be insensitive but they do look really cool. They add to your…" She waves her hand around as if she were cleaning a window. "Look."

"Thank you. I'll be sure to tell the artist." Another lie. That demon won't know a thing about Iris.

A quick heavy breath in place of a laugh escapes as she smiles, then it drops as another thought crosses her mind. "When was the last time he hurt you?"

I lean my head to one side, thinking about the answer and realising that it's been some time. "Six months? Maybe more?"

"Why do you think he stopped?"

I open my mouth to answer but don't actually have one ready.

"Sorry! Sorry, you don't have to answer that. I shouldn't have asked that." Iris cuts in, rushing through her words.

"No, it's okay, I don't mind. I think it might be because I'm getting older and he's probably grown bored of it." I look over to her and see that although she's got an answer from me, she still looks like she regrets asking. "He's been doing it since I was ten or something."

I shake my head as I realise how ridiculously long it's been.

Iris joins in on the head shaking, I can tell that she wants to say more but feels as if she'd overstepped a boundary that doesn't exist for her.

"I have to go now. But I swear the next time you see me, you'll see more of me—visually—I mean of my skin—of my scars, not other stuff." Now I'm the one dragging a hand down my face.

"Okay." She giggles. "I look forward to it."

She stays seated at the bench as I walk away early. This is the first time that I've done this and as much as I want to stay, I need to go.

Maverick's calling.

"You've been different since November. Is something the matter?"

Other than the fact that I've met Iris and that this particular job is immoral, no.

"No, I've just been feeling sick."

"Since November? Oh dear." His sarcasm matches the glint in his eyes.

If I don't cover this with some truth, he will find his way to Iris.

"The girl I brought in committed suicide and our last talk about it left me unsatisfied, so forgive me if it's taking a few months to recover from something that's my fault."

The silence between us becomes deafening. I've never been sassy with Maverick before, that's always been Kade's thing, so I can't help but smile a little. I do try to hold it back before he catches a glimpse of it, but I can't help it. Iris is obviously bringing out a new side to me, a braver one. I like it. I knew that she would be good for me.

Maverick stares me down as if I had killed his mood, something which usually would've scared me, but now I'm just mentally preparing for his punishment, ready to get it over and done with.

"You're dismissed. Find Kaden and bring him to me."

"Maverick, just—"

"I said dismissed." He has a cold killer look in his eyes now, but I'm more worried about the possibility of Kade taking my punishment for me.

I calmly leave the room before things worsen. Soon as I

was out of sight and my actions would not be heard, I sprint towards Kade's studio to warn him of what might come.

Chapter 9
Kassian
30/01/2017 (Monday)

He wasn't in the studio and he's not in the 'gym,' the two places he would be if he isn't at his shipping container.

God, please don't be there.

"Kassian." Kade's strangled voice calls out.

I turn around the moment his struggling body drops against one of his trolleys, knocking a few things to the ground.

Has Maverick already taken his anger out on him?

"My skin." He flutters his hands towards his neck-chest area. "It's burning!"

He tries to tear his clothes off and I waste no time in joining in despite not knowing what's happening. But he is in pain, '*burning*' and wants to get out of his clothes, so that is what is going to happen. I practically run on auto as I try to save my brother from whatever's inflicting pain onto him, but as soon as I see his second skin and a smile grow on his face, I stop and take a step back.

"Don't stop now. I need help taking off the skin on my back and there's no one I trust to have my back to then you."

I don't know what to say, or feel.

I can't help but do what I hate other people doing towards me, stare.

"As annoying as it is, there's beauty in the design, so I got it done. With it, you look enthralling and I can't have you upping me when it comes to looks, especially since we're supposed to look the same." He inspects his arms. "Now we can parade ourselves and see who the real charmer is."

My eyes swell with tears and before they drop, I swing Kade around so that I could embrace him. I don't know why he thinks I'm blind. I've been forced to live with these marks for so long, I can spot them easily. He's not fooling me; I can see beneath the tattoos he's layered on top.

I sniff as thick tears make their way down my face and onto his 'bare' skin. This whole time I thought that he was covering his skin and matching my style to not make me feel too alien, especially during the heat, but in actuality, he was taking my punishments for me.

"Hey, the tap you got on is going to ruin the ink."

I snicker, then hug him tighter. If he wants to call it ink, I'll go along with it.

Finally letting him go from a close embrace to holding him at arm's length, I realise I'm more fortunate than I had thought.

"After I help you with this skin, I want you to come with me to get mine coloured."

Maverick and his demands can wait.

Kade is both stunned and triumphant, making me want to see my plan through even more than before.

"I know just the guy." A smirk forms on his face, allowing his dimple to make an appearance.

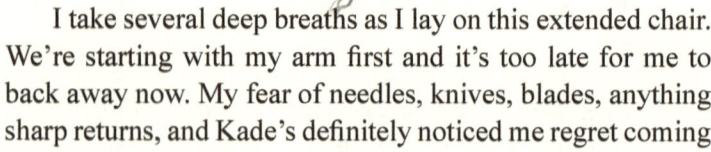

I take several deep breaths as I lay on this extended chair. We're starting with my arm first and it's too late for me to back away now. My fear of needles, knives, blades, anything sharp returns, and Kade's definitely noticed me regret coming here. He's just not saying anything because we both know that it's something I need to get over.

The man wipes the area down for the last time before bringing the machine to my skin. Kade wipes down my forehead as he gives me a gentle, comforting smile.

"Are you sure about the colour?" He asks a little too late.

I chose black. My scars, the art on my skin will be black. There's nothing more out there than it. Maverick and others will see how I now own them.

"I'm sure."

It's not bad at first, but I'm still taken back to the times where Maverick dug his designs into me. I start to shake my legs, vibrating them as I try to get through this process and my memories.

"What did you have to tell me?" Kade interrupts my thoughts.

I try to remember what I had to tell Kade despite the noise seemingly becoming louder.

"Which news do you want first? Good or bad?"

"Bad." It doesn't even take a second for him to think about it.

"Maverick wants to see you. I gave him a bit of attitude, then he dismissed me and called for you." I turn my head to face him. "I'm sorry."

He knew why I was apologising, there's only one reason why we would apologise to each other.

"Eh, don't care." He boredly brushes it off. "I'll deal with him later. What's the good news?"

"Iris's mate. The one I'd mentioned? Her name's Medisa. You should find her and be her friend, it could lead to more." I hiss as the man inks a certain scar, then continue. "She sounds as crazy as you."

An exaggeration, but needed.

If Kade actually sees it through, we would practically be together for life. Twin brothers with two girls who call each other '*wifey*,' that would certainly lead to interesting stories. And we would no doubt be an entertaining bunch.

"Do you want whatever it is you have with Iris to lead to something more?"

All of a sudden, the gun feels as though it's massaging me. There's no pain, there shouldn't be any pain anyways, I'd developed a high pain tolerance. And now with Kades question, I'm no longer associating the tattoo gun with Maverick's tools.

I nod to Kade's question then elaborate, my words filled with admiration as my mind constructs her features. "She's as perfect as one of your pieces. I can't help but be deeply immersed. She allows me to be free of the life we live and to be better when I'm forced to return to it. Every meeting I have with her, I'm surprised with how little it takes for her to make me feel better, make me believe that I could be a better person. And I want you to feel the same way, because I'm not leaving until you do, I refuse to allow this to progress without you experiencing the same thing."

"And you want me to experience this dream-like reality with her crazy friend?"

"Yes. Medisa."

"*Medisa.*" Kade purrs her name as if he's considering it.

Chapter 10
Kassian
31/01/2017 (Tuesday)

If it were up to me, I would find Iris today, show her how I highlighted what I used to keep hidden. I think she would love them, and if she were comfortable with it, I would approach her, show them up close so she can see the detail.

The workers in the house look at me differently now. Like I was Kade, or was making a big mistake by showing my own skin off. It makes me feel a little insecure, but then I remember how most of them saw my skin when it was newly grazed and secreting blood *if* Maverick had not graciously poured salt water over me. If I could show them my scars whilst they were healing—ignoring that I had no choice in the matter—then I can show them the designs whilst they healed from a procedure of my choosing.

Not having anything to do made the want to travel to London harder. How easy things would be if we were staying at one of our London properties, but no, Maverick has to have some sort of strange attachment to this one.

After idly walking around, I decide to check off something from my new list of things to do.

When Kade and I turned eighteen, we were introduced to the many buildings our parents left behind. Some of them are shared between the three of us, some of them are shared between us two, and some are just mine. One of my properties is here, in Scotland. I've only seen it in person the once but it was enough for me to know what I was going to do with it.

The plan is to buy the buildings next door, knock some walls down and turn it into a club. During the day it will be open to all, during the nights, as long as you have a guardian, you can come through and enjoy the environment I create. On top of keeping some kids and adults off the streets, I will also be getting them under my wings—not Maverick's or Kade's—and I would be making a fat chunk of money.

Dealing with people not wanting to sell their properties was a little more challenging than I thought. I could do things the shortcut way but that does not agree with my character development, so I am trying the civil way (first). Because of the stubbornness of the neighbouring properties, everything else is put on hold, so once again, I am walking around this place, only this time, I am looking for Kade.

"Kassian." Maverick calls out as I pass the dining room. It wasn't as a question to see if it were actually me, or to see if I had time for whatever he had to say. It was firm, as if my best option is to approach and listen.

Lazily stopping in my tracks, I chug down some water, wishing it were some sort of drink.

"Maverick." I say with no appease as I enter the room. This encounter is how he sees that I no longer care. I wanted it to be when the skin was removed and in front of an audience, but I guess there's some sort of dauntlessness to it just being me and him.

"I do believe I asked you to bring Kaden to me."

He's not even going to acknowledge what I'd done.

"Where is he?" He continues when I say nothing.

"Do you not have his number?"

God, it's like my teenage years have just started. It is only fair to be honest, he did rob us of them.

Maverick hides his disbelief well, and I would be satisfied, but the look he masked it with made me feel like a child again.

He clicks his tongue, a sign of annoyance.

For some reason he is holding himself back. Is it because I'm old enough to leave? I have more than enough money and shares to live a thousand good lives, I don't actually need him.

"I'm looking into doing my own thing." Perhaps it is the absence of reaction towards my tattoos, or the fact that he speaks to me like I'm alive to be at his beck and call, whatever it is, I childishly seek a reaction. Even if it is through prematurely exposing my plan. "I will still show face whenever I am needed, but other than that I'm done. I'm not staying here anymore and to be honest I don't see why this decision would affect you, I'm not exactly your prized winner anyways."

I shouldn't have said that last bit.

Maverick takes a deep breath. "When?"

I'm right, there's nothing he can do about this. "By the end of this week, we'll be gone."

"We?"

"Me and Kaden. We're going to figure things out on our own." I realise how naïve I sound after the words are spoken.

The perplexity that plays out through his laugh as he sneers, furthers my regret on how I went about this, but I don't show it.

"We're not cutting ties. We just want to live our own lives. And you know as much as I do that Kaden could never leave that part of your business. He needs it, even more than you do." It is vital that I mention us not cutting ties. Maverick needs that assurance otherwise we will never be able to get away from him.

He walks towards me, his head angled to one side as his eyes study me. "Good luck."

And with that, he leaves the room. No counterattacks, no disagreeing, nothing. Nothing but wished luck.

What just happened?

Chapter 11
Kade
01/02/2017 (Wednesday)

I open the door to Maverick's office expecting to be the one who waits for his brother, but no, he's already here. Usually I would not care, I am the one who pushes boundaries until I am reminded my choices affect Kassian too. But I've been busy and now that everything is set, I realise I care significantly less about my actions around Maverick.

He seems to already know this, I could tell from the way he's sat on the chair.

"Care to tell me why you chose to come today and not when I'd called you?"

"I'd rather just cut to the chase." He can't hurt us unless he wants to miss out on a chunk of properties and what have you. I made sure to create new wills and contracts and since I have Kassian's scars, it was easier for me to play the both of us. If we die, or go missing, our assets will no longer go to any River, unless we have a kid somewhere. Not to mention, if something were to happen to us, Nene, our grandparents, maybe even other Rivers will get involved and that kind of attention is not what he likes or needs.

Maverick gestures '*the stage is all yours*' with his hands, the calm before the storm.

"We're leaving. We have enough to our names to live like kings for generations, but I know for a fact that you will do whatever you can to make our lives hell away from you. So, I'm willing to do *one* more thing for you and then you have to leave us alone. I don't care what it is. Kill someone's son, sleep with someone's daughter, ten more matches, I don't care, but whatever it is, it *will* be our ticket to be free of you."

Maverick sits back in his chair, causing it to rock as though it were trying to put him to sleep.

"Okay."

I don't know how to react.

I expected more of a fight. If anything, him being quick to agree is more chilling. I can imagine the kind of monstrosity he would have me see through for our freedom, yet regret does not make an appearance.

"Amana Taheem. I want you to do whatever it takes to make her sign a Baronial contract."

I pull my brows together. "You want the last thing that I do for you, to be to make someone sign a contract? Whose daughter is she?

"She's someone who's given me a headache and I want you to deal with it." He throws a folder with her information on the table.

"I'll have it done by Friday."

The task is simple. It's just swapping someone's freedom for ours.

Chapter 12
Kade
02/02/2017 (Thursday)

This Amana girl is only sixteen, and from what I have on her, I know that she's not related to anyone special, she doesn't even *know* anyone special. The thought of what she could've done to royally piss Maverick off did pass my mind a few times, but I've dismissed it because like the many other times I'd been tasked to bring someone in to Baronial, I do not care. But then she is different, she's the last person I have to bring in, the last task before I could live my life the way I wanted and yet, she is a nobody. Which just makes it that much more suspicious as to why Maverick would want me to bring her in. Is she a trap? Is the information I have on her even correct or have they been doctored?

I've been tailing her all morning. She seems to be a decent person, every interaction is quick and polite, sometimes she even goes the extra mile to do something for a complete stranger. The more I observe the more my mind went back and forth on whether I cared enough to know *why* she has been condemned to this particular punishment. And since I don't think that I will ever get an answer, I push myself to approach her to get this over and done with.

Amana is the eldest of five kids. She uses most of her holidays picking up part time jobs to help out around the house and to fund the little things she wants in life. Her file says they are currently living in a house that has not been completed, subjecting them to live with mould and an unfurnished kitchen and living space. With a family of seven, that has got to be a pain in the ass, so my offer should feel like a miracle when I tell her about it.

I approach her as she wipes down a table, she doesn't notice me at first so I feel the need to be bolder. Sitting down at the table that she continues to wipe down should do it. It looks clean to me, so she must be some sort of clean freak, a downside to her future job.

"Hey." Her eyes grow with surprise but her tone is a welcoming one. I guess she has to be nice to a customer, even when they are interrupting her cleaning session.

"Hey." My charm should hook her in, it's never failed me before. I may be in Maverick's shadow, but it's not a hidden fact that we've all been blessed with good genes.

She glances at the clock on the wall behind her, then checks our surroundings as if this interaction is forbidden. "It's a bit early don't you think?" She busies herself with whatever's on the table to conversate for a little longer.

"I'm sorry, but I saw you from afar and wanted to come say hello, I hope you don't mind."

I didn't realise how green her eyes are, well, hazel, but more on the green side, something the picture Maverick has of her does not show off.

Noticing the lack of things she has to rearrange and clean, I spill some salt. "I'm Kade by the way." I tilt my head to catch her eyes. "And you are?"

"Is that your real name?" She questions with a smile.

"Yes. Why would I give you a fake one?" I pour more salt earning my hand a swat.

"Would you stop doing that? You're wasting the salt!" Though her voice is low and quick, she manages to get her frustration out through laughter. It sounds nervous, but also flirty and I'm not one to judge but given her appearance I thought that she would be more…dull.

"Would you finally tell me your name?" I lean in from my previous casual position.

Her eyes flicker between mine. "It's Amana."

I got her.

I can see it written all over her face. I have her, but why do I feel as though something is wrong? Maybe it's the little-to-no fight she put up? I was prepared to knock down some walls, but she has none up. I thought everyone had their own precautions built in place?

"Nice to meet you Amana." I give her another one of my bewitching smiles. "When d'you get off?"

She finally stops fidgeting with the table and stands upright. "I can take my break now if you want?"

This task is getting more and more easy.

"Yeah, alright, let's go. I can show you where I work."

Her face lights up a little, adding to her naivety which pricks me with guilt, but then I look at her eyes and although they're not exactly like Kassian's, they still remind me of him. And the whole reason I'm doing this, is *for* him. If he stays for any longer, the parts of him that are good would die, if he doesn't first.

As I let her into the office, she marvels at the interior for all of five seconds before speed walking over to the window. Meanwhile, I send everything I've collected to what I like to call '*The Sham Team.*' They should have everything ready in a few minutes, then I can get this over with and be on my way. Not that the task is difficult, I'm barely doing anything to distract her. Amana has all her (non-existent) defences down and walks around the place as though she were at a friend's home.

My phone and laptop ding, pulling my attention towards them. I open up her file to see my new resources. If she refuses the initial offer, they will make things easier.

"Amana? Would you be a dear and sit down for me please?"

She pulls a face as she makes her way to one of the chairs in front of my desk. "Are you about to interview me or something?"

I bite the inside of my lip whilst nodding, the charm slowly and prematurely dropping as I feel us approaching the end of this task. "Would you like a job here? We have an opening. All you have to do is sign a few things."

Her face drops all its expressions as she goes into some sort of shock. "What kind of job?"

"You'll be representing the company. Aiding several clients." I play with the pen in my hand. Twisting and flipping it in and out of fingers, *itching* to hand it over to her so that she can sign and free us of our bonds.

It doesn't take a genius to see that she is thinking about it, but due to my lack of patience, it rubs me the wrong way.

"You would work part time and your starting salary would be £2100 a month." That should be more than enough for someone her age.

"£2100 a month? For a student part-timer? What kind of clients are they?"

"High-end ones. Who love to give generous tips, sometimes triple your pay."

There's no way she could resist this offer, I could practically see her hand wanting to reach over and grab the pen.

She also has the same habit as Kassian, shaking her leg up and down until her brain made sense of everything.

"We also have a network that allows us to open up doors of opportunities for you." I rotate the pen on my thumb, how is she not making her move? "In turn, your family would also reap the benefits." I try another approach, being an older sibling must mean that she wants to look after them. I've witnessed this with others.

"I'll do it." She speaks.

Finally.

As I extend my arm out, I rotate the pen in my hand towards her. She must desperately need the money for her to not want to read the contract. This girl has done everything I want without too much of a push and as much as I hate to say it, I resemble Maverick and she has shown no reaction to it. So, what was stopping him from directly getting rid of a headache himself? Her file doesn't even have any sort of connection towards us, she's not even a perfect fit for who we grab for Baronial. Not to mention, she's not finding this suspicious despite having gone through an employment process once before. There are no harmful or calculated questions, she doesn't even have any demands. There's not one serious fault about her except for the fact that she's made her way on to Maverick's radar. And yet, her words of agreeance and the sounds of the pen marking her signature are music to my ears.

We quietly make it back to the lobby until she decides to speak.

"Thank you for giving me a job. I know that you don't know me too well but maybe I could tell you more and then maybe you could do the same?"

I hold onto my mask for a little longer. I should've been anticipating this. Several of the females I bring in, if not all, have tried to make advances on me. It's probably the reason why they were so quick and blind in signing papers. "I er. I actually have to pack up today. I'm leaving. You were my last task so I should really be thanking you."

Her face read '*What are you talking about?*'

"I also want to say that I'm sorry, I wish that things didn't play out like this for you. From what I know and seen, you are a good person and you don't deserve it, but it had to be done."

Amana's eyes flicker between mine, I can almost see her start to panic through them as she tries to understand what I've said. I, on the other hand, refuse to be aggravated at myself for saying too much. I wanted to apologise, so I did. That's a good sign, I still have it in me. But this can't last any longer, so I call over security to escort her out.

"Goodbye Amana. And good luck."

Chapter 13
Kassian
02/02/2017 (Thursday)

One of the last things on my list, one of the most important things after making a deal with Maverick, is to tell Iris more. I'm also going to help her out with her family in a way she can't refuse. I also need to show her that I've taken her advice, my scars are black, but I want it to be a cool reveal. I might just steal the way Kade done it so that she can come closer and help me peel off my clothes.

The park is not as full as I thought it would be, given that it's towards the end of the week.

I take my stand at the usual place, looking out to where Iris used to sit and scoff food down. I'm about to think about the *'who can eat the most wings to the bone in two minutes'* challenge we did, when I hear quick steps towards me. It's not enough to trigger memories as they aren't heavy steps, but I do turn around faster than the average person would.

I regret the reflex almost immediately. Iris stands a step away from me. This is the closest we've ever been and she's the one who chose to close that distance between us. Should I use this moment to perform Kade's act?

"Thank you for giving me the job but what the hell was that? And why are you sorry? And how comes you're here if you're leaving? Also, I don't want you to leave, I know that it's stupid and selfish but part of the reason on why I joined was because you were going to be there."

What is she talking about?

My heart skips a beat and not for the right reasons.

I know why it feels like we've skipped a chapter or two, I just don't want to go into it because it's not a yellow brick road. She's not actually mad and confused by my actions, she's mad and confused at—

"Kade! Hello?"

A ripple that mimicks pins and needles runs across my entire body. I have no control over how I just reacted but I do know that Iris has witnessed it and it only furthered her confusion and worries.

"I have to go." There's no sense of emergency behind my voice.

"What? Why? I—" She tries to cut in front of me.

"Get out of my way." I look down at her, making her jump a step back. I don't mean to be this way, but if I stayed any longer, she would experience more than a bad attitude. "Please." I soften my tone knowing that the damage has already been done.

Iris moves out the way with this confused, almost mournful expression and as much as I want to console her, I cannot. I don't know how long I have to fix this, *if* I could fix this, I just know that I need to leave right now. I run towards where I had parked my car. I do not have to go to the building to know if she's been processed yet. If her name is on the system, then there is nothing that I could do. If she's still being processed, I can save her before it's too late. Maverick wouldn't see her name, therefore wouldn't know of her existence, so there wouldn't be a problem when I burn her contract and everything on her.

I click and scroll and there it is. It's like the system knew I would look for her specifically. Her name and picture was displayed at the top, along with the date, time and the name of who had got her onto the system. I had a feeling before, but seeing it written down in bold hurt that much more.

'ARRIO'

Chapter 14
Kade
02/02/2017 (Thursday)

It's been a long-short day, and it's going to end with me being in my studio for the last time.

Hiring Amana was a somewhat breezy task. Usually it would take a few hours to get someone onto the system, but she was our golden ticket so I personally put her on myself as soon as she had been escorted out. I wasted no time. The long-winded part of the day are my thoughts on surprising Kassian with our discharge. I cannot wait—although I am being forced to as he is still not back from seeing Iris—to get out of here with him. Another thing that I want to do is meet Iris, the girl who unknowingly upgraded my brother which ended up being the push I needed in making all this happen. There's also that friend of hers that I am now more willing to meet. This entire time I've been respectful of Kassian's boundaries, keeping away from his time with Iris, keeping away from finding her and her friend, so, this better work out in our favour.

"*You* prick!"

I'm punched mid-turn, but I'm able to recover to dodge Kassian's other attacks.

"What the *hell* was that for?" I can't deny his punch actually hurt, and that's a surprise in itself.

"As if you don't fucking know." He circles me, preparing his next hit. "Maverick told me you had the choice to leave but at the cost of hiring someone. And you chose Iris. You hired her." His voice breaks. "Without hesitation."

"Iris? No, I—"

"You chose your freedom, *yourself*, over me and Iris, who has no idea what you signed her up for!" He destroys a trolley by kicking it over, but not before grabbing something and launching it towards me.

"Kassian that's not true." My mouth stays open to say more but I don't know what else to say. All day I felt something else at play, but I ignored it.

"No? Tell me. Were you not quick to jump at this opportunity?"

"Yes, but—" It was for the both of us.

"Were you not quick to get her onto the system?"

"I—"

"*Quicker* than usual?" He raised his voice.

I should've picked up on the similarities between Iris and Amana, I should've picked up on the coincidences, the gut feeling, but instead I forced the interpretation to be the excitement for freedom.

"I *finally* got rid of all my weaknesses in exchange for one that I would love for the rest of my life—" He holds back tears and it's not difficult to see the red in his eyes either. "And then you just had to come and be the jealous bastard you are and fuck it up." He charges at me and despite thinking that I am prepared for his moves, I am not. I'm not prepared to fight my own brother.

I won't fight him.

Kassian's never been one to resort to violence and now that he is, I don't know how to handle him. We've fought before, but that was different, that was forced. And Kassian wasn't a drunk raging animal that made me think I wasn't going to leave the place without some broken bones, if at all.

"Mavericks at fault! He's done this on purpose! He told me to—"

Kassian lands his punch then takes me with him to the ground.

"—I did this for us! We can leave!"

"I should have never told you!" He punches what I don't have blocked, forcing the air out of my lungs. "I should have never trusted you!" He gives up on trying to punch through the arms that blocked my face, and instead of stopping altogether, he finds a better way to take his frustration out; bashing my head into the ground, again and again and again.

Not once had I hit Kassian back, I didn't deserve to, it wouldn't be right to. But if I let him bash my head into the ground once more, I'm afraid I won't be able to wake. So, despite me being against hitting my brother, I have no choice but to put him down.

Before he slams my head into the ground once more, I muster up the strength to grab a thick wooden beam and hit him across the head with it.

He falls off my body and to the side, but refuses to back down. I see his deep ambivalence towards me as he tries to stabilise himself by gripping into my arms. I debate on whether I should hold him down and force him to listen, but even I know that it'll all sound like bullshit. It's not like I'm incapable of doing what he thinks I've done.

But not trying is a cop-out, so I do. "Kassian, I—"

He tries to get one up on me again but I manage to see it this time. I managed to see it despite the fact I was concentrating on the blood I made leak out of his head. I push him down, restraining him, but loosen my grip as he grimaces.

A look I've never seen on him before.

"You're dead to me." His words shake out with resentment as his face becomes devoid of all expression, putting the fear of God in me.

Just as he grabs onto a tool from the side, I bring my fist down with full force onto his face. His attack is slowed but not stopped, so I hit him again, finally rendering him unconscious.

Quickly moving to cradle Kassian, I trigger a time where I'd done so in the past, when we first came under Maverick's care. At least then I knew that if he woke, he would wake to be by my side.

My tears mix with his blood as I realise how brainless I've been. There's no undoing what I've done.

I hug Kassian one last time, then do what I can to stop the bleeding before calling Charles. When he wakes, I won't be here. And as stupid as I was in signing Iris into Baronial, it earned Kassian's safety against Maverick. It brings me solace to know that he's now free to do what he wants and has the strength to look after himself. He doesn't need me anymore, though if things had worked out differently, we would've been a good team.

Chapter 15
Kassian
04/02/2017 (Saturday)

One thing about Baronial, it does not waste time. It's already Iris's first day. I haven't had the chance to see her, to talk to her, to *explain* to her. Mostly because I'm not an idiot. I've announced my freedom but that just means that Maverick would be keeping a closer eye on me. He will be watching my every move to make sure I wasn't making a bold move against him.

As I still have access to the system, I am able to find out all I need to about Iris and her location. She's been put with a group today, a group that had a girl everyone knows I've been with, intimately, so it will not be shocking news if my appearance makes its way to Maverick.

Every part of me that would give my identity away is covered, I made sure of it. The suit covered most of my tattoos, the gloves covered my hands, my hair is braided back, two messy two-day-old braids and my eyes—a cut beneath one and a pink-purple bruise— are covered by shades. I have no doubt these coverings would make no difference, Iris has a sharp eye, which is why I will also be staying in the shadows.

She will not see me. She can't.

The four of them wait in the lobby. All 'exotic' looking, a requirement of the client. Iris is the only one wearing a headscarf, the only one who looks ready to take on whatever the day brings, assist where assistance is needed. The rest of them appear as if they already want the day to be over with.

No smiles from any of them, something they would put on in the room.

Iris seems to be the only one wanting to communicate, but due to their lack of energy, her eyes lean towards nervousness and her smile fades.

I want to tell her, tell her what to be prepared for, but I can't. If I interfere, Maverick will definitely find out and take it out on the both of us. He may even just take it out on Iris in front of me, then assign her a harsher fate to also satisfy the client. I thought the most difficult task would be to keep Maverick off my back today, but it's actually trying to stop myself from further getting involved.

I begin to comprehend what it means to be here. I will witness the before and after of Iris.

I know this man, this client. He's one of those people that invested the money he won from the lottery. Yes, he's into cars, girls, booze, but he's also smart and hungry, and those two things make a pretty potent mix. Why choose to spend all the money and indulge all at once when you can find a way to make the money come in for a lifetime?

He also happens to be someone Maverick wants to screw over. He just needs to find his weaknesses, other than the blatant kink for young girls overseas.

"Listen you bitch!" He raises his voice with so much outrage, it booms into the surrounding rooms.

"No *you* listen, you dumb fuck!"

I perk my head up. That's Iris.

He's raising his voice at Iris and she's raising her voice back.

I can't hear the next sentence or two because of the walls but I know that she's countering him.

A mistake she'll pay for.

A few bangs, scuffles and gasps are heard before she finally manages to swing the door open. I didn't realise I had been aggressively pacing back and forth, but thank God I was because my back had been to her when she exited the room.

As she escapes, I took in the sight of her, she was a mess but despite whatever had transpired, she was forcing herself to be strong and is fixing her out of place scarf. This is the first time I've seen her hair.

It's black, like mine.

The chaperone sent by Baronial is about to go latch his hands onto her, but I intervene. When she is finally out of sight, I address him, "We can't make a scene." I try not to raise my voice and show desperation. "I will go after her, you do what you can here and report back to me."

I find her three streets over. Her eyes are watery and red, her headscarf doesn't exactly look how it usually does, and she's hyperventilating. From the looks of it, she is trying to get herself through it instead of completely letting herself go, and I can't help but approach her. If Kade were here, he would call me an idiot. He would say that I don't have to do this, I don't have to care for everyone in the world, but that's the thing, Iris isn't just anyone.

She's my friend.

"Hey." I hold my empty hands up as I try the gentle approach.

She immediately flinches and takes steps away from me. When she processes who I am, she takes a small step closer. "Kade? What the hell did you sign me up for?" She fights for air with short breaths.

I don't have it in me to tell her the truth, what difference does it make if she knows. Kassian is just as responsible as Kade for this mess. The smallest silver lining in this, is that she thinks that I'm Kade, she's angry and blaming Kade, not me, and I won't ever correct her, not until I make this better.

"I-I'm quitting. I'm leaving. I won't go back. I don't need this job. I can find another one!"

My stomach drops.

"Amana." Her name feels strange to say. She hasn't introduced me to it, I only know her as Iris. "You can't leave." I try to say as soft as I can. "It's too late."

"What?" She shivers the word out.

"Your job is to distract the client or extract information from said client. Information your boss could use against them, information he could use to take them down." I stop listing what else Maverick could do with the information. She doesn't care for it anyway. "*It's a 'drunk men talk'* thing. You have to understand—"

She scoffs. "Drunk men talk? Do you know what he wants from us in there? What just happened to me? What *could've* happened to me?" Tears create a barrier over her eyes but she's more angry than sad.

Good. Anger is good. It'll make her stronger.

"I can feel my body deciding the colour of my bruises." Her voice is shaking. "And I feel dirty! Like it won't matter how much I wash and scrub and tell myself that I'm clean!"

For a moment I don't know what to say.

"It won't always be like this. It'll get better. I'm going to help." I nod nervously, almost to convince the both of us.

"You let me go through this. You want me to *continue* going through it?!"

"No! I—We *both* don't have a choice in this."

"I don't understand how you're standing there, treating this job like it's normal, trying to get me to stay!" She shoves me back as I approach. "I have a choice. I'm going to the police." Her voice is certain, like her decision is finalised.

I bow my head and take a deep breath.

"They'll go after your family, Medisa, and then you." I hear her breath hitch. "It's not worth the trouble, *trust me* on this." I realise my choice of words too late and I could tell from her eyes flickering back and forth that she needs more convincing.

Like someone who has studied her, I say her address, then think about what else I saw on her file. "One of your siblings is with you in school, the other three are in the primary school near the hospital." I let out a dry chuckle. "How convenient is that? An accident could happen but the hospital is right there, so everything *should* be okay, right?"

Her face turns into an expression I've seen a countless number of times, but that doesn't mean I'm used to it. If anything, it being on her face makes it that much sharper. But this is necessary, she needs to understand that her actions have consequences, now more than before.

I know the name of each sibling, the names of their classes and the name of their schools, teachers etc. and I recite it all to her like she were grading me.

"Baronial has clients just as powerful as that man, most of them have even more influence. It wouldn't be hard for them to do something to hurt you. The police would never have enough to even consider looking into your case."

"I don't believe you. I don't believe that it would be taken that far." She lies to herself.

I sigh, not wanting to take this further. "They have a contract with your signature, showing that you knew what you were getting yourself into. And if that's not enough, there are edited voice recordings where you could hear how eager you were to do this." I pull out my phone to play them to her. It doesn't matter what effect it has, as long as it stops her from going to the police.

I don't let it play all the way through, I didn't need to.

Iris is dissociating.

She slowly made her way down to the ground. Her face and posture gave her numbness away, confirming that she's been broken down and was dropping her plan of reporting what transpired.

"I will make this better. I swear it. You won't have to do anything, just stand and look pretty. You and your family would be protected, I'll make sure of it." I kneel down so that I could catch her faraway gaze. "Iris?"

"Stay away from me."

"Wh-what?"

She doesn't mean that. She doesn't know what she's saying.

"I said, *stay* away from me."

"You don't mean that, you're just in an emotional state right now."

"I should've rang the police the day I met you. I should've never approached you. *Dying* would even be a better option than meeting you, you piece of shit." She forces herself up to a stand. "I'm going to get through this." She sniffs as she nods to herself. "I know I will. I'm going to get through this and make sure that you get yours."

Chapter 16
Kade
15/06/2017 (Thursday)

I stumble down a path not really caring for where I end up, I've got what I need in my hand and more at the building. I can't say I know how many days have passed, they've all kind of blended into one.

When the sun comes up, I either wait for it to piss off, or I'm already conked out waiting for the darkness of the next nights sky. Not that I get that, the nights sky. This bloody area is lit up like some sort of club. But now, now I finally have found a path that's dark enough for me to be left alone with my drinks. It's the perfect spot, doesn't seem like people walk down here, doesn't even look like animals come here.

How did I not see it before? Her eyes aren't an exact replica of Kassian's but they are hazel *green*, like they were meant to meet and produce weird green-eyed babies.

Also I don't understand how I was *supposed* to know? What Muslim names themselves Iris? Iris does not sound very Muslimy. It doesn't even go with her look. I understand that her eyes are out there and in your face, but how was I supposed to link Amana to Kassian's Iris.

'*You're dead to me.*' Those aren't exactly loving last words but they will have to do… they will have to do except, I can't seem to get over them. Bloody idiot. Why couldn't he just listen? We were so close to having our own lives until he went ahead and blew up in my face as if I were supposed to have a picture-perfect image of Iris in my head. All that talk about whatever they did during their days together and he didn't want to give me a picture? A picture so that when I was out and did see her, I could avoid or protect her, not bloody hire her out to fulfil someone's kink whilst we run off into the sunset.

I'm forced into the wall as I lose what little balance I have after walking into someone.

"Sorr—"

They punch my gut before I get to finish my drunken apology. The drinks in my hand are snatched away from me and despite my lack of defence, they decide to stay and get a few more hits in. Perhaps they enjoy taking things out on people who couldn't fight back. Correction, *wouldn't* fight back. Although this was an unfair fight, the thing that I find most dirty about it, is the fact that it's chucking down. I'm not planning on going back just yet, which means I'm going to be beaten, bruised and wet for a while.

'*Good. Serves you right for what you've done.*'

They continue to kick again and again, three of them from what I can feel. Usually, this would be more than enough to trigger me into autopilot but for once, I truly do not care. The first group of people that tried it on me weren't so lucky. I had my fun with them, but who can blame me? I had just left my bleeding brother on the floor.

"Oi!"

The kicks gradually stop as someone sprints over. My eyes open, but my sight is blurry.

I blame the liquor and rain.

One person falls to the ground, a few grunts and hits and another joins me. The last of the group swears, I can't really hear him but it doesn't matter because he gets his arse handed to him. The new person in the scene, grabs and tosses them away, making sure to snatch the drinks from them.

"Wankers." He squats down to help me up. "You live around here?"

Not that I have a choice, but I'm in no mood to be engaging in conversation with this stranger.

"You took a beating, but it could've been worse."

The weighted droplets on my face and the ground around my ears is soothing enough to lull me to sleep. The rain forces my eyes shut, not that I mind, it's the best thing I've felt since leaving Kassian.

The stranger continues to talk. He's probably trying to keep me awake, but I have other plans and they don't include being conscious. They include being able to see our dreams, maybe even our past, which surprisingly I don't mind.

Chapter 17
Kassian
16/06/2017 (Friday)

It's been a while since I've seen her so it took a second for my brain to register that it is in fact *her* sitting a few feet away from me. She won't recognise me, I've made sure of it, so I could close the distance between us, but I want to play it safe, for now.

Her missing headscarf was the big difference. I shouldn't be surprised that she's no longer wearing one, she's a strong character but that doesn't mean she's going to allow people to use her to fulfil their questionable kinks. My brain feels funny after seeing her for the first time without a covering. It's like I'm trying to summon her scarf in my head to make up for the difference. Sometimes when I glance over, I swear that I see her wearing one, but then I blink and it disappears.

She looks happier now, better, despite the cruel realisation of what her job actually is. Something tells me that her buoyant attitude is more because she is able to provide for her family and was able to get them out of the hole they were in.

Her siblings have grown from the last time I've seen them, the last time being the sixteenth two months ago. I would check up on her more often but it would be inviting Maverick. So, even if it pains me to not see her as much as I would like, I will carry on visiting on the 16th whenever I am certain that eyes are off me.

A boy approaches her table and casually picks a few chips off her sisters plate. Her wide-eyed siblings look to each other then Iris for some sort of explanation and comfort. Iris herself looks as though she doesn't know what to do and he seems to continue to assume that his actions won't lead to any sort of consequence.

"You can go now." She holds authority in her voice and although she is sitting down, Iris looks down at him. I do too, he looks and is behaving like a rat.

The half-wit goes to pick up her drink but she beats him to it and splashes it all over him.

Her siblings get up as soon as she gives them a signal.

"You heard me." She doesn't get too close to him. He must stink, he looks like he does.

The boy pushes Iris back into her chair with so much force that her chair almost topples over. Luckily for the both of them, a few people were able to interfere and stop that from happening. The boy is guided away, but I'm not willing to let him get off that easy. After double checking that Iris and her siblings are okay and are getting the support that they need, I stalk the boy and the decent man who is escorting him out. Once he's taken outside, he's given a few words of wisdom then is left to be alone. No one else is on this side of the building and it's a busy day, so noise pollution is in my favour.

He mutters a few things then finally explodes, throwing whatever was in his hand to the ground. "Dirty paki! Who does she think she is?"

"I know right?" I cut in, not wanting to hear more. "One minute this country's pure, the next we're overrun. What has the world come to?" If any of my grandparents were to hear me…Maverick would become the least of my worries.

Agreeing with my false statement, he approaches as I scope the area to make sure no one's around. When our isolation is confirmed, I smash his head into the side of the wall.

Not enough damage.

He's on his knees now, gripping onto the sides of his head. "What the fuck! What the fuck?" He rocks himself to try and diminish the pain.

I grab onto both of his wrists, taking away his applied pressure as my eyes flicker between his hands.

"What are you doing?" He spits out, a little scared.

"Oh *you're* frustrated? No. You don't get to be. I just witnessed the fuckery you pulled inside and now I can't remember which dirty hand you used to eat that sweet girls chips."

"What?"

"Ahh. D'you know what? I suppose it doesn't matter. You did use both hands to push her sister."

The amount of his eyeball I could see double in size as he tries to pull his hands away but realises he can't.

"So, which one first?" Before he could even process the question, I fracture his wrist. His cries almost trigger me to take it to a level Kade would.

Still not enough damage.

"Lucky for us this part of London always has random crap lying around." I pick up a round door knob then place one of his hands on the pavement.

"Wait-wait-wait!" He's not really screaming anymore, more like pleading.

"You know, I think I remember what hand it was." I bring the doorknob with as much force as I can down onto his fingers. Not once, not twice, but enough times for me to see that his fingers would be fucked for life. Some of the meat around his bones are basically minced. Ugh, I would not want to be him, but I do think I understand what Kade means when he says that it's another type of satisfaction.

Chapter 18
Kade
16/06/2017 (Friday)

The unfamiliar smell of breakfast wakes me before the stranger cooking it does.

My sofa's been turned to face the open kitchen to make things easier for him to keep an eye on me. I'm not entirely surprised I am waking up here and not his house or even the pavement outside. But who is this person? And why are they comfortable enough to go through my things? If I had the energy, I would be mad at myself for allowing someone to follow me back, but since they're already here and I cannot travel through time, there is no point in wasting the little energy that I do have.

I sit up, unintentionally calling the stranger towards me.

"How you feeling?" He hands over a pint of water.

"Like I took a couple weak hits." I accept the water.

The stranger lets out a dry laugh, like he needs more convincing, like I haven't been through worse and survived.

'He doesn't know that.'

"Didn't look weak from where I was standing."

"And where were you standing? Why were you even there?" I consider the possibility of Maverick sending him and try to stand, but there's a wobble in my stance.

"I was just passing, then I heard the commotion." He holds up both of his hands. "You didn't allow me to take you to the hospital but you did mumble your address."

I scrap any thoughts of attacking him, mainly because

I am surprised I was able to remember my new address and instructed to be taken to it, instead of my old one.

"You have an accent. It's watered down, but it's there. Scottish?"

"Well aren't you observant?" I look past the gentleman and towards the drinks that survived the event.

"Don't even think about it mate."

"*Mate*?" Despite being tired and hurting, more emotionally than physically, I manage to take time and energy out to pull a face. "Who do you think you are?"

The strange man moves to pour the contents of the bottles down the sink, then makes his way towards the already plated breakfast.

"Well, since you don't want to go to a hospital, I've decided to personally nurse you back to health." He places the plate in front of a stool. "I also think that there is no harm in teaching you how to defend yourself." He puts down a knife and fork as if he were seating me at a restaurant.

I genuinely want to laugh in his face as he expresses his want to teach. He wants to turn me into a project? A hobby? How bored is he? How much time does he have? Somewhere along the lines of hiding amusement, my brain turns it into an offence. I can't help but want to prove him wrong, so I grab the steak knife and go for his throat. If I succeed, it's a bittersweet moment. The world loses a soul kind enough to waste their time on a stranger, but I also get to make my point of not needing a teacher.

As I launch the knife forward, he leans the top halve of his body to the side, avoiding my attack. He doesn't stop there, like most people would, instead, he grabs the wrist that failed my attack and pulls me forward. When I'm close enough he lets go, purposely sling-shotting his elbow into my nose. Out of the two of us, his shot landed, making me fall onto my back. But I refuse to give up. I hook my leg into his weak one as I swing round like some sort of turntable, instantly knocking him onto his back.

Somehow, we both mentally agree that was enough as we catch our breath on the floor.

"Your eyes gave you away first, then the positioning of your feet."

"You didn't hold my wrist tight enough, I could've easily gotten out of it if I wasn't still being affected by drinks."

"You're too slow."

"Your legs are weak." I shot back. We may have given up on physically attacking one another, but not verbally.

He looks at me with disbelief in his eyes but amusement around his mouth. When he finally lets out his chuckle, he joins me as I sit up.

"What do you mean my eyes gave me away?" I've never got to speak to my opponents before, mostly because they died, or because they were too injured to speak, so this is genuinely news to me.

"Your pupils dilate. Like you know what you could do to me and you see it play out in your head. You're breathing also shifts."

'Interesting.'

"I mean it when I say that I'm not slow." I lightly touch my nose where his elbow connected. "I'm just a little out of practice and am still feeling the effects of alcohol."

"From the looks of it, it seems like you've not allowed yourself to be sober." He looks around at the piles of bottles and cans here and there. "How long have you been drinking for? Since the ripe age of eight?"

"What month is it?" A genuine question that cuts his joke

short.

"June. It's the sixteenth."

"Five months. It's only been five months." A hard realisation. At some point towards the beginning, the days began to blur. But for it to have only been five months? It feels like it should've been years.

"*Only*?" He scruffs up his own hair. "Kid." There's compassion in his voice.

"*Kade*." My attitude makes an appearance.

The bored man stops himself from speaking words of wisdom, and instead chooses another way to try to get through to me. "I was able to pull you so quickly and with little effort because of how skinny you are. You're obviously not looking after yourself and you obviously have no one looking out for you. So if you want to stick a knife in my throat, you're going to have to let me look after you first. Let me help you gain healthy weight, until then, let's be friends."

"Are you some kind of paedophile in the making?" A pivotal question.

"I'm twenty-two! What are you? eighteen?"

"Yes. That's why I said '*in the making*.'"

He lets out a short borderline sarcastic laugh. "You do know how to be humorous, I thought you were going to be stoic forever."

"I was being serious, but now I've grown bored of the curiosity. I don't care why you're choosing to help me because I'm declining your offer." I get up and move towards the fridge.

"Well I decline your decline." The big baby continues to make a stand.

Before I open the fridge door, I sigh and lean my head as far back as it could go. "I woke up and tried to kill you. You didn't *die*. You haven't run out the building. Which could only mean that you somehow know who I am, or you're another type of twisted." I open the fridge door to view an empty fridge. He got rid of my drinks and has the nerve to cook me some breakfast? Was he even making the food for me or was he hoping that I woke after he ate? I pinch the bridge of my nose, I don't have the energy or the speed I need to take whatever I'm feeling out on him. "Which one is it?" I say the words slowly through gritted teeth.

"I don't know who you are and I'm not twisted. I'm just trying to help. Is help that unfamiliar to you that you don't recognise it when it's right in front of you?"

"Get out." I know what help is and it's not given without attachments, and I do not need more of those.

"I'm staying."

"I said, *get out*." That's the last thing I say, because my body decides to break down.

The stranger did not do anything to make me fall, that is made clear when a blurry version of him runs towards me. I do try to keep my eyes open but my lids do not listen. Every time I force them open the stranger's blurry body morphed more and more into Kassian's, just as his voice did when he called my name. For a brief moment it took me back to the ring, not when luck was on my side, but when I first entered to win us a proper meal.

Chapter 19
Kade
18/06/2017 (Sunday)

"Oi." I'm not one to be polite and let a person sleep whilst I move around, but in this scenario, I really do not have a choice. He's taped me into this office chair and no, not the regular '*wrap the wrists, wrap the ankles, wrap below the knees,*' no, he's taped my entire body, except my neck and above, to this damn chair. "If sleeping beauty doesn't *get up* before I manage to get out this chair, I *will* throw her out the window." I still don't know this guys name, but this building is tall enough to make his body splat when I throw it out. I'm just upset I won't get a good view of it.

He finally sits up and looks around through lazy eyes as though there were others in here with us. "Morning." He yawns out the word as he tries to smile.

"It's after twelve you cretinous being. Get me out of this." I wriggle my wrists but it's no use.

"No way. Do you know how many rolls I had to buy and use to keep you in place?"

"I don't think I asked, how many?"

"Ten rol—"

"Don't care."

He dropped his shoulders, obviously not appreciating my humour, then walked over to another chair, sliding it to be positioned directly in front of me. He's more awake now, far less likely to fall for anything else I try to pull.

"A quick rundown." He says as he grabs a bowl and

spoon. "I'm Bellamy. You've had your body cleaned out by my sister and her husband, both private doctors, no big hospitals. You been tied for some time, but it's okay because if you finish this soup and whatever else I feed you, I'll let you go." He sits down in front of me. "Choo-choo!" His tone's too cheerful as he snakes the full spoon into my mouth.

I purposely spit it all back out on him. "It's too hot."

It was not.

It was actually the perfect temperature and the taste was quite nice too.

Bellamy keeps his eyes shut as if he should've seen it coming, and he should've. I almost laugh at the sight of him as the thick parts of the soup make their way down his face, but I settle for a cheeky smile.

If I could use my legs I would kick his throat, or chest but then what? There's only so much a person can take, and he could easily end my life right here if he wanted to, but what's getting to me is that he's not. He willingly wants to waste his time.

He wipes his face. "Let's try that again."

I give in, but not without a devilish smirk and a tone to rub it in. "Choo-choo."

Chapter 20
Kade
21/06/2017 (Wednesday)

After months of no self-care, minus the occasional wash, my hair has grown to be too long. *Maverick* doesn't even keep his hair this long and he's one to follow through on tradition. I would say that I look or remind myself of dad, but truth be told I don't remember his face, or his voice. I just know that he had *long* hair.

"Are you sure that you don't want me to do it?" Bellamy pops his head into the bathroom.

I'd decided to keep him, not that I had much of a choice. The man was a fly in human form. He could choose to be anywhere in the world, he's what you would call self-made, and yet he's decided to stick around me.

When he cut me out of the chair, I'd done a background check on him and it came back clean. He has no tie to the River family, except for the unfortunate circumstance that brought him to me.

Bellamy also happens to be a good cook, which is a plus. He's been forcing me to learn how to make proper meals which isn't too bad, but I do enjoy making it a living hell for him. I used to be the cook when it was me and Kassian, we didn't have as many ingredients as Bellamy brings, or even the usual basics, but I was able to cook something up, so whatever skills Bellamy taught, honed whatever I already had.

Although it's only been a few days of eating proper food,

my body has started to look alive again. I've got my colour back and it won't be long until I get back into shape, maybe get even bigger and finally fulfil Bellamy's promise by sticking a knife into him.

Other than the pending fulfilment of a promise, I need to tackle my hair. It's been put off for too long. It's silly but hair is a big deal in the River family. It's one of our traits, basically one of our limbs. Cutting my hair to anything below four-to-five inches is outwardly parting from our name and I don't know if I'm ready to do that just yet. I wanted to do it with Kassian but that's not going to happen. I'm alone in this and keeping my hair long is not an option. Bellamy had taken down the bedsheets I used to cover the mirrors, so now I unintentionally catch my reflection and it's getting to me more and more.

"I need a machine."

Bellamy creates a smile by pulling in his lips as though he knew that I would rather a machine than scissors. Disappearing for a few seconds, he comes back with a small fabric black bag.

"What number do you want?"

Ignoring his question, I pick up the machine and drag it to the back of my head from my forehead. Not letting myself stop since there was no turning back now, I continue to shave the rest of my head. The aggression increasing.

"Holy shit." Bellamy takes a step back. "You sure a buzz cut was the move?" He asks like we had the power to turn back time.

I rub off the pieces of hair that didn't fall off with the guidance of the machine. Rotating my head so that I could see that I truly got rid of it all, I turn to Bellamy instead of viewing him through the mirror.

"Doesn't look too bad." I run my hand from the back of my head to the front. "My head feels lighter too."

"No it does not, but I think I prefer you with the wavy-curly inches."

I give him the most genuine smile I could create, then shut the door on his face. I'm not mad at him, I just need a wash, but watching his expressions change as I humour myself has become part of my daily routine.

"Any other crazy plans you want to fulfil?" Bellamy calls out from the other side of the door.

"Just one." I speak, mainly to myself, as I step into the shower, blocking out any words Bellamy could've given. This one plan is going to be a long one, possibly life long, but I don't care. I owe it to my brother.

"You want to make money to help people around the world to make yourself feel better about screwing over *other* people in the world, whilst also keeping track of your brothers crush so that you can help her where you can, to ensure that she lives a good life because her life is also one that you feel guilt towards." Bellamy says his own summarised version of the plan that I had *already* summarised, back to me in one breath. He takes another deep breath whilst I debate on whether or not I want to hear him say more. "Have you tried journalling? Maybe that'll help? And instead of that artist whose painting's slowly become distorted, yours becomes more clear, less demented." He rests his head back onto his interlocked fingers.

I say nothing. I do nothing. Nothing except grind my teeth. It would bring a sense of relief to take things out on him but it would also put me in the same position as before. He's kept me away from drinks for about six days, which is more than I can say for myself.

"Okay fine." He brings his hands out from behind his head. "What would you like me to do?"

"Keep me in check and be my business partner."

Bellamy drops his humorous side for a second, he's considering his options, perhaps even thinking of the best way to let me know he's not interested.

"If I do this, you need to be more willing to open up to me. No more keeping things in your head. The best way for me to keep you in check, is for me to know the whys. If you agree to this, I will do everything I can to make sure that you succeed, not just as your partner but as a friend."

I momentarily freeze. A friend? What a fantasy.

"Fine. I'll try my best to be more interdependent."

Bellamy's faint smile reveals that he wasn't expecting me to give in so soon. "Do you have a name for this business?"

"Aros."

He nods, not questioning why I chose that to be the name. "What will we be doing?"

"Investing in businesses, business ideas, inventions, art, anything and everything we can. I have contacts and I'm a good coach with valuable inside information. We'll have conditions and we'll take a cut." As naïve and adventurous as I sound, I mean it. One way or another we will have access to everything.

"I'm good at coding, I have my own business in it. We can bring them together and—"

"I'm aware of your successes. I done a background check."

Bellamy lets out a breath of disbelief.

"We have five years to make Aros have its fingers in every pot, but we can do it in three, two even. You'll be the face that the public sees if it comes to it, I'm the face that's hidden. It can't be any other way."

"Why five years?"

"She'll be twenty-one and out of a job. And I'll have my share in every type of business that she could go into, waiting to pay her back." Truth be told this isn't the reason why I started Aros, but I might as well use it to right some of my wrongs.

I'll be the River who helps and not the one who tricks.

"We need a gym in here." Bellamy speaks with no relevance to what I just said. "If you're trying to convince people to trust you, you can't look like...that." His finger hastily travels up and down as he points my body out. "You look like you offer the drugs you take and I can't tell if your new hair makes it worse."

I stick my middle finger up, momentarily being flashed back to the last time I did that to Kassian. If I do this for his Iris, I may bump into him. I know him, and I know that he wouldn't just let her go.

I'm almost counting on it.

Chapter 21
Kassian
24/08/2017 (Thursday)

The sound of one of those party-horns goes on for a lot longer than it needs to. I suppose it's because I didn't bother to open my eyes to check what it is that they want me to see.

This week has been one big boobs-fest, I mean, booze. Boobs too but the booze is what *really* helped. I have no sense of time if I'm honest. My club has hosted one Gatsby party after another this past week and any green eyed-dark haired girl or guy were told to shove off. I've had brawls, broads and have been way too bold with how many rules I could snap. Truthfully, the purpose of these parties, these never-ending drinks and assaults are so that I don't remember, don't have enough stability to want to think about anything, *anything* even remotely related to—

"Happy birthday!" Two lovely ladies scream at once.

I ruffle my hair then finally turn my body to see them.

Pulling myself up so that I could lean on the headboard to get a view of what they actually had in store for me, I almost get lost in a daze. If this were last year, you would never see me engage with the workers like this, but this year is different, obviously. The thinking before was '*don't take advantage when you know they're desperate for an escape,*' the thinking now is '*if she's asking for it amongst this shit-fest, why not give her some sort of release?*'

A tight smile takes over my face for a second. Kade would've loved me now, that dirty bastard would've thrown all sorts of parties, wilder than what I've had this past week. I know because he spoke about it, he *promised* it. This week may not have been one of Maverick's, but it still did not satisfy, mainly because Kade's not here. A few seconds more of those thoughts and I remember why.

The two birds put on their own show in front of me, starting the night with their own acts, luckily for me, I no longer care for being courteous.

"Ladies." I grab their attention. "Get over here."

Chapter 22
Kade
24/08/2017 (Thursday)

"Hey, you ready?"

"Yeah, just gimme a sec."

Bellamy's dragging me to a club, he says it's to celebrate Aros having a successful start with three businesses doing well, but I know it's because of my birthday.

It didn't take long for me to tell him things, we *have* been spending pretty much every day together since the day he found me. Though time together is no excuse to be loose lipped, which is why I only let him in when I was okay with it—Not just okay with the fact that I will be exposing us to a stranger, but okay with the fact that I will kill him if he ever told another soul—I told him about my birthday and twin brother, I've also mentioned Maverick. I haven't gotten into the details yet but I have no doubt I will give in and tell him everything. I understand what Kassian means now, about having a friend, it *can* be weightlifting.

As soon as I come into view, Bellamy pops a bottle.

"We just had the floor cleaned." My shoulders drop.

"It's not impossible to have them cleaned again, now drop that head back baby boy and get some of this." He raises the bottle above my head but doesn't tilt it until I'm ready.

I want to protest because this feels strange. Usually, I am the one pouring drinks into Kassian's mouth if not my own or someone who Maverick needs drunk. But so far, these new experiences with Bellamy have not been so bad, plus I need a drink, thoughts of my brother have been circulating this entire week. I sigh and can't help but smile as I tilt my head back allowing the first drink I've had in months to enter my system.

"Oh shit, you can drink!" He stops pouring the drink into my mouth despite me not being done. I could've chugged the entire thing.

I spot another bottle that's been tucked away like Bellamy made a last-minute decision to hide it. He looks ready to leave it behind, to smash it even.

"Is that one for later?"

"Oh, yeah, it's er, it's—"

"Just give me the bottle." I lazily hold out my hand.

Bellamy balances his weight on his heels then his toes, then clicks his tongue as he realises that there are two ways in which this would end. One, we fight for it. Two, he gives it to me while we're civil as I would win the fight.

He rummages through the bag that's made to hold a single bottle, then finally pulls it out. Bellamy tightens his grip on its neck as he plays with its trajectory, then finally holds it out towards me at an angle. The usual label is there, but so is a very messy attempt at calligraphy.

'To the unexpected friend turned brother,
-Bellamy.'

The date 1998, the year I was born.

"I didn't want it to freak you out or trigger you back into the spiral you were in, so I decided not to show you." He takes a deep breath when I don't say anything, then pulls the bottle back towards him. "It's too far, I know. I'll throw it out."

Without saying anything, or making my move obvious I rush to be in front of him. "I'm keeping it." I smile but hesitate with my arms. I lift them besides me as if I were about to create a snow fairy, but hesitate some more. I definitely look as though I'm malfunctioning. Feeling embarrassed I move to put my arms down but before I could get back to my usual stance, Bellamy wraps his arms around me.

"You're a little awkward with it, but we'll get you there." He taps my back twice before letting go of me. "Now come on, we got a night to enjoy!" He calls the elevator.

Before carefully putting the bottle away, safe from the drunk versions of ourselves, I quickly run my thumb over the etched 'brother' and allow myself to wonder what Kassian might be up to. He's probably paying a visit to our grandparents, or Nene, or even trying to develop some sort of relationship with our cousins, maybe even visiting one of the wonders of the world. Whatever it is, it won't be near Maverick's celebrations.

Cautiously putting the girl down, I quickly zip myself up and 'help' her with her dress. It's funny how before I could do what the both of us wanted but now, I am dizzy and am struggling with something as simple as a zip and twisted dress.

Her face is red and the black around her eyes has travelled down her cheeks. She's still a little drunk and despite her allowing me to be deep inside her a minute ago, she tries to cover her face with her hair. Her words are muffled and when I don't respond, she rushes out.

As soon as she left the stall, left the toilets altogether, I bury my head into the toilet, allowing most, if not all of what I had taken, to be spiralling around the bowl.

Trying to get up without seeing the room spin has proven

to be the hardest task of the day, on top of that, the music's bass feels as though it were coming from inside my head.

"Bellamy!" I say as I lean my head back. "Bells!" I know that he's around here somewhere, I saw him take a girl to the toilets, I also know that he won't be able to hear me, but it's worth a try.

I force myself up and make way to the sink. This place isn't exactly up on the hygiene scale but I've been in worse conditions, I'm sure a few gulps of this water won't kill me off.

The toilet door slams open and I half turn my head to see if my luck has improved.

It has not.

Bellamy was not the one to enter, it's just another pair not bothering to take things home. Not wanting to be an audience, I leave and stagger towards the ladies washroom. And somehow, somehow, it's dirtier than the men's. But this is where he is, not only do I know it because I saw him be guided in here, but because I could hear them. I go back and forth on how I should let them know that I am here. I could open their door, I could clear my throat and call out to him, or I could be a good friend and wait.

'Nah.'

Just as I'm about to interrupt their lasting session, a group of girls enter the toilets. From the looks of all their faces and the sudden halt in their steps, they clearly did not expect a man in here, but before any of them scream and get me kicked out, I quickly hold my hands out to tame them.

"My girlfriend's in there." I whisper as I put on the best act I could knowing that they've already bought the lie.

I hold back a grin.

"You poor thing. Come here." Two of them quietly approach me.

"I just—I just wanted to give her the world." My words create an inward shiver as I cringe, but I know that girls eat this shit up. If not the *'poor soul, I can help him'* part, then the revenge part.

"Aw." They extend the word whilst frowning, then one of them hits the door to Bellamy's stall. "You bitch! You don't deserve him!"

Without another word being said, two of them snake their arms around mine. Devilish smiles replace the pity they felt a second ago and all of a sudden, my mind is no longer on collecting Bellamy.

Chapter 23
Kade
20/09/2019 (Monday)

Finding out what University Amana accepted was not a difficult task. I roughly knew when the first semester starts, so I had stake-outs on her road. Not long after I had started, she unknowingly led me to her campus.

Today is the last day of her first week. She's not twenty-one just yet but something tells me that I will need to ease her into the idea of letting me help her. Something else tells me that two years should be enough time to convince her that I've changed.

"Show me your hands Kade." Her voice has matured.

I turn around with my empty hands slightly raised. She has her phone screen facing me, '*999*' ready for her to make the call.

"Why the hell are you still stalking me? And don't deny it I have proof, pictures of almost every time I've seen you."

I bite my bottom lip, practically hiding it from the world as I try to hold my smile. I haven't seen Amana since I got her into Baronial. She's been spotting Kassian which means I'm right. My brother is too sentimental for him to drop his first friend, which means that one of these days, I *will* be seeing him.

"You were the last person I signed into Baronial. The guilt I feel, that I have been feeling, is so extreme that it'll probably still be experienced after death." I drag the guilt trip out a little. She may not be wearing her head covering but that doesn't mean that she's abandoned her faith. One mention of the afterlife does not only show how severe the 'guilt' is, but also forces her to think of forgiveness and what have you. "I've been building an escape over the years and it's ready for you, if you want it."

"I don't care about your guilt."

I almost laugh, but it's nicely blocked by the current remorseful-saviour mask.

"And what makes you think that I want you to feel peace?" She continues, her voice not exactly raised but she delivers the message perfectly with her added attitude.

My mask does not slip, but it isn't exactly bulletproof either.

"Just leave me alone. Seriously, I'm tired."

"I won't. I may have been the person to introduce you to that life and I'm sorry, but I won't leave you until I've done what I can to make things easier. My company allows me to save those dumped by Baronial, sometimes even those who still have contracts."

She scoffs. "Getting me to sign is one thing, but coming back and asking me to trust you is hitting another nerve. Do you seriously think I don't have respect for myself, or that I'm dumb and desperate enough to fall for your shit twice?"

Her phone rings.

'*WIFEY<3*' replaces the '*999*'.

Panic is a strong look on her. Almost like a painting in a museum.

"You need to leave. She can't see you."

I think about my options. I could stay here and wait for her friend to approach, forcing Amana to introduce me and let me into her life. Or, I could do as she says and try again another time, try another route. One she would agree with.

I hold out my card.

"My details are on here. Call me for whatever you need, whenever you need it. I mean it when I say that I will help you."

Chapter 24
Kade
04/10/2021 (Monday)

"His name's James White. He's the head of year for first year finance students, which makes his job easier."

I play with the pen in my hand, spinning it on different fingers whilst also keeping it balanced as Bellamy gives me a rundown.

"The guy brings in a number of students to Baronial. If not directly through him, then through previous students he influenced to join. And not just that… he has records of those in his care. We need to bring him to our side or—"

"Kill him." People like him will never change. If they are willing to do these heartless jobs for some cash, the lower they go for it has no boundaries.

"Discreetly." Bellamy adds.

My lips curl into a smile. This agreeance would be more enjoyed if there were no complications. We've already hired over a thousand from Baronial, offering protection and guidance as well as a job. If that isn't calling for Maverick's attention, killing this man certainly will. There's also the thought of leaving him, which would give us an endless supply of people to take under our wing, allowing me to continue to create my own version of Baronial.

"I'll sort this out today." I get up to leave.

"Kade. Do *not* engage with her and don't stick around in hopes of bumping into Kassian."

He's no idiot, Bellamy. He wants to come off as this nice

guy, a therapist type of friend, but he does put his foot down when he needs to. He's also not wrong to tell me to stop trying. It's been made clear by Amana herself that she wants nothing to do with me, and I would be a version of my old self if I were to say I was waiting for me and Kassian to cross paths.

Goals have progressed and with it so have I, and I will not force a connection. I'm also not stubborn enough to disagree with the fact that the version of Kassian I love is different to who he is without me, who he is now. Hell, after what took place the last time I saw him, I doubt I even fully knew him then.

"I won't. I will be in and out of there before you know it." I click my tongue twice as though I were on a horse, then leave to get this over and done with.

I am able to lift him up as easy as a sack of potatoes, which allows me to slam him down onto his desk with a little more force than needed.

Jamesy whimpers as he tries to get his bearings, giving me enough time to grab a pencil. I slam him back down, getting him to stop moving, then angle the pencil near his eye as my weight holds him in place. Just as I am about to say my threat, I realise how blunt the damn thing is.

Kissing my teeth, I tap his pillow-like chest then look around for some sort of sharpener. And unfortunately for our meaty interest, he owns an electric one.

Whilst keeping my weight on top of him, I stick the pencil in the sharpener and roll my eyes as though this were a common occurrence. It used to be, but I don't like to get into that, it's temptation in disguise.

Once the pencil is as sharp as I like, I bring it close to his eye. "Will you work for me, yes or no?"

Even with a sharpened pencil to his eye, he hesitates.

"Let me rephrase. Do you want to die, yes or no?" My patience grows thin. I wanted this to be clean, to show Bellamy that my progress isn't an act, but shit, this guy is just not making it easy.

"It doesn't matter what I want. Whatever I choose will lead me to death, by yours or your brother's hands."

I smack my lips. He's right. And like everyone else connected to Baronial, Jimmy here needs to follow me out of respect, not fickle fear.

"Bastards." He spits out, it's obvious the intention was not for me to hear, but I can't help but have a reaction.

I sit him up so that his back was no longer on the desk. Patting him down, straightening out his clothes, I smile as his face remains fearfully confused.

"Bastards." I practically wheeze out the word with the biggest grin.

Confusion quickly turns to fear as I grab his wrist and slam his hand down onto the desk.

"This *bastard* is offering you a chance of escape, a chance of freedom and yet you stand here like the fool you are, thinking my brother's wrath is worse than mine." It takes everything I've got to not give him an example right here in this public space.

Students start pouring in, saving both me and Jamesy from myself.

"I'll be back for your answer." I leave the lecture hall, still shaking from the temptation of lodging a pencil into his hand, or eye.

I make it down the hallway and into the main seating area without the sudden urge to turn around.

"Oi-oi look who's back!"

"Giving fashion tips to Jim are you?"

"Get out of here before the girls see you!"

An aggravating group of males approach with their loudest volumes, making me turn from an invisible passerby to somewhat of a celebrity.

"Too late, I can already feel your girls eyes on me." I make a joke, but little does he know I've had more than her eyes on me. If I remember correctly his was the strawberry blonde.

They speak more uselessness that I pretend to be engaged with, with small remarks and gestures. I look around as they refuse to let me go and spot Amana. She's too into whatever is being said for her to spot me.

I excuse myself from the wild crowd and walk towards the entrance. I could go around, away from where Amana is sitting and exit from behind her, but why would I do that? I try not to stare as I walk past, but I can't help but give a glance here and there. She's almost at the end of her Baronial contract, and it's been two years since I've made her the offer. Surely things have changed and she's thought things over?

I glance over again and notice that she's looking directly into my eyes.

"Kade." Her invisible friend becomes visible as she calls out to me as though we know each other.

"Yeah?" I look between the girls who I now stood beside then settle my eyes on Amana. I did not expect her to discuss me, let alone fill her friend in on whatever has happened. It's a risk, surely she knows that? Old me would already have files on her friend with enough to get her to sign her own contract.

"I was just telling her about you, she was saying your name not knowing that it's yours because A: she likes the name and B: she likes your clothes." Amana explains as though this behaviour of her strange friend made sense.

How do I respond to this?

I want to laugh as this is what it took for us to have a 'normal' conversation—to have one of her friends be present—but what if she is calm and visibly unbothered by my presence because she has a trick up her sleeve? She's been collecting pictures of Kassian, why else would she need them if not to do something to us?

"Hey-er? We'll talk later."

I zone back in and before things are dragged out, I nod in agreeance to Amana and politely smile at her friend before moving away.

Saying that I can feel their eyes on me would be an understatement, and I'm doing everything I can to stop myself from walking right back up to them. I had hoped for Amana to change her mind, for her to approach me for some sort of support, but now that she is civil, I can't help but think that there is an ulterior motive to her behaviour.

Before I could think about where to go next, a text message appears on my screen.

'Meet me outside on the right side of the building at 4:30 -Amana'

She's finally putting my number to use and now I have to wait hours to find out why.

I lean on the wall that separates the university from the

pavement as Amana hurriedly walks over to me. As she is the one who called for this, I wait for her to speak first.

"You can pay me back now."

I pull a face as my chin is pulled back into my neck.

"You're going to hire my friend, keep her away from trouble whilst making her have the time of her life. She won't be working for you for long, just until we graduate."

"Why would I do that?"

"You *owe* me. You stalked me, offered me help and freedom and now I am asking you to help and free my friend."

"Help and free her from what?"

"Her life, and what her life would be if she were to give it to Baronial."

"They've approached her?"

"*They've approached her*." She's already beginning to lose her patience.

I look to the side for a second, this does change things.

"You need to make her an offer she can't refuse. Offer more money. I'm willing to give a cut of what I earn to make up for it. Just please, help me help her." She looks desperate, a change from her usual hostile self.

If I help her friend, Amana will become happy and if she were to bump into Kassian, he will know about what I've done and most likely want to approach me.

I think it over then scoff, this is not a difficult decision, I have the means to provide for thousands of people, what is personally looking after two more?

"You don't have to give a cut of your earnings. I will pay her more than enough."

"And be her friend. I'm picking up more shifts, milking them for money before I leave. The time that I have outside of work would be left to catch up on university so that I can graduate this year. She's going to need someone to be there for her when I can't be."

"You don't have to work. I can give you a job as well and pay you just as much, if not more." I owe her that much at least, though she doesn't need to do all this for money. If she could just move on and accept Kassian, he would take care of her, I know it.

Now Amana scoffs. "I work now to make enough for my family for when I leave. I'm not planning on staying here, especially with you. The *only* reason I'm trusting you with Medisa is because I have no choice."

'*Medisa*.' The friend Kassian spoke about?

I take a deep breath. "So how do I become her friend?"

"It's easy. You just need to be funny, be able to understand and make innuendoes, be someone who helps and stands up for people—that one might be hard for you—be a foodie, a movie person, teach her new things, guide her, talk to her—"

I raise my hand, cutting her list short. She's asking for too much, a dog has less needs than her friend. "When do I approach the girl?"

"*Medisa*." Amana says sternly.

"Right. Apologies. Medisa."

"In about half an hour to forty minutes. I have a client I need to meet and you can't let her go home until she's accepted your job. I'll meet you guys after and work with what's left to do."

Great.

Today went from being an in-and-out thing to staying here all day, now taking the role of a babysitter.

"And if she declines?"

"She won't."

"And if she does?"

"She doesn't exactly have many options, you just need to not screw up your side of things. Also, she's a Muslim, so don't be a creep and get too close."

Innuendoes are a yes, close proximity is a no. The girl needs to get her shit straight.

"And if she wants that?"

"She won't."

"And if she does?"

"*Your* job is to keep her distracted and away from anything that could suck her up into this. *Her* goals are to make money, graduate, leave and be as connected with our religion as possible. And that does not come with wanting you. She's not an idiot, nor is she someone who easily develops a crush or is swayed. She has standards and you are nowhere near them."

'Yes, because I am way above them.'

If Kassian's happiness was not enough to get me to agree, Amana's confidence in her friend is. Pre-Bellamy Kade would agree just to prove that one statement she made, wrong. Her not-so-easily-swayed friend would have been blown into so many positions that she may even add contortionist to her list of achievements.

"If anything, *you* are the one who needs to not develop something towards her." Amana continues to yap. "You're going to be acting for these next few months, if you could do it to ruin someone's life, you can do it to help someone." She begins to walk away, visibly sick of this conversation.

Dramatically sighing, I pinch the bridge of my nose.

'It's just for a few months Kade. You've been through worse.'

Chapter 25
Kade
04/10/2021 (Monday)

"Girls, have you seen a light skin South-Asian girl about way big?" I hold out a flat hand marking a rough estimate of her height. "Long black hair, black clothes, mustard boots."

"Oh yeah, she went into the Gardens like two-three minutes ago." One of them quickly answers whilst the others idly stand around, gawking as though I hadn't asked a question.

"Thank you." For not wasting my time like the idiots at the architecture department.

I walk into the Gardens from its main entrance. If I didn't have to find this damsel in awaiting distress, I would be busy marvelling the university's latest attraction, or, I don't know, resting back at Aros.

It doesn't take long for me to find her, she's pretty much sitting in sight looking up to the sky. Her neck is strangely too long and thick for her head and her sense of surroundings is atrocious. She hasn't bothered to check who came into the Gardens. I could easily drag her away into one of the darker corners of the campus.

Getting comfortable at the nearest archway, I wait for her to notice me.

She does not.

I think of the time and the things I could be doing and decide that I no longer want to wait for a girl who seems to be in la-la land. I clear my throat, hoping that it would be enough for her to bring her extended neck down.

It's enough.

She views me as though I am a figment of her imagination then begins to make the most bizarre expressions I've ever seen in my life. And I've seen how Maverick reacts to things that entertain him, this is almost on par with that, if not slightly more disturbing. I could at least *identify* most of his expressions.

It takes a little time for me to get used to the sight of her. She is quite odd looking. Not necessarily ugly, but I also don't have the words, or time, to properly articulate how she looks or how I feel looking at her. Her looks just command some sort of… fascination? Perhaps even annoyance?

All of a sudden, her expressions are compressed into one as she supresses a laugh and breathes it out through her nose. I don't make a comment yet, she may consider me rude and demanding and I can't afford to fail this side quest almost immediately, it would hurt my pride.

Her eyes make their way up and down my body as she drops all joyful expressions promptly after noticing that I am *still* standing here. If I didn't know from Amana that this girl is quite the character, I would assume that she's blatantly sizing me up.

Her expression changes again.

Now I see regret, maybe even a little worry, whatever it is, she's still not addressing me. And I can't wait a moment longer, so if she won't say anything, I will.

"I've done two rounds in this campus trying to find you. I ended up asking some students and they said that they saw a girl walk into the Gardens." Letting her know why I'm here should be a good way to start things. I also make sure to smile, and to hide away my laugh to avoid offending her.

'Better a laugh than hostility.'

"Are you laughing at me?" She gives an impression that she's not actually offended. "I was making faces 'cause I saw you and started to take the piss in my head."

My head involuntarily pushes back into my neck. I did not expect her to be upfront about her abnormality.

"You were making fun out of me in your head? What were you saying?" I move closer, momentarily ignoring Amana's words of advice about proximity.

"Don't worry about it." Her top lip disappears as her lower lip protrudes out even more, then before another second of that expression passes, she switches it up to a curious look. "Why were you looking for me anyways?"

'Is she under the influence?'

"Amana texted, letting me know that you're here alone and that she has another half hour to an hour to go, so she—"

"She wants you to keep me company." She gasps as her eyes widen and her hands cover the lower half of her face. "Look at that we're already besties, finishing each other's sentences 'n all."

I gasp to match her sarcasm. My muscles almost cramp from the smile I force my face to hold as I think '*what a little shit.*' I hold myself for as long as I can before a genuine— but wry—chuckle—practically a scoff— escapes. She really does not understand how lucky she is, swift steps forward and she would be in a position she cannot break out of, a second more and her jaw is loose, then her hands would really have something to hide.

I position myself to be directly in front of her on the other side of the arch. This should be a good amount of distance between us.

"Let me reintroduce myself, I'm Kade. And I've been wanting to say since our encounter in the morning, that I'm sorry for making things awkward." Making it seem like she's been on my mind all day should work, girls love stuff like this and on top of that I'm showing I have manners and care.

This has to work.

Once again, her face morphs into another look.

'What the fuck is that facial expression?'

I decide against commenting on her weird look and instead pause to wait for her to say something. '*Oh no, it's okay, really,*' or '*yeah that does ring a bell*' or even '*no-no I'm the one that made it awkward…I'm Medisa by the way.*' But she refuses to speak, her eyes can't decide whether they should stay on me or on our surroundings. I don't even think that she was following what I was saying or has noticed that I've stopped talking. No wonder Amana called me to help, forget Baronial, this girl wouldn't survive the world.

I question whether I have enough patience for this, it's rhetorical of course but it's something to fill this pause.

"So…" She speaks, finally. "Where you from? You British?" A poor attempt of some sort of accent comes out her mouth, on top of that, I sound nothing like it. I may sound more English than before, but my accent is *not* like that.

Putting my thoughts to the side about the accent she put on, I distract myself with her question. How do I answer this? It's not exactly a straight answer. I guess I could say where my parents are from, and where their parents are from, but that's too long and too intimate.

Taking a deep breath, I look up to the sky.

This doesn't have to be difficult. I don't have to answer with detail. "I'm made up of almost every country in the world."

"O-kay." She extends the word, looking around as if *I'm* the looney one. Her facial expression then does that thing it was doing before, reacting to whatever her small smooth brain thought of.

Keeping calm and collected is quickly becoming another difficult task. She is unknowingly playing with fire and I'm supposed to just take it because a younger version of me decided to sign on her friend—who happens to be my twin brother's first friend—into my older brother's not so friendly business.

She supresses a laugh, but doesn't have the decency to hide that smile on her face.

"Alright that's it." I realise my words come out a little too serious so I lighten my tone and have on a 'fake' but 'amused' expression. "You need to stop having conversations with yourself and let me in on the jokes."

"I know this don't make sense but the word 'slag' came to mind." One of her hands does a poor job of hiding her smile whilst the other flaps around.

Watching her eyes glisten as she childishly spoke through giggles, then noticing her face drop as I do not match her energy makes me think about how shielded she must be. I bet everyone around her protects her from any sort of negativity, her own—only it seems like— friend does. If I were sick like Maverick, seeing her go from this to whatever Baronial turns her into would be classed as a satisfying watch. And from experience, I would give it a month for the change to play out, maybe even one disturbed client.

"Hear me out-hear me out. You said every country in the world and my mind just flew to the word slag." She explains how she reached the word, but it is something I had already known.

God, it wasn't that hard to connect the dots. What kind of idiot does she think I am?

I can't make her feel too embarrassed or be someone who's not compatible enough to be her friend, so I pretend to be offended in a way where she knows that I'm really not. "Are you calling my mum a sla—"

Her phone lights up on the side and I couldn't finish delivering my humorous line because she wasted no time in answering it.

Medisa begins to pace as she speaks to whoever's on the other side of the line whilst I struggle to get past the fact that she didn't even say '*do you mind if I take this?*' or '*I'll answer that later.*' Which means that whatever I'm doing isn't working. She isn't swooning over me like they usually do.

I stalk her with my eyes and try to put my good ears to use. The caller cannot be heard but Medisa's thirst can. It doesn't take a genius to realise she is being offered a job and since I've already been briefed, I know that it's someone from Baronial. She says her thanks several times, too many times than needed then hangs up. By the time she turns to me, I'm already stood in front of her, eager to know what's on her mind now.

"Is everything okay?"

'*Shit.*'

A watered-down version of Mavericks accent came through. Hopefully she didn't realise.

"I got the job." She's in disbelief, her voice almost muted. Angling her head up to me she searches my eyes before speaking again. "I got the job." She repeats louder. "*I* actually got the job." Moving past me, too stunned to stand in one place, she holds her finger down on her screen to send Amana a voice note. "They want me to come in to sign a few things but scream for me baby 'cos I got the job!"

I try not to hold a '*get me out of here*' expression as she begins to literally extend the word 'whoop' several times down her phone. The only thing that does help me bring about a smile and proud face is the fact that I find her pleasure in getting the job at Baronial comedic. If only I was able to let things play out and witness her face when she finds out what her job requires.

"Whooping instead of screams. Interesting."

She stops walking back and forth then stretches her neck up to view me, defining her jawline more than her usual stance does. "Is it?"

A rhetorical question.

"*Sorry*, sorry, that came out rude." Though I have not moved one inch she holds her hands out in front of her as if to keep a distance between us. "Er, yeah, fun fact, for some reason I can't scream. Don't think my vocal cords are strong enough or something." She awkwardly rushes through an explanation, her mind still on the way she addressed my statement.

She's kidding? She doesn't know how to scream? She's the perfect person to play with *if* I were Maverick. Finding out what gets her there would be the perfect game too. I scan over her closer than usual, trying to figure out what her tipping point would be, then realise I've left too large a gap and must be making her uncomfortable.

'*Ah, what does she like? What does she like?... Innuendoes.*'

I adjust my weight between my elbows as I lean back on the bench, preparing myself to sell the words as ones I like, rather than words that are being forced out of my mouth to please her low standards. "Bet I know a few things that would make you scream."

Out of the many things I have done and said in my life, this is the one that has repulsed me the most.

She turns her head towards me with impressive speed, disgust plastered all over and I can't help but smile. Maybe her standards aren't as low as I originally suspected?

"How original. What, are you ten?" She sizes me up, no admiration behind her pretty brown eyes.

Playing on my theory, I lick my lip inside before I give her some sort of smirk. At first, she continued to give me nothing but disgust, but then she began to observe me more than I have done of her. After what I assume is her being done with making a judgement on my physical appearance, she comes back to looking me in the eyes. The top half of her face continues to show disgust whilst the lower half gives in to a smile.

"Astaghfirullah." She says through a quiet scoff as she scoots away, shaking her head.

Usually I would approach the girl or I would reach out and pull her closer than she was before she had moved away. But none of those would work on this one, and on top of that she's a Muslim, granted she could be on her knees for multiple reasons but it's best to assume that she's a devout one. *Without* a head covering.

'Not exactly a good example of faith yourself.'

"I was thinking of things like spiders and clowns, what were you thinking of?" I purposefully slow down my blinks as I deliver a confused but curious tone. My lips slowly stretch into a mischievous smile as I notice her picking up on what I'm doing.

"Oh, you know, slowly torturing me and then eventually ripping my heart out." She springs back into action as though she remembered there's a conversation that she is a part of. And her ideas aren't exactly far off what I usually would be doing, which does cause a split second of intense staring into her eyes to see if she knows more than I thought. "What else would I be thinking of?" She mimics my tone of voice then slowly flutters her lashes, hitting me back with a waggish smile as now I have to be the one answering.

'Touché.'

It couldn't be more obvious. I was not impressing her. Pushing forward with anymore jokes like that and I would be leaving with nothing and this whole thing would be a waste of time. If I allow things to continue like this, I may as well kiss this chance of forgiveness goodbye.

I angle my head up as a chuckle escapes in the form of a sigh. "How am I doing?" My face shows her for the first time in this interaction how disgusted I am by my own actions.

"You got points for matching my energy, points for the sarcasm, points for being somewhat interesting and then you lost some for the first sexual comment and then trying to be smart about it."

'You got points for matching my energy, points for—' I stop mocking her in my head as I realise, I actually like the way she's summarised our interaction without giving me a headache.

"Amana had said you liked innuendoes and such."

Once again, she dramatically turns to face me, I guess blaming her friend—her *only* friend—isn't the way to go.

"I do like innuendoes and…such."

Her consistency in copying my words, mannerisms even, are a constant reminder of Kassian. I may as well slap a wig and contacts on her and call it a day.

"Too early then?" My eyes and brows slightly scrunch together.

"*Way* too early for the kind you went for."

"Apologies. I'll wait a bit for the next one." I joke but it gets nothing but a horrible sympathy smile and a few slow nods. Her lips can't be seen anymore, as though they're holding in more of her words, and her gaze is no longer on me.

Not to have a stick up my arse but *why* is she not swooning over me? Usually people can't take their eyes off me or they say anything to keep a conversation going, but she hasn't dropped her 'act' of wanting to be done with me as soon as possible. And now I have to be the one who starts a conversation, *again*.

"So, what lucky place gets to have a special character like you?" She seems to like honesty, ironic really but I'm just going to have to play on it and right now, though I know the answer, I am curious to know how she replies.

"Baronial?" Her response is more like a question than a solid answer, like she's asking me if I've heard of it. "Don't ask me what they do because honestly I have no idea, I just need the money and they offered plenty."

Telling the truth seems to be something that comes easy to her. Others would not be so open with a stranger. Maybe it's because she assumes this would be her only interaction with me?

Her eyes travel over me and before she regrets her decision on telling me anything at all, I intervene before they do another round. "If good money is what you need, I can get you a job at my workplace. You'll be more comfortable and there's a lot of benefits that come with it."

"Say a benefit." She boredly shoots back, not giving me time to think about what I just said.

"Me. You'll get to see and spend time with me." Although I say this as a joke, I do mean it. No one but Kassian and Bellamy gets to spend time with me and I happen to be someone who's learnt a lot of lessons, so why wouldn't someone want to learn from me?

She scoffs almost perfectly in time with the start of a few drops of rain.

"This better not be some sort of pathetic fallacy, my life is already shit thanks." After sluggishly pointing up at the rain, she lazily salutes with two fingers then turns and takes a step away from me, no doubt thanking the timing of the rain so that she doesn't have to respond to my proposition now.

Without thinking, I grab onto her forearm as I take a large step towards her, then turn her back around to face me. The distance being closed between us does not help her. Her height and build puts her at a disadvantage and though my grip on her isn't too heavy, she cannot escape it. Before she begins to panic or use our belongings and the rain as an excuse, I move away to hide them under the bench. And to my surprise, she stays still. I thought that she would put up more of a fight, Amana certainly would, but she just looks confused.

The droplets become more intense as I make my way back to her. Though it's just the beginning, Act 1 with Medisa has already gone on for long enough and I am starting to give in to my impatience.

"We're not leaving until you take the job!" If only I'd approached Amana the same way, someone like her would've sensed something was off and would run away, changing the course of what has already played out.

"You're *crazy*!" She has a punch packed in the word. "Did Amana put you up to this?!" Her question and how she seems to be close to the truth makes me laugh as I block her path with my body.

"Oh, you have no idea!" The words escape amongst the laughter, then all of a sudden, I stop. I look over her once more deciding if I really wanted to do this. This girl's my golden ticket back to Kassian and yet a part of me is actually thinking this over. So, instead of pushing her further, I put her fate in her own hands because God knows that I can keep us here for as long as it takes. "You taking the job or not?"

She squints because of the rain, her dry hair now being soaked waves. Her eyes flutter between mine, her mouth slowly opening as she thinks of her answer.

Just as I suspect she would finally talk, a voice shouts across the Gardens, "What the heck are you guys doing!" Amana stands by the door. Her hands act as an umbrella for her face and she has one leg warm inside whilst the other holds the door open for us to get in.

After viewing Amana for herself, Medisa twists the top half of her body back towards me, her long hair swings as it follows the direction she chose to look. "*Fine!*" She yells like she's being forced to agree. "I'll take the job." Her words lose the attitude whilst she looks defeated, maybe even desperate instead of her other stubborn look.

She was so close to not being involved with me, so close. It only took one appearance from Amana and that was it, she's sealed her fate. There's no need for me to say more and there is no need for us to still be outside in the rain. So, using our belongings as an escape, I grip onto them and head towards the door Amana still holds open.

As I approach and walk past her, she has this expression on as though she were waiting for me to make one wrong move. She didn't need to say anything, her face alone delivered the threat. Subtly of course, no doubt to hide any suspicions arising from Medisa, but I saw it, loud and clear and whether I meant it or not, I gave one back. One that read '*this is on you.*' I will play the part that she wants me to play but I will not be responsible if anything were to happen to Medisa.

Leading the girls to the library was as comical as it could get. They may not be using their voices but they may as well be. Each turn against a reflective surface gave away snippets of their facial conversation. They are obviously what people call '*two peas in a pod.*'

If it weren't for the development of my relationship with Bellamy, I would question Amana's sanity. Why choose to waste energy on someone who is not blood? I could end this right now. Spare myself my own time and energy by turning around and exposing Medisa to her friends double life and what was to become of her own if she were to choose Baronial instead of Aros, but, where's the fun in that? Also, if Bellamy were to find out about how I've discarded the broken compass he's been working on, he would leave, and he's the face of Aros.

'For now.'

Getting comfortable on the leather seat as the girls walked in reminded me of a scenario I've been in one too many times. I snap out of the moments in Baronial as soon as Medisa sits next to me and Amana takes a seat opposite us.

Amana's eyes jump between me and Medisa more times than I care to count. She waits for either one of us to say something as though our relationship's been a catalyst and we've grown so close, finding we have much in common— No.

"I'm going to go get you guys some tissues, hot chocolate and maybe some food?" She gets ready to leave when she's finally lost hope in us starting a conversation.

"Take my card." If she's going to use me, she may as well do it properly.

Without even a courtesy sigh, or verbal decline she practically runs away.

I guess I could dig through the information I keep of her from Baronial, bank details should be included.

Her little bipolar friend has surprisingly been too quiet. What thought is she deciding to act on now? I look down to my side, surprised I did not notice her shivering beside me. How far am I supposed to extend this act of kindness? Am I supposed to tie her shoelaces too? Button her shirts and zip up her jackets? More and more I realise why Amana is trying to protect her, she can't even look after herself when her life *isn't* being pushed in all sorts of directions. People like Medisa fall into holes even when they are looking at what's in front of them. She's not worth the time or effort.

'But Kassian would do this, he would help her.'

Before, it felt as though I were only humouring Amana, but now I feel more of the need to fix how Amana sees my brother. I guess I could be the one who teaches Medisa where to step, and how to get out of a hole. Having Medisa under me, of being—dare I say it—a pupil, an apprentice who would learn and gain experience through me doesn't sound too bad.

"You don't have to be so tense you know? You can allow yourself to shake. It's not every day sit like a model." Even whilst we sit, she needs to look up to me.

Involuntarily, my eyes roll until I view Amanas seat. Her friend will end up getting ill and dying before I get to redeem myself or Kassian. The windows are closed but the room is cold, meaning the radiators are either off or not working. It's unlikely that she carries around spare clothes and today happens to be a day I have not bought any (a habit that's close to being lost).

There are students plotted here and there across the library, she can take some of their clothes and sit closer to me until she heats up.

"Yeah no, you don't get to do that. If I can't have conversations in my head neither can you."

I look down at her again like she's someone who has a habit of talking when their voice doesn't want to be heard by other people. Coincidently, not wanting to hear other people happens to be a 24-hour thing for me.

"You need to take your clothes off and be given heat. Since we don't have towels or blankets and the radiators not working, you need body heat."

I'm no idiot, I know that she wouldn't agree to pushing up her somewhat naked body against me. But how funny would it be to watch Amana's face change as she spots the sight of us?

"Er?" She extends the word as she—I assume, no I guarantee—struggles to form full sentences in her mind. Must be a frequent struggle if you ask me. "You're still taking the jokes a bit too far."

"I'm not joking." I'm about to explain the rest of what I was going to say but she cuts me off.

"Oh, then I suppose you would prefer it to be your body heat, no? We're not living in the bloody ice ages. Coming at me with some sort of medieval method of survival." She moves to a chair next to Amana's.

I try to hold in my laugh, but a small sound still escapes, reminding me of my past with Kassian. When Nene and Dede—may he rest in peace—would visit, I would convince Kassian to drink until he couldn't stand because Maverick couldn't punish us whilst they were with us. The sounds of squashed giggles and hiccups were the best even when we were punished after they had left. I don't think Medisa heard it, which works out in my favour, but she does notice my face, pushing me to take things a little further.

"Ice ages and medieval methods huh? Your history teacher needs to be re-evaluated."

"Ugh. What a piss-take. You know what I meant."

I do know what she meant, but seeing her get riled up is something I have found to be amusing.

She gives me a facial expression that would translate to a hundred different curses, her pretty brown eyes overshadowed by her brows before she finally looks away in frustration towards the window.

"I don't know what you mea—" I stop myself as she continues to look away even while I try to make another joke. I don't outwardly sigh, but I do feel an intense need to. Bullying her for the next few months shouldn't be how I make time go by faster. "I wasn't trying to offend you. I was trying to help you. I was going to keep it to myself but you wanted to know—"

"So, you decided not to lie and gave me what I wanted?"

There she goes again cutting me off. She's not even aware of how lucky she is to even be able to get away with it, making my poor attempt of an apology much more difficult.

"I do enjoy giving females what they desperately want." I go back to saying things she would not want to hear. If I can't take things out on her the old way, I can do it through a new one. Yes, it's true, I do love the hold I have over women. I love watching them crumble from the overpowering sensations they feel when I say or do the simplest actions. Watching them come back and beg for more, ridding self-control and respect for themselves and others is some of the many things I love. And now, insinuating that Medisa is one of them, will be one of the many ways I touch her nerves without taking things too far.

She scrunches her brows, no doubt unamused and ready to pounce. "I wasn't desperate you bastard."

"No, but you do deserve the truth." I reply almost instantly, swapping the smug look for something more intense. If this doesn't spark her curiosity and lead her to what is being hidden from her, then I don't know what will.

Reminding myself of what I could lose to Medisa finding out, I pace my breaths in a way she would not notice. If I don't get a grip, I will end up spoiling this for everyone.

"You're so weird." She shakes her head and body as she speaks as though she were getting rid of the feeling.

All this talk and she still hasn't done anything about being cold and wet.

"At least take your socks and shoes off, you could get seriously ill."

"What about you? Why aren't you taking things off?"

'She has a point.'

I stand and strip the top half of my body. If I have to sit here semi-naked to get her to change then so be it, I don't personally know anyone here and I'm already successful.

"Okay, okay! I don't need to see all that."

I stop removing clothes and walk out the room, already spotting whose clothes I'm going to take. His hoodie is placed behind him, I could easily snatch it up as I walk past. He wouldn't notice it's absence unless he sees her wearing it. Even then, if things were to get rowdy, I could knock him out cold blindfolded.

"For your hoodie." I hold out two folded fifty-pound notes between two fingers.

"Shit, I would've gave it for fifty." He hands over the hoodie, all his teeth showing.

I prematurely stop a chuckle. "And I was going to steal

it." I grin as his face drops before striding back towards the room.

Medisa puts her phone down as soon as I walk in.

Placing my wallet back into my pocket, I hold out the hoodie towards her. She politely declines like the little brat she is and it takes everything in me to not put it on her myself.

I go back to stripping the top half of my body whilst Medisa's eyes look everywhere else. Hers were obviously trying to find a distraction, unlike the eyes back at Baronial that wouldn't dare look at me out of fear. The sound of a zip being done up was some sort of signal for her, giving her the 'OK' to look in my direction.

Taking out a pair of fresh socks from my bag, I hold them out to her, but she continues to decline my offerings.

"So, let's just say I get the job at your workplace—"

"You will." I almost roll my eyes and hold them in place.

"O-kay then. *When* I get the job at your workplace, you can't be touching me the way you did in the Garden. It's haram."

"I'm sorry, I forgot you're a Muslim."

She pulls her brows together again, not as close or aggressive as before, but enough for me to know I've said something I shouldn't have. I may as well just tell her that her friend gave me a quick rundown earlier today.

"It's okay. The next time you go to touch me just remember that you're not my husband, so you don't have them privileges, but, if we're ever in a serious situation feel free to get me the eff out."

I cut a laugh too short. "Is saying '*eff*' you trying to be a good Muslim?"

"Yeah. Well, a better one than before."

"Right, because God doesn't know that means 'fuck.'" I

realise too late that I'm attacking her for no reason.

Her facial expression turns from a thoughtful one to one that read '*what the eff is your problem?*' and in attempts to fix the tone I just set, I speak out before she thinks low of me. "But He does know that you're trying."

"He knows I'm trying." Medisa says at the same time.

I shouldn't get too involved with conversations like this. I do not pray to God unless Nene and Dede treated us with their company, they are the ones who say a few prayers and try to spread His teachings. I did try to participate, I said '*Amen*' but even that felt like a chore. The last memory I have of actually being excited and taking part in whatever religious act it was, was when Mum was still alive. And even then, I hate it. How shitty is it that I remember more of that, than I do of her actual face or her voice? Sometimes I dream about them and in the dream, I *know* that it's them, but when I wake up and try to draw their faces, their features become a blur.

Another thing I have Maverick to thank for.

"I'm sorry for calling you a bastard." Medisa apologises out of the blue.

"And I'm sorry for offending you... multiple times."

She finally abandons her go-to facial expression of scrunching her brows together, and smiles after what seems like forever.

"I'm Medisa by the way." She leans back in her chair.

"Hello Medisa." My smile is genuine. We're finally getting somewhere.

Just as she were about to say something, Amana walks in wearing tissue rolls on her sleeves with a bag of hot food in one hand and hot chocolate in the other. The smells mix together as they travel the room and I must admit, I am hungry.

Holding myself back from getting the food out myself, I

notice Amana searching my body, then slowly take her seat beside Medisa.

"What happened?" She looks between me and Medisa and I finally understand why she is delaying the food and drinks from entering any of our systems. "Don't think I would hesitate in chopping your fingers off." She looks to me with burning eyes as she says this and though it's not directed towards her, Medisa pulls her hands away from opening the bags. "Did you touch her?"

I can see how other boys would be intimidated by Amana. I know myself that I haven't acted too out of line, but if I were not myself, I would probably start to question whether or not I actually touched her friend.

"I didn't want to get Gunnah so I just moved away from him." Medisa speaks before I do. "Gunnah meaning sinned." She addresses me before looking back to Amana, giving her a smile that did not compliment any of her features. I suppose it's her 'puppy' face because after that Amana got comfortable and began handing out what she had bought for us.

Despite Medisa's save, Amana continued to try and burn a hole into my face. I took it as a sign to start a new conversation. Something normal people would talk about.

"I know that Amana's from Pakistan, but where are you from?"

"Pakistan." They answer in sync.

It's been a while since a River has married someone from there, I try to follow the tree back to when that might have been but I give up as soon as it hits grandparents and the number of kids they had. Also, my knowledge in our tree isn't too great.

"Pakistan's quite diverse huh." I try to carry the conversation since they both went silent after responding.

"Aren't all countries?" Medisa presses her lips together, forming a thin line, then, like an owl, she tilts her head to the side, questioning my intelligence.

"I suppose most are." It's true most countries have different tribes, villages, cities, states where certain features are more prominent. But these two, they must be from polar ends of Pakistan and yet they've managed to be like-minded.

Medisa goes quiet and I could tell that she's gone somewhere in her head. I doubt she would even notice the lack of conversation between me and Amana which means she would hardly be paying attention to a conversation we would be having.

"How's work?" I ask.

Amana's eyes widen as she stops chewing. She makes a quick glance at Medisa then looks to me. "It's okay."

"You saw Mr. Avery today huh? I know because he requests that those who visit him wear that shade of lipstick you wore earlier." I whisper the lipstick part as I lean over to retrieve some tissue. "Has he been giving you any trouble? I can deal with him if he has."

Picking up Medisa's wet tissue she positions her arm back then launches it at me. I understand why she may be feeling some resentment towards me, but I *am* trying and I'm not used to people taking advantage of me like this. So, I pick up my own wet tissues and launch one at her. After this, I somehow trigger her further, earning more tissues being thrown my way. In the midst of this, Medisa wakes up from her thoughts and joins in, tag-teaming with Amana.

"Wait, think of the cleaners!" I pull the sympathy card.

"Cleaners?" They speak in sync again, then look to each other as if they couldn't believe what they were hearing.

"*Think of the cleaners.*" Amana mocks, pairing her annoying voice with a repulsed expression.

"Kade we're going to clean this up ourselves." Medisa shakes her head as she looks at the tissues surrounding us.

Both her and Amana start to clear away, their actions pushing me to take over and help. I could tell that Amana would use this activity to push me away so that she could have some alone time with Medisa so, I beat her to it.

"Amana, could you put this in the bin please?" I hand over a bunch of wet tissues and she takes them without fuss.

Turning to Medisa who was busy picking at the bits of wet tissue stuck on her wet clothes, I decide now is the right time to try again. "Medisa put my jacket on, it was covered from the rain so it's not too wet."

Her head almost drops back.

"There's no point in wearing something dry on top of something wet." She speaks to me like I'm an idiot as she continues to be stubborn.

"I'm not *telling* you to wear it with that wet top, I'm telling you to—" use your brain and "—take your top off and wear it." My tone is stricter, like I'm speaking to a child, but it's better than the other options.

Sighing, she looks to the side where our things are placed. "You got issues." She says as she finally moves to pick up my jacket.

Amana comes back ready to sit down but stays standing as she notices Medisa heading out.

"Where you going?"

"To wear this ugly jacket." She holds up one of my favourite pieces to Amana, who follows her out the door and towards the ladies room.

After giving them no choice in how they were getting home, we finally get to my car at 23:15.

Medisa strangely calls shotgun for the back seat instead of the front, pushing Amana to sit in the passenger seat. And Amana didn't seem to mind, in fact after our conversations in the library she seems to have loosened up. It's because Medisa is with us, but regardless, I can see more of why Kassian liked her.

"So Medisa, you'll be a scout at Aros." I almost immediately feel Amana's large eyes on me. "You just need to find people for us to invest in, of course there would be more to your job, but we need to see how you are with this task and then more will be given. You'll be paid £2500 at first, with commission."

I purposely spew out a number that would grab Amana's attention. If she could see how easy it is for me to provide for Medisa, maybe she will give in and accept my offer. But she provides no reaction, not even a hint of jealousy.

Maybe I should up the number?

I turn onto a road that would allow the girls to see more of London before we get to the boring tunnels and highway. Looking into the mirror I notice Medisa's face, she's definitely having another conversation in her head.

When I get to a red light, I look at her through the mirror again. This time she has on a dumb smile, like she couldn't believe what's happening. Her smiles then turn into giggles, grabbing Amana's attention. Surprisingly, her reaction to her friend mirrors mine, which in some way does not help.

"You know, you look at me like that a lot you know, which is weird because if anything I should be looking at you like that. I literally just met you today, the girls think that you're some sort of mafia man and now you're here with your fancy little car and accessories telling me that you got me a job with high pay *and* it's more convenient for me. Well shit, I might just start believing the rumours." Medisa talks to me through our reflection.

This girl really is something.

I haven't seen her take anything, so this is how she is sober. And about the rumours, there's been many things spread about me and that's the one she chose to mention?

Once she is done with her little monologue, Amana lets out a cackle and I realise I'm actually entertained.

"Little?" It's never been a word to describe me, not even to say I am Maverick's younger brother. "That's not a word I would use to describe myself. And I *know* you've heard rumours that nothing about me is '*little*.'" I stare at Medisa through the centre mirror, expecting her to say more, but she stays silent.

She must be tapping the floor or something, because other than the noise from outside there are these strange rustling, fidgety noises.

"I'm not in the mafia." I say more seriously when no response is given.

Her eyes hold no amusement as she lazily hangs her head to one side. "Let a girl dream."

Medisa's unconscious body drops her head down.

"She's going to wake up with a sore neck." I try to make conversation with Amana.

When Medisa was awake, Amana's act did not feel fake. It was as though I were experiencing her as anyone else would, but now, with Medisa asleep, she no longer needed to entertain, so she kept to herself.

"Maybe next time have a jacket *and* a pillow ready for her?" She turns around to pick up Medisa's head, placing it back onto the headrest.

I ignore her comment and ask her what has been on my mind. "You two are close, there's no doubt about it. So why is it you haven't told her about Baronial?"

"What good would that do? She has no power against people like that. If anything it would just put her in danger. If she'd known, she would've acted out, maybe even treat me differently, like I'm something that's fragile. And I didn't need that, I just needed to be treated the way she has always treated me—turn here."

I turn into the road as directed causing Medisa's head to hit the window for the fifth time. I hold in my laugh as I park up and could see Amana doing the same, then out of nowhere Medisa gasps, before falling back to sleep.

The ends of my lips are pulled and are kept that way, it's been a while since I've grinned this hard. Amana is in shock but also holds back a laugh with her hand. After a few seconds of not being able to take it, I let out my suppressed laugh—quiet enough for Medisa to not be disturbed, but loud enough for me to let it all out—waiting for Amana to do the same.

She does not.

She continues to hold back her laugh and fails to keep a serious face.

When I quieten down, Amana takes one good look at Medisa then looks towards me. "Don't mess this up." And with that, she opens the car door and leaves, trusting me to be alone with her other half.

'Idiot.'

Chapter 26
Kade
05/10/2021 (Tuesday)

"No."

"I've already hired her."

"No."

"She starts Tuesday."

"I said no."

"Yet you haven't said why?"

Bellamy stops punching the bag so I stop holding it in place and begin to punch it myself.

"Have you considered it being a trap? If not from Amana herself then from your brother?" He holds the bag in place.

"You think a girl would be able to take me down?" I laugh as I punch the bag a few more times.

"This girl, Medisa. Even if she's not against you, she'll bring attention towards us. Someone may check to see why she turned them down when she was so eager."

"Yeah so?" I punch the bag some more, being not as worried as Bellamy as I've already assessed any risks and have come up with multiple solutions.

He huffs then moves back to his previous worry. "I'm not an idiot Kade, I know that you want to see your brother. But Medisa is a risk I'm not sure I'm willing to let you take. He and Amana could be honey trapping you."

Now I blow a dry raspberry.

"Relax *dad*. I've already been told I'm not to touch her or spend too much time with her. I just need to distract her for a few months and pay her well. Besides, I'm not much of a pillow-talker anyway."

Bellamy sighs. "If I suspect her of anything, she's gone."

"As much as I am touched by your sheer protection, inspecting her will be difficult when you'll be acting as the CEO and I, her colleague."

"There was no need for you to lie about Aros."

"Yeah well, the truth would just come with more questions and perhaps even curiosity. Like how her friend knows someone so powerful and is only now deciding to use him." This fake position would also allow me to spend as much time as I can with her.

Bellamy thinks things over. He's not on board but there's not much that he can do to stop this, so he's trying to figure a way out to at least put his own mind at ease.

"We're swapping offices as well." I add. "Getting close to her gives me and Amana a reason to talk to each other. Eventually she'll give in to her biology and forgive 'Kassian.'" And yes, maybe Kassian would forgive me too. He'll see that after all this time, I tried to make things better.

"Did you at least sort out the situation with James?"

I stop punching the bag and let out my own sigh. "Shit. I got distracted and let the bastard escape. Maverick's probably been told I approached him by now." I've never been distracted before, but to be honest, I'm not too scared of the damage my mistake will do.

Bellamy rids his hands of the wrap, readying himself to leave and sort the situation out himself, but before he leaves me completely alone, he stops at the door.

"There's nothing else I need to know about?" His eyes tense a little as though he could sense that I'm keeping information back.

"No. That's pretty much it."

"You weren't triggered?"

"No. I must be cured." I cheekily smile then go back to punching the bag before he feels the need to inquire.

Chapter 27
Kade
12/10/2021 (Tuesday)

I examine her office.

We had to clear out a room we used to store a few things but now it looks like someone with no personality decorated it. There's a desk, a mini library, a chair for whenever she has a guest—preferably Amana, and a few plants to keep her happy.

Bellamy's gone to pick her up from the station. He wants to see how she is when she's not with me, see if he could spot something I didn't. Prior to this arrangement, we went back and forth on whether or not I should've accepted Amana's request of occupying her friend. I thought that we had moved past it from when I first mentioned hiring Medisa, but Bellamy went and done his own research only to find nothing on her. She has no social media presence or any type of bread crumb trail that we could follow. If I hadn't met the girl, I would agree that it was strange, but there wasn't enough hours in these last six days for me to translate that to Bellamy. Eventually, we met in the middle and agreed that Medisa has one week. If within the week we suspect her of anything, we'll shut it down, if not, she can stay and reap the benefits I'll provide. Bellamy is determined to figure out what her deal is in the few minutes that he will be spending with her this week. Apparently, he only believes one sob story in his life—mine.

Just as I'm about to move, the elevator doors open, revealing a glossy Medisa and an already-sick-of-it Bellamy. I was readying myself to put on an act but with this sight, I get all the help I need. Both mine and Medisa's faces mirror each other, the biggest smiles grow until she comes to some sort of realisation and drops hers.

"Kade, answer any of her questions, show her some examples of what we want, inform her on what's in the area and give her a tour of the floor."

"Yes sir." My lips lift from the side hidden from Medisa's view. Bellamy does not find this as amusing as me, but that can easily be seen as him being the grumpy, stressed boss.

Once the doors shut, I look to my side at the girl who's already trying to keep it together.

"C'mon, let me show you around."

"Wait. Take this." She holds out the jacket I had given her the day we met.

"You can keep it." I've been watching movies where the main genre is romance these past few days, and I'm pretty sure this is a move one of those male characters pull.

"Just take it."

"You don't want it?"

"No, I have a lot of jackets."

"Don't you want one of mine?"

Her shoulders slightly drop at the same time her eyelids do. She looks half asleep until she rolls her eyes, giving her that possessed look.

"Fine. I'll hold it for you." I take it and begin the tour before she walks out of here.

We go to the washroom first. There was no need in renovating it as Bellamy and I had done a fine job at it when we'd first done everything. The next place was another room we had cleared out for her. Amana had said that Medisa's trying to be more connected with their religion, and what better way for me to get on her good side than giving her a room for her to pray in.

Taking things a step further, I took time out of my days to research some of the basic rulings to avoid digging myself a hole. I also wanted to nail the pronuncations of words to One: avoid sounding like a fool and Two: to get on her good side. However, to my disappointment, she barely acknowledges it.

The rest of the tour is not what I had expected. She's quieter than the Gardens, less expressive and doesn't seem to have the need to comment on anything. At first, I thought that it was me, so I dropped the seriousness I have towards Aros, but she still stayed somewhat mute. This is when I found myself wanting the Gardens Medisa back.

I summarise what Aros is, which did get some sort of approval from her, I assume it's the whole '*oh they actually help people*' side of it, but then she goes back to whatever her thoughts busy her with.

"I'm sure you realised downstairs—" I highly doubt it. "—But the elevator is something that can only be accessed by me and Bellamy, and now you. So don't go around telling people the access code." I thought this would get her going, but I am wrong. She really is in no mood to talk, just a few nods and expressions. Which makes me wonder, is this how the brat is on a normal day?

As we walk towards the offices, I begin to think that Bellamy has said something to her. That has to be the reason for her muteness and sweating. I chew the inside of my mouth, if what I do fails, Gardens Medisa won't make an appearance for a while.

"*Damn* Medisa, what do you eat?" I swat the air in front

of me, squinting as though the smells she produced effected my eyes.

Her mouth drops as she struggles to find the words, then she finally lets out a proper giggle, unlike the polite ones she was giving before.

"Leave me alone." Her giggles transition into a fake cry.

I gesture for her to follow me into Bellamy's office. Inside, she overtakes me and walks towards the window as though she's never seen buildings before. And just as she's about to get too occupied with the view, I clear my throat.

Turning around, ready with an attitude, she sees what I want her to and drops her planned intentions. Her look of obviously being in some sort of trance takes over, making me hold onto an eyeroll. If she keeps this up, we will barely share five conversations between us these next few months.

There's not much to look at so I don't know what's with the marvelling, it's just Bellamy's cologne collection, laid out onto a platform as though they were drinks. Some people collect trophies and medals, others stamps, but Bellamy, he collects limited edition cologne.

"You might as well try them all to see which one covers up the stank." My eyes flicker between the collection and Medisa's face as I squeeze onto my nose, blocking any of her fumes from entering whilst simultaneously offering a nasally voice.

"That's it." She mutters with annoyance. As soon as she picks up each and every one of them, trying them all with at least three-to-four puffs each, sometimes picking up the same bottle twice, I knew that this was what would make Bellamy be okay with becoming a murderer.

Watching her try as many as she can, like she had a time limit is funny, but watching her slowly realise that I'm not reacting the way she had suspected—as well as imagining her reaction to the cologne belonging to Bellamy, her 'boss'—has me laughing hysterically to the point where I actually feel as though I need some sort of support to stand.

Just as I think that this couldn't get any more entertaining, Bellamy enters as soon as Medisa slows down from the lack of explosive reaction.

I continue to laugh.

His face is much better than what I had pictured, and Medisa transforming like the gremlin she is does not help the situation either.

Bellamy's face continues to stay frozen like he's walked in on me spilling Medisa's guts. Obviously, my lack of composure is a sick playlist to what he witnessed and now he—and Medisa—are waiting for me to stop.

I try to stifle my laugh as his eyes look between his collection, Medisa and me—who should have known better.

"A word Kade." Bellamy speaks through his teeth, refusing to break eye contact with her. I'm sure his eye just twitched as well.

Poor girl, I didn't even face a smidge of his wrath this early on.

Medisa, being part-cartoon, leaves as fast as she can, but not without tripping and knocking over more of his beloved items. She noticeably panics some more as she moves even faster, and instead of a straight walk into her office, she walks straight into the glass door frame, leaving a stain with the continuance noise of things still toppling over.

I can't help but snicker, a snort might have even escaped.

Bellamy stood like he was frozen in frame, his eyes forced shut, occasionally twitching when things continued to fall over. When he sensed that Medisa had reached her desk, he turns to me, noticeably pissed. Bright side, she doesn't stink anymore which is something that I know he can't stand.

"So what d'you think?" I say, my tone too happy for his liking.

"I think it's best I don't say anything at the moment." Bellamy talks through a somewhat clenched jaw.

"Why's that?" I can't help but grin after the fake concern.

His eyes turn to slits but I refuse to drop my smile. If I'm not allowed to express myself the way that I would like, things like this will have to do. He knows that, which is why he's not gone straight to kicking off. That, and Medisa is still here.

After a few seconds of holding his eyes shut, he takes a deep breath.

"Look, I didn't know she would do that. One or two puffs maybe, but not that." I try to have on a sincere naïve face but my smile grows back.

He takes another deep breath then pinches his nose. "If she is someone that is supposed to trap you... I can't tell if she's bad at her job, or too good."

"What do you mean?"

"You haven't noticed how odd she is? How her behaviour switches from animated to nothing, how she rambles but suddenly switches off? She gets nervous but also has this weird confidence about her."

"Those aren't exactly things that I needed to have my full attention on to notice." I respond, but he's right. She could be fooling us into thinking that she is too incompetent for the task Bellamy suspects her of. "But let's not be too rash, we still have the week to figure her out." I speak before he does.

I must admit, a part of why I wanted her to be here is because of her odd behaviour. To me, conversations are like tunes you've already heard. You have an idea of how it would go, unless on a rare occasion someone changes the tempo or adds their own lyrics. Medisa is that rarity, in fact, she changes the melody entirely.

I look into her office and all doubts of her *almost* disappear as I see how she tries to 'discreetly' watch us—her hands are over her face as if she were hiding herself, but her fingers are slightly apart, allowing for her to look through and into my new office. I could barely see her eyes, but I know that she could be looking.

Is she dumb? Or is she just really intelligent?

I walk into her default office with bags of food.

Thanks to Amana, I don't have to use my brain to figure Medisa out. When I have a question, or would like to save time, I ask Amana. The most recent question being something along the lines of what Medisa likes to eat, or what the safest options are, and she replies with '*halal burger meals, noodles, pizza, wraps. Anything with flavour, preferably spicy and with some crunch.*'

"Bellamy is coming down to join us." I warn her as I remember how getting him to agree to this was a task in itself. He's still a little sour from the cologne situation.

Medisa's face struggles to choose a reaction.

"Think of it as tradition." We've never done this before, but she does not need to know that, just like she doesn't need to know that this is a way for her to get on Bellamy's good side. Which is something that may not happen today as her office seems to have absorbed his scents whilst also spewing it out and around us. Her only hope is to pray the smell from the food is strong enough to overpower it.

It is not.

"The food is halal so don't worry about it when you see meat."

She helps me out with the food; taking them out the bag and placing them in front of where each person would be sitting.

Bellamy walks in, trying not so hard in not showing his distaste for this casual gathering. I look to Medisa to see if she's noticed or appears to be uncomfortable but she seems to be allured. Even when he walks over, she does not look away. Then my eyes follow hers and I see her ogling his arms and chest now that he's unbuttoned a few of his top buttons.

I clear my throat.

"So, how's the day been so far? Enjoying it?" I blink unnaturally as Bellamy takes a seat beside me

"It's okay, nothing I can't handle."

Unbelievable. Not only does she give me a bland answer, she doesn't even bother to look in my direction. Her neck seems to have developed some sort of stiffness which is why she continues to look at Bellamy, who I know is in no mood for talking.

"Since when did Kade start working here?"

And now she wants to talk about me, but not to me? I force a couple chips into my mouth to stop myself from being a pest.

Bellamy doesn't know what he's allowed to say or what lie to spew as he's still under the impression that Medisa knows more than she's letting on. He's not convinced that Amana didn't tell her *best friend* her job of five years.

"Since a bit before my nineteenth birthday, isn't that right Bells?" I cut in before he spoke, winking at him to carry on the jokester façade as I stuff my face some more.

"Isn't that right Bells?" Medisa mocks, her expression exuding disgust before her hand slowly lowers the chips from her mouth as she realises we heard her.

Once again, I am both amused and disrespected. I could punish her by staying quiet, let her drown in embarrassment from how awkward things would be but, this is also a good moment to get on her good side.

"Isn't that right Bells?" I mock the voice she had put on, distorting the words even further.

Medisa, of course, does not see this as me saving her, she sees it as disrespect, so she continues, distorting the question even more, so much so that she creates more sounds than words. But before she's able to complete the sentence, she clears her throat. I follow her eye line to see that she is once again looking at Bellamy. And if he didn't wish to not know me before, he certainly does now.

Before things are addressed, Medisa stirs the conversation away. "I'm sorry if this question is rude but, do you come from money? It seems like it would take a lot to start Aros, or at least get it to where it is right now."

I pull my lips in. Not three seconds pass before a smile comes through. I look to Bellamy, *waiting* to hear what he comes up with.

"I inherited some money and put it towards investments. Then I met Kade who helped create Aros and then stayed to see it grow, he had the idea to have multiple divisions and—"

"Next question." I cut in. He was giving away too much truth, no doubt payback for one of the things that has happened today. I'm all for babysitting this girl, but I'm not for telling her too much, if anything at all. "Medisa, what are your plans after graduating?"

Maybe it's because of my tone switching, maybe it's because she is thinking of her answer, but it goes quiet. She chews on a few chips, a good method to delay and allow her to think of an answer.

"Put it this way." She pauses again. "Aros's success was due to its multiple divisions, right?"

I nod, my lips pulled in, almost to say '*well done Junior.*'

"Well, like Aros I don't think that I'm going to get far if I stick to one thing. I want to have multiple things happening at once. My problem is that I don't know which one to start with, and my problem used to be being able to fund it, but now, hopefully I get to stay here a while longer while I figure things out and save money up." She looks to Bellamy with a look that would have most people wrapped around her finger.

'Oh, she's good.'

Bellamy excuses himself, and I know for a fact that he's thinking what I'm thinking.

Medisa looks towards me with concern in her eyes.

"He's just having a bad day. You'll be able to read him soon enough to know that he actually likes you."

Her shoulders drop a little, she is not fully convinced, but it's enough.

"Come, let's go get some fresh air." I stand and before I could do it myself, she packs the food and gets to the elevator before me.

She begs the elevator to open its doors by pushing the button more times than necessary, if anyone else were here they would assume I held her hostage.

As soon as the doors open, she gets in as I continue to take my time in walking over.

"You're twenty." I say once the doors shut. I could tell the conversation's still on her mind so I give her textbook advice. "You've got time, just focus on yourself and stop looking at how everyone else's life is playing out."

"I know not to look at others progressions but I feel like I've wasted my youth, you know?"

'Somewhat.'

"I had *so* many ideas and goals when I was younger but I kept shutting myself down before I even began—"

"Don't you think looking back at the past, like the way you are, is repeating your mistakes? You're wasting your time, bringing your mood down, what's happened has happened, what are you doing today to change the course of your life for the better?" This conversation was so close to perfectly mimicking a conversation me and Kassian had in the past. He felt guilt for the both of us and almost always let problems outside of his hands get to him. It was stupid. He got himself worked up for no reason.

Medisa does not say anything, her eyes wondered back and forth and instead of being offended by my judgemental tone of voice, she stayed quiet, almost as though she were actually listening to me.

"But one life isn't enough to achieve *all* my goals."

I refrain from face palming.

"It is now that you have me. C'mon, I know a place where you can tell me about your goals, then I'll figure out a way to make them come true." I lead her out the elevator, seriously considering breaking her into telling me the truth of why she is here.

Theories of what her true motive is, is influenced once again when I spot her 'discreetly' sending messages.

Chapter 28
Kade
14/10/2021 (Thursday)

"Do you see how she watches us? I can't decide if it's curiosity, boredom, or her waiting for us to slip up."

Bellamy and I both look into her office, making her panic and do a shit job of pretending to be doing her work. Sometimes she doesn't even bother hiding the fact that she's watching us, but it's difficult to tell if she's zoned out or not.

"We shouldn't personally be looking after her. I'm going to get her a job in Junaid's company. He'll look after her and he's trustworthy enough to give reports and loyal enough to not question us."

"We're not giving her away. She's mine to deal with." I sway on his office chair. "And I'll bear the consequences."

"That's the problem!" He raises his voice, but not enough for Medisa to hear him. "You'll bare the consequences, *you*." He points at me with all fingers.

When I don't respond, he rubs his forehead and sighs.

I understand why he worries. It was him who got me out of addicting habits and dark indulgences and it was not an easy task. But if I've made it this far, surely a test is due? See if I slip back into the old ways? Yes, this may be me wanting this odd situation to provoke me into turning back, but it's also something I can use to prove to everyone who knows me that I've evolved. I'm no longer Maverick's version of a colosseum lion or even a bloody gladiator.

I walk over to Bellamy and place my hand on his shoulder. "You should know by now that I know what I'm doing. I have backup plans if things do go to shit. Now please, go, deal with your side of things with Aros then go home and treat your girl."

His lips part, shocked that I know a girl is staying with him.

"Yes, I know about her. Yes, I know that she's the girl from the club and no I don't have cameras in your house, although if you do want to put together a movie, I don't mind giving feedback."

Watching his face go from being surprised to pure disgust as I made the last statement is how I know I successfully got his mind off Medisa. If his mind is still on her, he's not as worried because I just reminded him of how attentive and prepared I actually am.

"Now if you would excuse me, I'm going to ask Medisa to spend lunch with me."

"Are you Bi?" Medisa spoke out of the blue.

There is nothing that has previously been said that could have allowed her to make this connection or to even ask this question.

I almost choke on my drink. "What?"

"Do you like Bellamy more than a friend? More than a boss? Do you want him to order you around in other rooms other than the office? Do you—"

"Please stop." If I allow her to go on, the images in my head will become vivid and intense. I have to admit it is funny she has these suspicions but it is also very much sickening. He's not blood but he is close to.

I pull a face that would read '*Ew*' in her language.

"Because if you do, then I hope you know that he groomed you. Eighteen or not when you met him, it's still a little fresh from being a child don't you think? I mean, I'm twenty and I still kind of feel like a kid. And I'm a woman, we're supposed to develop before you guys."

'Supposed to.'

I hide away a smile and bite my tongue. She really does ramble and shockingly I do not have the urge to knock her out to make it stop.

She's curious about mine and Bellamy's relationship? No doubt because of the observations she's made.

"He's like the brother I've always needed."

"Damn. I hope I stay here long enough for me to develop that kind of relationship with him. Who knows, he may be sick of having a younger brother and may want a younger—more intelligent sibling...a sister if you will."

I kiss my teeth.

First an overpaid job and her list of requirements and now she wants my relationship with Bellamy. If she's not stopped, she will ask for the world soon.

"He's good thanks, you stay where you are with Amana."

"Who said I can't have both?" She jokes, but it's not a good one.

"Alright stingy." My playful tone of voice momentarily stuns me for a few seconds. I've heard it before. Someone's addressed me in the exact same way, only thing is, it feels more like it was a dream then something that happened when awake.

"Don't be jealous, you could be levelled up to be my best friend if you act right."

"Best friend? What are you five?"

Someone kill me before I am put through the pain of being in any sort of relationship or contact with Medisa after she graduates.

'If she graduates.'

"I take it you don't have any friends?" She squints whilst raising her brows, slightly nodding to coerce me into agreeing.

"I take it you don't have a life?" I say, only because she needs to be someone who can dish it out *and* take it.

Her mouth resembles a small 'o' but then she quickly recovers. "Ugh, you got me. The plan's actually to marry rich, kill him off, and then live off his hard-earned money." Her seriousness is wrapped in sarcasm, but given how both me and Bellamy still can't tell things with her, I can imagine her being able to pull that plan off. "Anyways, we're actually lucky to have someone like them. A lot of people don't, and have to get by, by themselves. We might not be attached by blood, but she's there. Amana's my person."

"Yeah, and Bellamy's mine." So back off.

A part of me is still trying to make sense of this 'memory' that now lingers like it were at the tip of my tongue of who said it.

Before too much time passes, I say more. "I genuinely don't know where I'd be without him." Probably would've made my way back to Maverick after being drunk out of my mind.

"Probably off somewhere being useless and a hassle to someone else." She makes a dig at me with no ill intent.

I scoff and lower my voice. "Understatement of the year."

Looking out into the distance I wonder what Kassian has achieved these past few years. What great things has he done that I had planned for the both of us to experience together?

What has he been doing with his assets?

"Speaking of friendships..." Once again Medisa grabs my attention. She sits weirdly now, clearly hiding something in her hands. "I genuinely hope that we become good friends—"

So this whole conversation on Bellamy, Amana, persons, is just her long-winded way of saying that she wants to become a friend of mine.

'How inane.'

"—I thought you were a little shit before...and I still do." She mumbles the last bit, but not very well.

And I choose to ignore the '*little shit*,'—that's called 'growth,'—and the last time I checked, achievements are rewarded. Now do I want to force Medisa to face her deepest fears, or do I want her to bring Amana in and force her to interact with 'Kassian'?

"But I could tell that you're a good nut." A smile stretches out after she says her interesting set of words.

I dramatically shut my eyes and hold them there, exaggerating the disbelief. And without my say so, a laugh escapes as though I were holding my breath. "You were doing so well until the '*nut*'."

"That's what she said!" She's quick to shoot back, causing me to try and stifle another laugh.

It's not funny, but how fast she is to say it, as though she wanted to get it out before I did, is.

"Anyways I didn't even get to the best part—"

Finally, she takes out what she's been badly hiding: an oddly shaped desk lamp. I can't tell if it were a tree branch design, or rivers, but it brought back any suspicions on her.

"—It's for your desk. I know that you guys stay later than me and like to have minimal lighting, so I thought that this would be a good thank you gift."

A thank you gift?

"You know, for the job? I actually like it here. I was scared of working before and was desperate, but then you helped me out even when you didn't really know me, so thank you… Seriously."

She's giving me a gift for helping her? She's *thanking* me for helping her? Is this a trick? One of the steps leading me into a trap?

"Don't grip it like that! It'll break. I made it a long time ago from cheapish material."

"Thank you." I raise the lamp with no bulb. "But you should really be giving this to Amana."

"I got her a gift too, don't worry. I know what she's done for me." She replies as though her answers have been prepared for her.

'*I know what she's done for me.*' Does she though? Does she know what I've done? She wouldn't be giving me a present if she knew what I had done to her friend, what I could've done to her.

My stinging eyes flicker between her clueless ones. Here I am playing a friend whilst her real one is being booked left, right and centre to be able to make enough money so that the both of them could leave and be comfortable.

This has to be some sort of trick.

She's acting.

She's been acting. There's probably a mic in this 'gift'. I should kill her right now. Kill the both of them for even attempting to make a stand against me. No wonder why Amana was so quick to letting Medisa work with me and not someone else. She's waiting for me to screw up somewhere, waiting for one last push before she does us over. I should do something to Medisa and then her. But then there's Kassian, and his Iris, and Iris and her friend.

For fucks sake.

I need something strong. Something expensive.

Something *now*.

"Lunch is over."

Medisa senses something not being right but by some miracle she does not fight against me. And thank her God for that, as I'm no longer stable enough to handle her, or any form of rebuke.

My mind tries to convince me to update my sins, to go back to the storage container and rejuvenate before I have to handle another day of this sorry-ass redemption. It doesn't matter how much Bellamy has turned my head the other way, it doesn't matter how much he finds a new alternative to be added to the list of things to keep me 'sane', I still want to go back. Because at the end of the day I know what keeps me going, I know what feeds me and I know that I should have never considered doing this soft approach shit, I should've forced Kassian to hear my side of things the moment he woke up from getting his arse knocked out.

Chapter 29
Kassian
14/10/2021 (Thursday)

I did start to think life was getting a bit boring, a bit repetitive. That being said, things have progressed, there's no denying it. I've allowed change to rid me of any weaknesses and all my investments are doing well. I could have everything that one may want but I still feel as if I have not been in my own body for years. There are a few times where I've made an appearance, usually it happens when I hallucinate or take my emotions out on someone. Other than that, I've just been a desensitised watcher whose body is on autopilot.

Maverick requested my attendance.

That's what he does now. He requests, he doesn't demand. What a joke. Anyway, I've been fond of no longer being controlled by him so whenever I can, whenever I feel the need to laugh, I do take the piss with his time. So, here I am, days after the day he wanted me, making my way to my big brother.

"How nice of you to finally join me." Maverick comes out of nowhere.

"Yeah, what d'you want?" I say like I don't have all the time in the world.

"It's Kaden."

My heart ups its pace as I take control of my actions again.

"He visited one of our universities and threatened a scout. Whatever method he used seems to have made this James

White grow some and make ridiculous demands." Maverick continues, ignoring my sudden change in appearance. "Protection and a raise?" He spits out, almost laughing.

I know that scout. I know him because I know that University. Iris goes there.

I pull myself together and feed myself hope in knowing that Maverick will assume my slight reaction to his words is because of our brother, and not a girl whose employment created a ravine in mine and Kade's relationship (which then made him lose Kade himself).

Why after all this time is he appearing out of nowhere and contacting a Baronial scout? What is he up to?

"I need you to deal with it. If I send anyone else and they bump into Kaden, they could stray. So, you go and handle James, frame your brother if you want. I don't care, just don't let this situation get out of hand. I don't want this scout squealing to the wrong people." He walks away from me as if he has a list of things to do, not even bothering with courtesies.

There are many '*wrong people*' this James could go to, but I know that Maverick is specifically thinking about Kade. Though I have not made an effort to see what he's been up to, nor have I cared, I knew Kade was alive. And if there's one thing that I know is bothersome enough to be considered a fear for Maverick, it's Kade taking him down and robbing him of everything he owns.

Chapter 30
Kassian
15/10/2021 (Friday)

Arriving at the university's building with the early students, still transitioning into a hangover allows me to blend in with the majorities zombie-like behaviour.

I put a face on for Maverick yesterday, but soon after, I spiralled as my thoughts showed no mercy. If Kade had visited her university, there's a chance he saw her and a chance that she saw him. Two people who in the past I wanted to introduce to each other, were *coincidently* at the same place at the same time. What if he saw her and ruined my image some more? What if he decided to take his anger out on her?

I can't imagine how he's strung her up.

Admittedly, I also drank to deaden my nerves. It's been a while since I've seen her, but now that I'm here, standing, waiting for my coffee, I wish that I had the confidence I've got for everything else, to be able to find and approach her. But guilt eats me up every time. It may not have been me who got her into Baronial, but it sure as hell feels like it.

I fight the urge to not spit the shot of coffee back into the cup. It's literally liquid static but I need it to stay awake so I walk over to the sugar, straw, tissue stand and just as I'm about to rip into a sugar packet, I am nudged.

"Hey, what you doing here?" A girl stands close to me.

Her comfortability in approaching me, then going on to nudge and talk implies that we know one another, but I struggle to recall. Usually, I would ignore and move on, maybe even do something to get rid of the ease she felt in approaching me, but I can't help but feel like I know her.

Have I slept with her?

"Hey." I stretch the word as I search my mind on where I might have seen or met her. And just in case she is someone, I pull her in for a hug.

Her being surprised by my actions makes me think that we are not as close as I suspected, which then furthers my curiosity on why she seems so familiar.

"Are you drunk? Why are you hugging me? And what's up with your eyes? They look—"

"Hungover. And because I want to. Why can't I hug you again?" I'm almost proud of my ability to actually listen and answer her.

She leans away from me, her confusion mixed with annoyance. "You got a trim?"

"Yah. Do you like it?" I did cut my hair yesterday to mimic the most recent picture Maverick has of Kade. Not because I like it, but because if Iris did see Kade, she can't then see me and notice the differences. A smart girl like her would put things together and I'm not ready for that revelation yet, hence why I've also covered my tattoos.

The girl in front of me specifically said 'trim' and not 'cut,' so she must be someone who entertains Kade when he's around.

"Why are you putting on an accent?—"

In the time it took for me to realise how much I've already messed up, her expression went from being annoyed-confused, to her shaking it off to move on.

"—Never mind, listen."

Now that she was two steps away, I can see her features properly, making a fuzzy version of a memory appear. Whilst she rambles on about something about yesterday and apologising and comfortability, I push my head back into my neck, then I lower it as I force myself to blink and to properly inspect her features. I *do* know her. She's lost some of the baby fat on her face and is wearing makeup, but it is her.

"Medisa?" I murmur after a long pause and I don't need her to speak for me to know that it is her. Her facial expression gives away that much.

"Hey, Wifey!"

I know that voice anywhere. It's Iris.

Shoving past me, Medisa wakes me up enough for me to leave before Iris sees me.

Barging into a place called 'The Gardens', I pace as I piece together what could've happened, no longer needing the coffee to wake me up. If Medisa—Iris's friend—knows Kade, then Iris has most definitely met Kade, or at least knows of his existence, perhaps has even forgiven him for what he has done. There's no other explanation as to why she would allow Medisa to be near him. Unless of course, Kade the fox, purposely befriended Medisa to get to Iris. And Iris being who she is, doesn't have it in her to tell Medisa how much of a cunt he is.

Judging by how she approached and spoke to me, I would say her relationship with my brother has already developed. And he's not the type to entertain without some sort of motive.

Is he living the life I should've been living?

I sit down on one of the benches thinking about what to do next. The scout can wait, I'm sure Maverick would be interested in knowing the details of what his dear brother has been up to anyway.

I wait around until lunch, that's when most classes are out and about. When she hadn't arrived at the canteen, I knew that she would be out, ordering food from outside. So, now I wait next to the exit, she's going to show up here at some point and when she does, I will be the one to approach her.

Not long after, I spot her saying goodbye to a group of girls, Iris not being one of them. I want to say that if I had known she would leave the building two minutes before lunch ends, I would've dealt with the scout, but truth be told I wouldn't have. My anger towards Kade does not diminish my hatred towards Maverick, ergo, his needs and wants can wait.

Wrapping an arm around her shoulders, trapping her besides me, Medisa's shoulders stiffen then drop as soon as she sees me. Her brows are pulled together, screaming irritation, especially since it's all I can see being this close.

"Are you still hungover? You owe me when you're not, I'm not letting this slide." She unwraps herself by pinching my sleeve and lifting my arm, handing it back to me.

"Where are you going?"

"Aros."

Her comfortability of talking with an attitude surprises me, I'm almost stunned that Kade allows her to speak to him this way. Personally, I'm not too bothered by her tone as it's obvious something has transpired between them. If anything, I am almost glad someone is brave enough to be this way with him.

"*Why* are you following me?"

"*Why* can't I follow you? Aren't we friends?" I need to know what she is to Kade. Is he using her? Does he even know who she is? Who she's friends with? Medisa doesn't respond to my questions so I try to play on her nurturing side.

"You can't expect me to drive in the condition I'm in."

"You drove here, didn't you?"

I can't help but smile, which eventually drops as I realise how I was right about her being good for Kade. If things were different, this realisation would be much more healing and less of a piss-take.

As we enter the station, I take mental points of the journey for when I return, meanwhile, Medisa doesn't bother to entertain. She just looks as if she's thinking about running away from me.

At some point in standing around waiting for the train, she switches up, her face exposing her motive on wanting to start a conversation. And despite the strong urge to get her to spit her words out, I sit this one out. It's best if I don't navigate our talk. I need to see how she communicates with Kade without my influence.

"If you knew that you were busy today, especially in the morning, why did you drink to get yourself this drunk?"

Good thing I'm not actually drunk. There are easier ways to say what she's just said and she chose one of the wordier ways.

"If I tell you the truth, would you do the same when I ask you some questions?"

"I will. I promise." She's sure of herself but if she is the company Kade is choosing to keep, I do not trust her one bit.

"How do I know you'll be telling the truth?" I search her eyes.

"How do I know that *you'll* be telling the truth?" She searches mine and there's no doubt in my mind that she is determined to extract as much as information as she can.

"I have no reason to lie to that question. Now." I close the distance between us, lowering my head so that she has no choice but to look into my eyes. "Tell me. Is it fair for me to say that you owe me if I find out you lied?"

"That's fair, but I'm telling you, I won't lie." She's almost offended by my distrust in her.

Letting out a single '*ha*', I tilt my head closer towards her. "I'll see about that."

A train arrives besides us but Medisa does not make a move towards it. I check to see when the next train would be coming then decide it will come too late for my liking. Yes, I would like to know more about what Kade has been up to, but I don't want to be around her for longer than I need to. So, I grab onto her and drag her into the somewhat packed train, finding a place for us to stand in front of each other.

As the train jerks forward, so does Medisa. I was anticipating her fall from when I noticed her stick-like stance, but her being Iris's favourite friend forces me to grab a hold of her.

"Hold onto my hoodie." I may have been touchy-feely with her before, but I am not keeping my arm snaked around her for the rest of the journey.

Medisa's eyes express how she felt for her only option at this point. There are no bars for her to hold onto, they are covered. There is no part of the train that she could lean on, they're all taken.

Taking her time in going through her non-existent options, I let go of her.

"I'm not saving you next time and I won't offer again." I go back to viewing the top of people's heads.

Her internal battle doesn't last long.

Medisa gives in by barely holding onto the parts of my hoodie that were baggy enough for her to hold a fistful. After that, she doesn't talk or look at anyone. Her head is kept down as if she felt shameful, or even embarrassed.

"I didn't drink to get myself drunk. I drank to ease my mind." I confess.

She angles her head up but I don't bother looking down to her. My head already hurts, I don't want my neck to be the next sore thing.

"I have to take care of some family I haven't seen in a long time…it brought back memories." My mind might be mine, but it does not show me mercy. Yes, my thoughts were flooded of Iris but they were also—as much as I hate it—were of Kade. Not of the backstabbing, but of him before. How perfectly wild he was. How tired he must have been from pulling the weight for the both of us, but still found energy to entertain me, to momentarily distract me.

"What kind of memories?" Medisa's quick response snaps me out of wherever my thoughts were going to lead me.

"That's another question Desdemona." I lower my head so that our eyes could meet, slightly pissed at her interruption. "You willing to take that risk?"

Clicking her tongue as if my underlying tone of threat does not affect her, she answers, "Not sure… Was that your question for me? 'Cause, I answered truthfully princess."

Her fake smile and slow blinks tick me off. Not to mention *'princess'* is not on the same level as *'Desdemona.'* There are levels as to why I give her this name, I almost want to educate her but there's no use in wasting this opportunity.

"Clever girl. You just might be able to work this all out."

Medisa's brows are pulled together for a second before she wiggles the skin on her forehead with a few fingers.

I've never seen that motion before. Was she trying to summon useful thoughts, or is she worried about wrinkles?

"Could've used that brain to work out the memories clearly weren't good ones." I add.

By how she has been so far, I would say her brain is actually half of what the average person has. Yes, she did notice my hair and eyes, but it doesn't seem like she has the capacity to take things further to connect or create theoretical dots.

"My turn," I continue. "Before you manage to get another answer out of me."

What to ask, what to ask?

I lower myself to get my lips as close to her ear as possible. "What situation were you in that made you *desperate* for a job?" I slowly ascend back to a normal stance as I take in her eyes. I'd been connecting dots myself. Medisa's name is on the list of potentials, I checked. Medisa not being recruited and Kade being around her, has to have some sort of correlation.

"My family. They don't get along with me—"

"You're going to have to give me more than that. Right now, you sound like you're stealing my story—"

"I'm *not* lying." Her mouth is stretches out, almost mimicking a smile as she delivers her offended tone. "I got a job because I don't have it in me to sit around waiting for something better to come anymore."

I almost don't know what expression to wear. Should I smile for my brother or should I grind my teeth? I questioned why Kade has chosen to keep her close and now I know that he must see himself in her. Being abused and not having it in her to wait for a hero, yeah that's Kade alright. He couldn't be arsed to find another way of escape so he chose to push me and Iris under the bus. Question is, is Medisa doing something similar?

I scoff. "Interesting."

Medisa turns her head to face me. "What the hell is so interesting about that?"

We hold each other's gaze. As she waits for an answer, I think about how tragically poetic this all is.

After searching my eyes, tired of waiting for some sort of response, Medisa turns away. Minutes go by, stops come and go and she still remains silent.

She catches me staring but can't seem to decide if she wants to be timid or annoyed. At some point she moves and for a split second, I thought we had to get off, but then I see where she's going and it's to a couple of seats that have been emptied by passengers.

I sit down before her and watch how her facial expression changes from hopeful to '*really*?' I suppose she wanted to leave me standing.

Pity.

I do try to wait a little longer but I cannot stand the noises anymore. How people do this every day without fail—to even pay for this—I do not know. As I tap her foot with mine, again and again, I begin to think that I should've forced her into my car.

Finally, Medisa looks up from her phone, at first curious as to who is tapping her, then her polite expression switches to a rude one. Holding a shrug and raising her brows she—almost rudely—asks, '*What*?'

"How long?" I don't bother speaking close to a whisper like she did.

"Twenty minutes." She enunciates whilst speaking closer to her normal volume.

Leaning back, continuing to analyse her, I try to figure out what Kade's thinking. What's Medisa's role in his plans? What is his goal here?

"Are you going to keep your eyes on me all day?" Her attitude continues to surprise me.

"I'm going to keep my eyes on you for a lot longer than that."

Medisa takes us into a building in an area where I'm surprised Kade has set up camp. I didn't know he got given a building here.

The elevator we are now using can only be accessed by her and Kade. And since she thinks that I am him, she is being oh-so open with how to get in.

There are only three floor buttons, the top one obviously being Kade's floor. I move my hand to press it but she instantly smacks it away.

"What are you doing? You're drunk—"

"Hungover—"

"You're not in your right mind is what you are—"

"Am I ever though? Why can't we go up?"

"Er, *hello*? Bellamy?" She stretches out his name as if it would ring a bell. "Your boss is up there."

I almost snort. "My boss?"

The elevator doors open to the floor Medisa had pressed.

"Oh my God, I can't be arsed for this. I don't care what kind of relationship you guys have, I'm not letting you go up there like this when he's probably in a meeting or something."

I follow her, but not without analysing everything and anything. Every little detail of this place, confirms that Kade has been here, he probably even lived here for a bit.

Medisa directs me into an office that's not really Kade's

style, then shoves bottles into my chest.

"Sober up." She speaks to me like I'm a spoilt child.

"My office is a joke."

She pulls a face. "Yeah, well you can take that up with Bellamy when you're better."

Again with this '*Bellamy.*' Who is that? What's his connection to Kade? Is Kade working here as a cover?

I should leave before the real Kade or this Bellamy shows up and ruins everything. I've already taken the piss with my luck by coming all the way in.

"Actually, I'm going to get going now. Thank you for bringing me here and giving me water—" She opens her mouth but I continue to talk. "—Don't worry about Bellamy, I'll talk to him later and don't worry about me, I'll call a taxi."

Medisa looks as if she's contemplating it, almost as if she's going through some sort of internal war until she finally allows herself to use words. "Do you want me to come with you?"

"Nah, I'm good." I reply too quickly then move in for a hug.

A hug she dodges.

"You seriously need to stop forgetting that you can't touch me."

"I will. The next time you see me, I'll be sober and will remember everything." I turn to leave, still in a rush to get out before anyone who is able to recognise Kade sees me.

Just as I'm about to walk away, I realise I'm leaving too many loose ends and need to tie at least one of them, so I turn back around.

"Oh, and Medisa, I'm sorry about how I was today." I use the acting skills I've been honing over time to try to make her pity me. "Can we pretend today didn't happen…please?"

She heavily sighs. "Fine. But you owe me lunch then."

I smile, her lack of ability to put things together continues to be an advantage. "Deal."

Chapter 31
Kade
18/10/2021 (Monday)

"I messed up." I confess to Amana. "Your friend is triggering. I don't know what it is, but she conjures things up in my mind even if it's not her intention."

At first Amana was worried, but now her head is slightly tilted to the side, her eyes close to slits, as though she is drowsy and is saying '*Seriously*?'

She heavily sighs, already deeming this meeting a waste of time. "What did she trigger? What did you do?"

"I'd rather not talk about it." It would be the biggest joke for me to talk and seek comfort from this girl. It's already slightly depressing for her to be okay with this and wanting to know what's bothering me. "I've called you to help me with damage control. I need more than '*be the funny understanding guy*.' Tell me the places she likes. I will take her there as an apology."

"Cook for her—"

She can't even do that for herself?

"—maybe make it something that you both do, that way she'll learn and have fun—"

A child. That's who I have to make friends with. A child.

"—If you don't have time to cook, I will do it for you, but then you have to eat with her—"

Do I have to feed her too?

"—As for a place she likes. There's an ice rink-bowling place near Kensington Palace, you can take her there. Skating makes her laugh so hard she loses her voice, so, if she does have a problem with you, that place would definitely make things easier for you guys to make up."

"She laughs when she skates?"

What a nutcase.

"No, she laughs when she falls. She can't skate."

'Course she can't, how silly of me to assume she has at least one skill.

I huff.

'It's only until May Kade. It'll come and she'll go before you know it.'

Chapter 32
Kade
19/10/2021 (Tuesday)

I wait for Medisa in her office, leaving her with no choice but to interact with me. I would search her space to pass time, but I've already dismissed the idea of her working undercover (after checking her homemade lamp for some sort of camera/microphone). Besides, her office is still a little empty, there's not many spaces where she could hide something (ignoring the hours of footage I went through to make sure). As for the fact that Medisa does trigger me, I've decided to be more open. Perhaps her company will allow me to remember more over time, perhaps it will even open me up to not be a paranoid freak who thinks everyone and everything has a catch.

"Our offices aren't that similar for you to mistake mine for yours."

I turn around, glad to see and hear her act as though nothing had happened. Amana must've spoken to her.

"Hey, I got us the day off. Convinced Bell he doesn't need us today."

Her shoulders drop and her face mimics the expression Amana pulled when I met her over the weekend. "Ugh, seriously, you didn't want to let me know before I left my house?"

She's not even the slightest bit curious on how I managed to '*convince Bells.*'

"Actually, I've made plans for us and I didn't know if you would come if I told you whilst you were home."

I've been informed Medisa tends to be lazy whenever she is able to.

"Plans?"

"Yep, it's a surprise. But you'll like it." I move towards her.

"Do you want to bet on that?"

"Isn't betting haram?" I've done more research. Mostly to humble her when she does step out of line, a little because I want to be respectful, but also because I want to see what I can push.

"Oooo look at you doing your research." She waves her hands and sways her neck. After she's bored of those motions—which does not take long—she dramatically sighs, dropping her shoulders. "I could've made some serious money here."

"C'mon. We haven't got long." I laugh through my words then walk out of her office.

Medisa tags along half a step behind me, definitely thinking about what I've planned for us. So far, her mind seems to be on today and not the last time we've interacted.

I open the passenger door for her, making Medisa gasp too loudly, and too real for someone like me to not be on edge and check our surroundings.

"You're gonna let me handle your car?" She reaches for my key, giggling.

I let out a sigh disguised as a scoff after realising there's no real danger. Then, I hide the keys behind me. "Get in. I'll give you something to handle."

Medisa freezes as her jaw drops. "Uh- Astaghfirullah.

As-Tagh-firu-llah." She holds a finger out and repeats the words again and again, each time her lips curl as she tries to be serious.

It doesn't take long for Medisa to giddily smile her way into the passenger seat.

"It's about an hour away, so feel free to get yourself comfortable and eat the snacks." Despite not knowing if Medisa would be okay with travelling with me, I packed the car with her favourite snacks and beverages.

"Do you have any bread and cheese?" She picks up two packets of crisps as I reverse.

"This isn't your local corner shop—"

"Looks like it though. Ohhhh." She oddly sways herself as if she were dodging punches, her hand curved around her lips, her thumb resting on her chin. "Bars-bars. Mic-drop."

I pause to allow myself to process how many more weeks of this I have to endure. Then, I respond to her eccentric behaviour with sardonic laughter and a blank expression, further emphasising how unamused I am by her attempted joke. And instead of her backing down, her lips twitch up until she bursts and lets out hawk screeches and tea kettle laughs.

Hitting the breaks as her laughter genuinely shocks me, I turn to inspect if she is mentally okay whilst also questioning if the sounds even came from her. Her ability to not scream is obviously some sort of mental block, because her chords and lungs definitely allow it.

Whilst I look her over, Medisa is busy slapping everything and anything as she tries to calm her laughter-turned-giggles down.

"That's concerning."

She's mental.

I turn my attention back to driving. "I only got snacks

because we're going to be eating properly later and *no* that is not where we are driving to, that's a separate plan."

Medisa nods, turning her attention towards the packets she's chosen—flavours which Amana told me she likes—and how silly of me to assume that she would consume them like a regular human being. What I thought would have been the quiet part of our journey has now turned into Medisa scrunching the packets to turn perfect sizes into crumbs. She then professionally mixes and scoffs them down.

"Who eats crisps like that?"

"What-do-you-meannn?" Her words came too quick in defence as though the way she ate was the norm. "This is one of the best ways to eat two flavours that go well with one another. Try it." Her hand jolts as if in the second she decided to feed me, she also decides not to. "Err." Removing her bottle from its holder, she replaces it with the crisp packet. "There, try it later when you can." Her smile goes from '*ha good thing he didn't notice my hesitancy,*'—ignoring my great vision—to a face that looks as though it's about to inquire.

I move my attention towards the road.

"Has anyone ever told you that you look like a pretty boy?"

"What?" I did suspect a question. I just made the mistake of hoping for a decent one.

"I don't mean to sound perverted and I don't know if '*pretty boy*' is an insult, it might be. But what *I* mean is that you have feminine features, but then you don't, but then you do. I don't know…I don't know if it's your eyes or lips or your skin but yeah…"

I pause. "That's one way of distracting me whilst I'm driving."

"I could think of another." She shoots back, cheekily

raising her brows whilst her chin is slightly pushed back into her neck. "Astaghfirullah. Anyways, you got manly features too. Like the space between your nose and lips is defined—I haven't seen that on a girl."

"I think you're staring at my lips a bit too much."

"Don't act like you don't stare at mine, Cole."

'Who the heck is Cole?'

"Anywho, a better way to put it, is that if someone were to ask me to describe how you looked, I would say a lighter skinned Scar in human form...Scar or his son—one of them." Her eyes quickly travel up and down my body when I turn to read her expression.

"Scar is a pretty boy?" Though I don't waste my time in front of a screen, I do know who she is talking about. We watched it with my parents.

"Oh my God. I didn't mean pretty boy in a bad way. You *still* look scary and intimidating but—yeah, I give up. We'll come back to this when I have the words to properly articulate myself." She holds her hand out like she were pressing a pause button on the conversation.

Barely stifling a giggle, I mentally admit I admire her lack of denial when it comes to her knowledge, in this case, her lack of vocabulary. Also, she thinks that I'm intimidating? That's news considering how she behaves like I'm just any Tom, Dick and Harry.

"I think I know what you mean and I'm not taking it as an insult. I just wanted to hear more about what you think about me and how you got to that conclusion." I realise that I'm not actually paying attention to the road, I've been driving without being conscious of it.

Medisa nods and opts to sit silently for the rest of the journey, but now I don't have it in me to be quiet.

I want to talk.

"Has anyone ever told you that you switch between talking formally and informally? Or that sometimes you rush through your words and may use a word the wrong way, but we still get the gist on what you're trying to say?" I felt my smile form midway but I also realise I don't care.

I glance at Medisa to see if she shares similar emotions.

"My apologies. If I had known that pointing out your looks would make you point out my flaws, I would've simply called you a little bitch than compare you to such characters."

The way she has somehow created a problem, is *so* ridiculous I cannot even bring myself to laugh.

Without thinking, I pull over, the tires screech as I dismiss everything else. "I'm not pointing out your flaws. I'm pointing out what I like about you." I realise my tone is too strict so I lighten up a little. "You silly girl."

"Oh, well that's embarrassing...for me." She brings herself to timidly look me in the eyes. "I'm sorry I called you a bitch, I don't actually think that you're one. I just wanted to hurt you in some way and that word came to mind."

I bite my lower lip and raise my brows. '*Bitch*' is the word that came to her mind to insult me? I feel as though I need to prove how much that is not true.

Now Medisa peeled her lips, more because of nerves than trivial thoughts. "You didn't have to stop driving to tell me that I was wrong by the way."

"I did. You needed to see it on my face that I was telling the truth." I'd picked up on the fact that Medisa relies on her eyes and not entirely on her ears. Even now, she was trying to read me whilst her fingers aggressively peeled away at the soft layers on her lips.

After a few seconds of facing her, Medisa lowers her

hand and clears her throat as she adjusts and views whatever's happening in front of us. I'm making her uncomfortable and yet, it takes me a long second after her adjustment for me to get back to facing the steering wheel.

She really does have pretty brown eyes.

"You've yet to show me a real flaw Medisa."

Her need to insult me the second after she felt insulted does not count. Me and 95% of the population are the same. Is it a flaw? Maybe. But so long as that percentage is above fifty, I class it as the norm.

"Really? I just showed you one and I could name a few if you want?" She doesn't believe me, almost as though I am someone who would lie to be in her favour.

I shake my head, deciding to move away from the topic of flaws. "Get some rest, you being tired will not be a valid excuse later."

A cheeky smile grows on her face as she stops peeling her lips. Her face doesn't hide the question *'what are we doing later?'*

"Get. Some. Rest. Medisa." My tone of voice does not hide my amusement... neither does the slow curl of one side of my lips.

"Just say that you don't want to talk to me."

"Alright." Easy-peasy. "I don't want to talk to you... There." I say more to myself.

"Wow." Medisa picks up the packet she'd left for me and begins to tunnel the crumbs into her mouth, and I can't help but smile.

Petty girl.

We arrive a little later than I'd intended, but it's okay, our spots are guaranteed. Like the night I dropped her home, I am crouched outside the car, beside her. Despite her humour, or her issue with authority, she looks innocent whilst sleeping. And as conflicting as it sounds, she looks both troubled and at peace.

I turn on my phone to view the time again. I can't let her sleep for any longer, not when so much effort went into today.

"Medisa, we're here." I try to wake her with a gentle voice than gentle hands. Just as I think that I have succeeded, she loses consciousness. "Medisa c'mon." I raise my voice and slap the sun visor up into place, my patience slowly slipping away.

The sound of the visor slapping back into position wakes her up.

"Did you put the visor down while I was sleeping?" Her voice travels through a yawn.

"Yep. C'mon, ask me any other questions when we're inside. We're a tiny bit late." Though I urge her to hurry, I stay crouched in place.

"Cute." She stretches then gets out the car, ready to follow me in her sleepy daze.

I move around the place like it were mine—a behaviour that comes naturally to me— and walk straight towards the ice rink.

"Oh, me and Amana have been here before. It's so fun. She's so good at skating." Medisa's use of '*so*' is hard to ignore, *so* is her habit of bringing up Amana whenever we do something remotely similar to whatever they've experienced together. Or something that they would like to do together. Or something that Amana may have an interest in.

'*Or, or, or.*'

I've never been here before but from the looks of things, this is definitely a place Kassian would love, perhaps even build himself.

"Jessie! Hey man, I'm sorry that we're a little late. Could you still let us in?"

I don't know why I bothered to ask, we both know he has no choice but to let Medisa and I in. He was given a rundown beforehand. Not too much, just that Medisa's a girl who knows nothing, so he should keep his mouth shut and act as though we have a normal friendly relationship. In reality, Jessie is someone signed into Baronial and then into Aros. I've messed him up (Baronial) and sorted him out (Aros) but how things turn out for him overall, depends on the smile on her face.

Medisa looks on edge but still manages to shyly greet him. Is his appearance making her this timid? Why is her voice like that? Does she think he's cute?

"You guys still have some time before it's open to the public. I put your shoes to the side over there." He points over to where the shoes are. "Penguins are on me and if you need extra help with teaching, feel free to give me a shout, I'll be around here somewhere."

Not that I am ecstatic over this, but I am not allowing Medisa to seek help from someone else, especially Jessie.

"Cool." I am done with this interaction and though Jessies acting skills are close to flawless, I could tell he feels the same, he just has no choice but to go along with it.

"Let me know if there's anything else that you need."

"Cheers." I grin at him, I wanted top-notch acting, and he delivered. Medisa has no clue. Even as she walks back over to us, she seems to have her mind on something else and not the fact that I basically own Jessie.

Her eyes stalk Jessie as he busies himself elsewhere and I fight my tongue to not ask her to get a room. Then, as soon as Jessie is at somewhat of a distance, she turns to me.

"We can't do this, I can't do this, I can't skate!" She speaks through loud whispers as I piece together her thoughts and worries being about skating and not the boy she just met.

"We can do this, *you* can do this, I can teach you."

"No Kade, you can't touch me remember?" Her brows turn to slopes as she comes close to a frustrated pout.

"I know, which is why I'm going to skate besides you and only interfere if it looks like you're going to have a bad fall."

Her shoulders drop as she realises there's no escaping this. Momentarily using her eyes to look around, I could tell that she is trying to find a way to make this easier for herself.

"I need a penguin."

"No, you don't. Having a penguin longs out the process and doesn't allow you to push and believe in yourself. You just need to throw yourself out there and trust yourself... and me." I almost cringe at the use of the words '*longs out.*' Her puny brain is rubbing off on me rather than growing into mine.

She grabs her skates without fussing then walks over to the bench to put them on. "Did you book us a private lesson?"

"No, I got Jessie to agree to let us in without a worker." There wasn't much to it, it's not like he had a choice. I quite literally am in charge of what happens to him.

"Oh, that's actually on brand for you." Medisa grabs our shoes and walks away before I can say anything.

On brand? Does she mean being efficient?

She walks straight over to Jessie. I can't exactly hear what is being said, but I do see his expressions. He better not be saying too much and she better not be straying from her faith, I should be the only exception, we're colleagues, who is he?

"I should be thanking you for—" He notices me and makes it too obvious. "—For being a fan of skating." He smiles after that pathetic transparent excuse then turns to leave.

Medisa turns around and makes her way back to me, and only now do I realise that I chose to stand too close. She chooses not to bring up Jessie's obvious pivot or the fact that I am stood too close, and instead decides to walk over and grip onto what separates the ice rink from us.

"I'm not letting you stick to the edges. You're going to go start off in the middle—" She opens her mouth to utter some words of disagreement, but I cut her off. "—I'm not hearing it. I'll take you to the middle myself if you try escaping."

"That's haram."

"God is forgiving."

Her jaw drops in shock, but her lips slowly lift to a smile in which she does a poor job of hiding with one of her hands. And before I let myself get carried away and forget my place, I look around for someone to hold and take Medisa to the middle.

"Excuse me!" I call out to a woman who skated like it's as natural to her as breathing. "Hi. Do you think you could take my friend to the middle?"

Before Medisa kicks up a fuss—which I doubt as she wouldn't want to be an inconvenience to the lady skating over—I lower myself to talk into her ear.

"Remember to bend your legs and keep them that way." I pull myself away, not caring to hide the satisfaction of this all.

"Uh—" She struggles to find the words and whether it's because of mine or because of the rink, I don't care because she's no longer trying to find a way to not skate.

"C'mon Hun, I'll get you there safely." The woman reaches out for her.

I skate ahead to where I would like her to drop Medisa off, then watch as she brings a wobbly Medisa to where I am. It doesn't take too long for her to reach me. Her postures a little off and her arms are out like she's weirdly asking for a hug, some parents may even translate it to uppies.

"Are you seriously not going to give me any tips?"

"I only have the one." I grin, she walked into that one. "Stick to what I said and try to figure it out from there. If in the next five minutes you haven't worked it out, I'll help some more."

Taking a deep breath with her eyes to the ice below, one would think that she's about to start, but no. She finds my eyes again. "Can you close your eyes or look away or something?"

I shake my head.

Giving up on waiting for me to look away, Medisa squats a little lower and begins to move as though she were on a scooter.

I don't celebrate.

She might be moving, but anyone could spot her unease and we're not leaving until she becomes confident. At the moment, I could breathe too close to her and she would fall over.

Not moving as normal people do when they skate, she jerks a few times, but I don't interfere, I watch as she fixes what she assumes is the problem. And when Medisa finally glides for a little longer, she looks up and raises an arm to get my attention like I haven't been watching this whole time.

"Hey I'm doing it! I'm—" Her body dives into the ice, and in an attempt to save herself, she pushes herself backwards, giving me just about enough time to reach her.

I don't have seconds to think, so I grab what makes sense. I gather a fistful of her clothes that would normally be resting on her chest and pull her up to a normal stance. As soon as I have her standing, I let go and have my arms out in case she were to fall again.

Not knowing how bad her fall would've been, Medisa gasps for air as her laughter takes over. "Did you just pull me back up using my bra?" She spoke through what seemed to be a combination of an asthma attack and chuckles. Her body bends over as she struggles to get her words out and when that doesn't work, she slowly shakes her way down into a low squat. "When you said that you were going to interfere—" The desperate gasp she makes as her laughter suffocates her could come from a horror movie. "—I didn't think that you were going to use my bra as a *harness*!" She continues to be in hysterics, grabbing onto her chest where her heart lies. Tears gather but do not fall from her eyes.

As she wheezes and adjusts her bra, I stand by—I admit—still shocked from how fast it all happened.

"I don't know if I should feel violated or not." Her giggles just about calm down as I process how close she came to injuring herself and her reaction to being saved.

"Well sorry for not using the milliseconds I had to sit on the side and think of the best non violating way to save your arse." The situation plays out in my head, and now that it's over and we know the outcome, I begin to feel tickled and have the urge to laugh out what I now feel.

After Medisa recovers from her derangement, she sets

off almost instantly, leaving me behind as she goes back to skating as though she were on a scooter...

'Weirdo.'

Medisa's almost completely lost her voice from all the laughs and voice raising, so I've made it my mission to warm her up. It's the least I could do after making her fall a few times. (Not my fault she hadn't learnt to strengthen and stabilise her balance).

A man around Bellamy's age has his jacket hooked onto the back of his chair. I could swipe it off but since I can't be arsed dealing with the consequences, I take out my wallet.

The £200 I hold out grabs his attention. "For the jacket."

"It's worth more than that mate."

'Not after your monstrous body's been in it.' I force a smile.

The place isn't too busy, so it won't be as big of an outrage when my itching fingers break his beer bottle and jam it into his neck. Jessie can clean up after me and a wrapped-up Medisa walk out.

I look back to a distracted Medisa then to the stench in human form. 'Clean-up' will be harder without the usual people and today was supposed to be a day where I make things up to her, not create more problems.

I add another note then take the jacket without permission.

"Am I supposed to eat that?" Medisa jokes as I approach.

"They didn't have hot chocolate and I didn't want us to leave without you experiencing something first." I hold the padded jacket out for her to grab. "Put it on, this will be fun."

Her eyes travel behind me, as though expecting the original owner to snatch it back. When her worries are set to the side, she takes the jacket.

"What we doing?"

"Medisa, trust me, you're going to want to do this." After about an hour of her barely skating, I say this is something that is well deserved.

Tapping my foot on the ground, I wait and restrain myself from helping her zip up the jacket that drowned her.

Once she is ready, I pinch a chunk of the jacket.

"Can you feel that?"

She attempts to look at me over her shoulder. "Feel what?"

"Good, you can't feel me, which means whatever we're about to do isn't going to be haram."

She sighs with more disappointment than usual. "Me chilling with you right now is haram."

"Well then you definitely need to do this, can't waste this already sinful day without experiencing this." I move towards the rink and motion for her to follow me.

This time when we enter the rink, we carefully make our way over to the far edge.

"Put your back to me and hold your arms out like the letter 'T'."

She does as she's told but her leg remains stiff.

"Bend your legs."

Adjusting my hands on her jacket, making sure I have a good grip without actually holding onto her, I take off. Eventually, Medisa, perhaps without even realising it, begins to put more of her weight onto me, leaning back more than she was when we first started. I had already taken her around five times, speeding more and more, but once I noticed the time, I was the one to stop the experience as we still had two more things to do.

"When did she leave?" I rush around the kitchen.

"She's still here, and she's already put everything into containers and the drinks in the fridge." Bellamy dries his hands, already having washed the used dishes. "Do you need help carrying them down?"

"Nah-nah I'm good. Just make sure she leaves without being seen. Medisa can't know that she's here." I stack the containers into a bag then do the same with the drinks. Holding the door open with my foot I turn to Bellamy. "Thank you."

He looks at me weird but I haven't got time to find out why, Medisa is waiting.

Just as I'm about to have my other foot out the door, I turn to him again. "Tell her I said thank you as well."

"So it's working?"

"So far it's been good, yeah." I nod my head. "I'll tell you about it later, foods getting cold." I lift the bag of food in my hand as though he hadn't noticed.

Riding the elevator down is a risk I'm willing to take. If I am caught and it comes down to it, I'll just tell her that Bellamy let me store food in his personal kitchen, and she won't question it because she's never actually been upstairs.

There's no sign of her in our offices, so I go to knock on her washroom door.

I get no response.

Travelling through the rest of the floor, peeking into each section and room, becomes more and more dull as my brain refuses to put two and two together.

My heart picks up its pace.

Has she left?

The day was going so well, but now I feel as though I need to make a trip to the shipping container. Lord knows the gym upstairs won't be enough this time.

Just as the thought to drop the food, pick up a real drink and then leave comes to mind, I open the door to the games room. Medisa turns to me smiling, and the view of her was enough for me to get rid of the heavy feeling in my chest.

'And the need to add something to the Gallery.'

"I thought you left." I sigh in relief.

"Not till my belly's full."

Still feeling relieved, I don't take notice of how we somehow managed to get comfortable on the floor. No matter, we have a good view, good company and good food.

Whilst Medisa is distracted by the sunset's colours being reflected onto the building in front, I organise the containers and drinks. Medisa then prematurely looks down wanting to help and I almost snap at her to look away.

"Don't look until I say. It's not ready yet." If she helps me in what is supposed to be a part of my apology, her actions will basically diminish it and I will have to do this all again.

Momentarily moving away to manually turn off the lights so that they did not light the room when they detected movement, I come back and make sure that everything is in place and within arm's reach. "Okay, you can look now."

"What the hell? Did you make all of this?"

"I made the roast and the noodles but had help with the rice." It's true, I did make the food, but it was a team effort. Amana made the rice and suggested the other dishes. I marinated the roast and had the noodles on heat all day. Bellamy was the one to put the roast in the oven and to actually fill the containers.

Does Medisa need to know all of that? No, no she does not.

"When did you make them? Who told you about the chutney and yoghurt combo? Where did you even keep all this?"

Ah yes, the chutney and yoghurt was also made by Amana, to accompany the rice.

"Sometimes cooking is therapy, so could you please dig in and compliment me, they won't stay warm forever." It's true. Cooking can be like therapy.

"Is Bellamy still here? We should give him some, no?"

Dramatically sighing as though her question adds hours onto the day, I type a bunch of random letters onto the notes app like I were a child. "I'll see if he's still here, but he's not eating till you've tried everything."

Medisa looks over the food once more, deciding what to start with first. I don't move to fill my container until she's filled hers and I'm not planning on eating until she takes the first bite.

"Who the hell helped you make the rice? Do you have an Asian girl I don't know about?" The expression given with her questions is unexpected, but proud, like I had gone against whatever assumptions she came up with.

Maybe this is her being jealous without being too obvious about it? I laugh through my nose, which is basically blowing air—huffing—which sounds like I am proud or even impressed (another thing Medisa has rubbed off onto me). "What century are you living in? We have access to something called 'The Internet' you know? Also, Bellamy's not here." I say as though he responded to the text I hadn't sent.

She eats a forkful straight after she hears of his absence.

Her fork is actually something I had picked up on from

before. Medisa does not use spoons. She likes using forks no matter what the food is.

"You need to send me the link 'cause this is one of the best roasts and rice I've ever had, and that's saying something 'cause I've had a lot."

'She likes my roast.'

Forcing myself to snap out of it, I fill my container with the same selection of food as her.

"You know the best way to eat rice is with your hand, and before you say 'that's dirty' or messy, just try it, trust me—"

Not that she notices, but I instantly put my spoon down.

"—And don't act like you don't eat burger and chips, or pizza with those same hands."

"I would never say those things." If there's one thing I don't like, it's individuals who are not open-minded. It's like choosing to be in a cage that you've constructed and it makes no sense as to why someone would do that? Even Maverick, who thinks that he is above everyone, is open enough to try new things.

Noticing Medisa chucking food down as though she weren't allowing herself to properly chew her meal, I deduce that if she's that eager to eat, she definitely didn't say her little line.

"By the way." I decide to bring it up. "You didn't say that thing that you say before you eat."

"Yes, I did." Her voice is sure but her eyes say otherwise.

"No, you didn't."

Her shoulders drop. "No...I didn't."

Covering my smug look by feeding myself more handfuls, I go from one thought to another, and now I'm wondering how Medisa feels. Did she enjoy herself? Did she like skating with me? Did she get proper hours of sleep or were they completed in my car? Is she enjoying herself right now?

My mind travels down another route after remembering how she was with Jessie, and how different she is with me, and I find myself wanting to know more. Like, is she with someone? Does she have someone in mind?

"So, Medisa, let's talk boys." Not really subtle but I couldn't care less.

"Let's not." She funnels some more food into her mouth.

"Don't girls like talking about boys? *Obviously* not all the time, but I'm sure it pops up every now and then." I play with my food by gathering some rice into a corner to make it easier to pick up.

"Only when there's one to talk about."

"Well, *is* there one to talk about?" I busy myself with a bottle of water.

"Nope, you're the only boy in my life." She dramatically delivers her line whilst extending her arm out and aggressively biting her lips.

Though I know she is joking, my heart drops at the fear of her developing some sort of attachment towards me. The thought of her being around me for longer than what I had agreed on, sends shivers down my spine.

"Nah I'm kidding, I'm not interested in anyone. Never have been." She seems to make a mental agreement to have one more finger-ful before taking a break.

"You don't want to get married?"

"Are you interested?" Medisa's answer is too quick and too curious for her to be joking.

It's almost like I've stepped into uncharted territory.

"No, that would be haram." I place a water bottle closer to her.

"Oh, *sorry* Mr. I-do-my-research." Medisa grabs the bottle but just as she's about to open it, she stops in her tracks. "I like the idea of marriage and what-not, but it just feels like I won't get that. I always have something else going on *and* whenever I hear about boys or actually hear a boy talk, it furthers my uninterest—the shit that you guys come out with is ridiculous. It's like there are no real men anymore—and don't even get me started on 'Muslim boys'—especially the ones online—ugh." She takes a sip then forces more rice into her mouth.

'O-*kay then.*' There's clearly more to unpack.

"No-no, do go on, I wanna hear what you have to say." I adjust to get more comfortable as experience reminds me that Medisa can go on, and for once she has more than a pinch of my interest.

Points are made for hypocritical boys, disloyal boys, delusional boys and I hear it all, but I can't help but push it a little to the side and focus more on how passionate Medisa is about the subject. She's not as dumb as she's made herself out to seem. I knew her eyes and ears catch onto things others may dismiss, but this was on a level that I admire. For her to never give in, never be fooled, surely that would lead to the worlds saddest scam for when she finally does. It's not that I don't think that there aren't any good men out there, there are, it's just that they're a dying breed. If it isn't any of the points she's made, it's some things else and I don't have time to clarify faults when the list is probably getting bigger as Medisa speaks.

At the end of her rushed squeezed-in-a-minute speech, Medisa's breaths become heavy and I almost want to laugh at the fact that she chose to get her point across over oxygen.

"Damn." I react more to her behaviour than her words. "They sound like every other prick, only difference is they use your religion as an excuse for their behaviour—"

"Exactly, exactly!" She switches position, almost ready to jump over the food and get in my face.

'You wouldn't complain.'

"They just give Islam and practicing Muslims a bad rep. Even on things like drinking, some of them—And some girls, would be like *'oh that's just Islam being too strict, we're stopped from doing anything fun'* like no you idiot, there's a reason why things are haram, God is literally trying to protect us. Honestly, the way they act is another reason why some—mostly girls, I think—want a revert—which by the way is another thing that pisses them off and it's hilarious." She waits for me to say something against anything she's said.

Her curiosity to where I stand in a matter that has got nothing to do with me is a little endearing.

"Why do some girls prefer reverts to Muslim-borns?" I push her to talk more about this one-sided passionate conversation because it is somewhat entertaining and because there is a chance, however small that if things play out well, Kassian may consider 'reverting' *if* his relationship with Amana develops.

"*Muslim-borns.*" She quietly chuckles, almost calming herself down from previously trying to get all her words out at once. "Because when a revert sins by… let's just say drinking. You would be more understanding as it's probably a habit that they're still trying to get out of, whereas a Muslim born person has been told from young what to stay away from, so when they do it, there's literally no valid reason, unless of course it's forced down their throat. Also reverts tend to be more knowledgeable, so they could teach you something you don't already know. Oh-oh and—" She extends the word a little. "If a Muslim can guide someone to the religion, he or she will be granted rewards for every good deed that person does, and some say that it basically guarantees them a spot in heaven."

"Great. So reverts are golden tickets?"

"*Good* reverts are golden tickets." Medisa confirms whilst I try and remember the interactions between 'Iris' and Kassian.

Was Amana just trying to convince him to join a religion like I was trying to convince her to join Baronial?

That doesn't seem too far-fetched.

Medisa looks me up and down, then stares at my skin for two seconds too long.

"And some reverts have tattoos." She poorly mumbles as she scratches the back of her ear.

"What about tattoos?"

Her expression and eyes that look everywhere but me, lets me know that she is thinking of how to form a comprehensive explanation. "We believe that our bodies aren't really ours, that our bodies are entrusted to us by God—a gift if you will—to hold our souls—our spiritual beings, so we should look after them, hence why certain food and drinks are haram and why we can't get tattoos or certain piercings or even do stuff before marriage. We'll just be damaging our perfect bodies slash souls and inflicting unnecessary pain or confusion." She stops to see if I'm following, and shockingly, I am. "That's why if some people are crazy serious about their love for tattoos, but also religion, they *may* seek out a revert for them to marry."

I replace the somewhat finished rice and roast container with the container filled with noodles, buying me time to go over everything Medisa's said.

"I don't know if I'm scared or admire that sort of dedication. Here try some noodles."

Truthfully, I would like to move away from the conversation. I don't want to taint the relationship between Amana and Kassian by thinking that she only spoke to my brother because she was basically a scout too. Meaning that it was never genuine, making the fallout between me and Kassian continue to grow its pointlessness. Not to mention what I would do to/ in front of Medisa if I let the thoughts continue.

"For real. Anyway, I probably should've asked before I ate the roast, but I'm just going to ask now just in case. Is this all halal?"

I tut a few times.

"I would never feed your Gift something haram." Unbeknownst to her, Amana reminded me more than she needed to about how the ingredients need to be halal. I was almost going to purposely go against her demand to spite her.

Medisa makes a sound from the back of her throat, a type of laugh I've never heard from her before. "Shut up." She cringes the words out.

Feeling warmth from within, I think back to her relationship with Amana, and Amana's with Kassian. I wonder about their conversations, the things they would do together, and I find myself wanting to know why they are so close without blood ties or work relations. Kassian gave me his answer, but I want to know what it is for Medisa. What made her like Amana?

"Can I ask you something about Amana?"

She hums her approval, her shoulders slowly shrivelling.

"Why do you have such an attachment towards her?"

Medisa's expression gives her away. I read '*that's out of the blue.*'

"Err, she's my first real friend and she stayed despite me

being a little different."

"What d'you mean?" I know that Medisa's not normal, I just want to hear what she knows is different about herself. Maybe she reveals something new?

"I," She extends until she comes up with more, "didn't really do much before her, just observe, and maybe feel a little anger or sadness, jealousy—"

Jealousy? Anger? Towards who—what? Why?

"—but she opened me up to feel more. Don't get me wrong, I wasn't boring, I just didn't talk as much, so where I picked up on things and let it pile until I did something, other people saw outbursts. And then after Amana, I started being a little more external with my thoughts and feelings."

Medisa still observes, and has moments where she doesn't feel the need to talk, and if this is her 'improved' and I feel some type of way about it, am grateful I didn't know her when she was in that phase. Perhaps I have more than one thing to thank Amana for?

"My parents and siblings thought I was demented when I was younger—"

O-kay.

I try not to have on a *'where did that come from?'* face.

"—Even took me to a therapist at the ripe age of eight— maybe seven, to get the 'psychopath' diagnosed."

I'm sorry what? How bad were her outbursts? And why have I never seen one...

'It's not completely out of your hands to bring one about.'

"But I was *way* too aware of the situation, so I put on an act lol."

So she can act well enough to fool professionals, unless of course they took her to some shoddy-could-not-give-a-shit start up therapist.

She shoves noodles into her mouth, but they are longer than she expected. Instead of using her teeth, she glances over and if I were well mannered, I would look away but for some reason, entertainment purposes or not, I refuse to take my eyes off her. Medisa then decides to inhale them, and when that doesn't work, she remembers the use of her teeth. Then there's me, watching as she struggles, having no idea how to react.

Politely clearing her throat, she continues as though nothing happened. "Speaking of tattoos—"

We were done with that conversation ages ago...

"—What are yours about? Any stories? The smoky one that leaks onto the area near the end of your collarbone kinda looks like three roses."

Depressing, draining memories and thoughts of my life with Maverick flash before my eyes. If I give in to them, they will sabotage my mental state and this fake relationship I got going on with Medisa, and we haven't even gotten round to me apologising yet.

"I'll tell you the stories another time. Right now I want to know what you think of the food and what progress you've made towards the future you want." I know for a fact that she hasn't done anything so this should move us miles away from whatever conversation she planned on having.

Medisa stuffs two more forkfuls. "These noodles have set the standards way too high for any other ones. You sir, have trapped yourself with me for the rest of your life, because now, whenever I crave this bad boy, you will be the one that I come to."

I smile, not just because she likes the noodles I made, but because now *she* is the one trying to change the subject.

"Are you going to tell me what I did to deserve this good

day?"

My smile slowly drops as I am reminded that she is not as ditsy as I thought. Medisa's held the purpose of today at the back of her mind, just as I have kept it at the back of mine. One would hope—Bellamy—that her ability to be considering and wait for the right moment to deal with a matter, is rubbed off onto me.

"How I treated you last week wasn't right. It was out of the blue and I'm sorry, I didn't mean to be an arse but I—"

"You had things going on with your family I get it—"

"What?" I automatically leer at her.

Where did she get this notion?

Does she know more than I thought?

Her face shows her panic, like she knows that she slipped up. "Er-I I just assumed it was something to do with your family because when I act out, out of the blue it's usually because of mine."

Medisa's a good actress. It's to the point where I'm not even sure if she is acting.

Logically thinking, Medisa previously thought I had been groomed by Bellamy, so I think it's safe to say that this is something she somehow put together.

'You're making excuses.'

"Oh." I calm down with the expressions and tone. "Well thank you for giving me some space and for being so understanding."

"Don't expect space next time. I was fighting the urge to run up to you, to beat whatever you were holding in, out. Dunno if I could hold myself back next time."

"Do that. Don't hold yourself back next time." Medisa may be the next person to push my boundaries and succeed. Not because of who she is, but because of who she knows.

Her relationship with Amana, and Amana's with Kassian, almost makes Medisa untouchable.

"You better remember this when that '*next time*' happens. In fact, forget that, there better not even be a next time. I know that we're not close and that we barely know each other, but you can talk to me. I'm not the type to spread it round and I've been told that I'm a good person to talk to."

"You are a good person to talk to. *And* be around." I can't say where those words came from. I suspect it's in my nature to be a charming liar.

Medisa humorously scoots away from me, tickling a laugh and succeeding in getting one out. I'll deny it to others, I try to deny it myself, but Medisa is quite funny, in a weird way.

"I can't believe you did all of this to apologise to someone you've known for like a week." She begins to clear up.

"As *disgustingly* cliché as this sounds, you're not just someone Medisa. I could tell from before that you're different." Not knowing how she's different won't kill her. In fact, it would give her a better life according to Amana.

"You're starting to sound like every other guy now."

"I'm aware. Makes me feel sick. But I hope you know I'm being serious and have no ill intentions." No ill intentions as of yet, who's to say I won't want to kill her one day.

'*And actually see it through.*'

"*I'm aware.*" She mimics my tone with a cheeky smile.

Not wanting to sit back down, Medisa walks over to the ping pong table, picks up a bat and motions for me to do the same.

I start the game with no intention of being competitive. "Now that you know the truth behind today, tell me about your future plans, what have you decided or done?"

Medisa misses the ball as her face goes back to looking like she's been caught.

"Oh c'mon. You didn't think that I fell for your little topic change and forgot about it, did you? Good job by the way, *loved* the deliverance. However, I genuinely care and want to help, so, get talking." I serve another ball.

She pouts a little, not in a cute way—although it can be read like it—but in a '*shit what should I do*' way.

"You know what? I should probably go catch up with my prayers and then if it's not too late, we'll talk about it." Medisa slowly backs away towards the door as though her moving slower than usual means that I cannot see her.

Just as she gets a sense of being close to the door, she whips herself around and pulls it open like her life depends on it.

I allow for her to feel as though she can escape, but just as the door opens wide enough for her to get through, I slam it shut. It's a little like playing with my food.

With my hand above her, holding the door shut, she stands there, probably thinking about what to do.

"We're talking about it, *today*." I say knowing damn well that she will run away after her prayers.

Medisa's shoulders dropping give away a lot. Today, in this context, it shows defeat as she turns around.

I back away before our lack of distance makes her uncomfortable.

"Truthfully, I don't have anything to say. My mind has been a little occupied lately and it's kinda embarrassing that you're more on this than me." She bites her bottom lip in a way where it almost looks as if she's trying to chew it off.

Disregarding what Medisa thinks of me—I am not '*more on this*' than her—only because if I give it more attention, I will laugh, I move to open the door.

"I don't have anything to say, so you're kicking me out?"

"Kicking you out? No. I'm helping you out. Going blank, being busy or holding yourself back while trying to make a big change are all normal. I'm just showing you that it's way easier if you're upfront with me. I'm not going to punish you."

Her lips curl into a smile which I've now identified as her risqué mind having a thought.

"Punish me." She cocks her head slightly to the side, her deliverance wavering between a question and a request.

I think about it, I do, but then I think about how I just spent the day trying to get on her good side, and if I do something now, I would most definitely would have to do more for Amana's apology because of Kassian and blah blah blah.

Can't be arsed.

But I do admit, this human oddity I'm forced to look after can be a little compelling.

"Go pray." I keep the door open.

Medisa walks past with her cheeky eyes fixed on my stern ones, there's no evidence of any attempts of her trying to hide the face she's got on.

"Oh, and by the way, before I forget to say it." Her tone makes it clear that a new thought has popped into her head. "I loved today. But to avoid continuing being a hypocrite—the whole giving Muslim boys shit for sinning when I'm here chilling and eating with you—we need to keep hanging out, outside of work hours to a minimum, if not stopping completely...unless you're comfortable with my dad or brother being in the room with us."

I could not even begin to fathom the switch up. Do I understand how she came to it, because of her explanation? Yes.

Do I understand the timing of it? Not so much.

"Give me their numbers."

"Ugh, could you take this seriously please." Her deliverance alone is too friendly for her to be asking for her request to be respected, nevertheless, I am being serious. "The whole reason I'm earning money is to get away and be a better Muslim, not worsen. So this is the last time…okay?"

Ah yes, Amana did mention Medisa's faith being a serious goal of hers. Based on her actions and words in all of our interactions, I would say that she's taking it slow and steady.

"Okay." I agree because it's what she wants to hear, but now I have the task to come up with more ways to spend time with her.

Chapter 33
Kassian
22/10/2021 (Friday)

Kade or this 'Bellamy' not being inside the building last week was a lucky outcome on a stupid decision made on my behalf. So now I've been waiting in my car for my brother or the other guy to show up. So far, no one but Medisa has gone up the elevator.

After waiting until a little after lunch—when no one came—I walk over to the elevator and let myself in. Soon as the doors open, I make my way to my brother's supposed office. It really isn't his style, there's not one thing in here that I can confidently say is placed by him. Maybe the cologne collection?

"Did you guys have a meeting?" Medisa stands at the doorway.

"No-no I just woke up feeling a little poorly." I'm working on how Kade would talk. So far, Medisa gives no reaction so I assume I'm doing okay. "But I feel better now, so here I am." I raise my hands as if to show off the office.

"Cool." She balances on one heel as if to pivot away but then decides to look back inside. "I was going to make a dead joke about how you were avoiding today so that you don't mess up and feel the need to spend a whole day apologising again."

"The *whole* day?" The words slip out.

"Was it not the whole day?"

I pull my lips in, forcing a tight smile. "It was...it didn't feel like it at the time, but it was."

"Alright, calm down." She motions '*settle down*' with her hand.

Before I have the chance to get into what she's just revealed, Medisa half pivots away from me then turns back.

"Okay, I know that it's been a few days but before we move into another week, I just want to say thank you for buying my favourite snacks—"

Her favourite snacks? What is he trying to achieve?

"—For holding me whilst skating—"

What?

"—For the meals you cooked—"

He took time out of his day to cook her food?

"—And for the time after."

What did they do after?

"I know you're probably like '*why is she bringing it up?*' but it's because I kept feeling like I hadn't properly said thank you and then on Wednesday and Thursday, you and Bellamy were occupied with things." She moves her weight from her heels to her toes. "So yeah, thank you again…just in case you didn't hear it the first two times." She murmurs.

"No problem. But know that I'm waiting for my very own apology day." I make a joke, hoping for her to laugh on her way *back* to her office.

She does not.

She fakes a '*ha-ha*' then shoots a serious look my way. "By the way, I'm gonna give you a list of movies and shows to watch so that we can talk about it after we've had our work discussions." She walks away before I can protest, not that I will, I think it's good that she wants to waste his time.

Her strange behaviour is not hard to ignore when I now know how far things have gone between her and Kade. I bet he himself doesn't even realise his actions. Sabotaging whatever this is now would be a waste, it would be better to let their relationship marinate, perhaps even escalate things myself every now and then.

I take out my phone, aware that my emotions are once again pushing me to do this. This isn't what I had planned. I admit, curiosity did bring me here again, but not because of Kade, but because of Iris. I could update myself through Medisa. It's not enough to see her from a distance, I need to know what she does when she's not working. Is she exploring like she wanted to? Is she trying out new places, meeting new people? Has she changed her mind on her future occupation? What movie-like things have they experienced? I need to know. And if Medisa talks about her as much as she did about Medisa, I will know.

Maverick answers the call.

"Just in case you still wonder why your dog hasn't come back, it's because he's found another owner. Two in fact." Propping my feet up on Kade's desk, I sway on his chair.

"Give me names."

"Ah-ah, not so fast. I have my own plans with how to deal with this."

"Kassian." He calls my name, his tone a warning. "Come back to the house."

Chapter 34
Kassian
16/12/2021 (Thursday)

I admit, as time went on, I very quickly began to dislike Medisa. While she did share stories of her and Iris, I couldn't help but hold distaste towards how oblivious she is, which then of course grew over time. My opinions of Medisa is truly what allows how we would deal with Kade much easier. Sure, this isn't her fault, but why is she allowed to have this much fun with my brother when me and Iris are still suffering from his decisions?

Maverick wants Kade back, sure, but his interest in Medisa and Bellamy peaked almost instantly. He wanted to know more about them, he needed updates just as much as I did and we've agreed that when it comes down to it, he will be gentle with Medisa. I can't say the same for Bellamy and I wouldn't dare try to convince Maverick to give him the same special treatment. Maverick's whole thing was to keep us brothers close. He doesn't know the words I spoke to Kade the day he left, he doesn't know what happened period. He assumes Kade not coming home is due to Bellamy keeping him away. Hell, I even think it.

Regardless of what date marked the last day of the semester, today was always going to be the date I revealed myself to Medisa. Today being a Thursday and not a Friday does bug me a little as it's a day shy from being perfection but nevertheless, it's close enough. The fact that she will dig around after my reveal and get caught in some sort of trap that will ultimately bring her to Maverick is sublime. Especially since I won't have to do much after tipping the snowball.

I don't know what Kade's punishment is, or if he even has one. But I do know that once I start exposing Medisa to what he's kept hidden, he's going to have no choice but to stop acting. Eventually, he'll realise he has no moves to help the situation, one wrong move and Maverick or I would stage an accident and then, and then he'll *really* feel what I did; powerless.

I want to say that I've grown, that I'm better than this, but how is that being anymore fair to myself than Kade was back then when he made his choice. Why should I deny myself even a lick of satisfaction?

Someone trips and falls beside me. Without too much effort—looking down at them—I see that it's Medisa. She has a weird habit of trying to scare Kade and given that she hasn't backed down, I can say my brother isn't bothered to pretend that he doesn't make use of his senses.

"What are you doing here? Is it because I didn't come in the morning? I asked Bellamy if it was okay for me to come in later and he didn't seem to mind. Anyways we're all supposed to meet at the station remember? To go see the lights?" She rambles, obviously trying to move away from her failed attempt.

Coming out to her needed to be perfect, needed to be away from anyone she regards as familiar, and hearing of this link up between the lot of them puts a slight dent in my plan. I need to find a way to get her away from the lights, away from them.

Her eyes focus on mine. "Your eyes are kinda red and the actual colour part is different. Something you wanna talk about?"

One thing about Medisa, she makes use of her eyes. Another thing about Medisa, she's not confident enough to call things out so she either keeps it to herself or she disguises her words as a joke.

"They're contacts." I lie as I stand up.

"They look good but your natural colour is already unique looking <u>May God bless you.</u>" Another thing about Medisa (and Iris) they have a habit of talking with terms from a language they do not speak.

"Yeah, I just wanted something different today." I move towards the revolving door, almost abandoning her with how fast I move away. And if leaving her behind *was* the goal, I would've failed as we now stood to the side waiting for the doors to empty.

"Shall I call Amana to see if she's free right now—"

"No." I do not want her to be here today, or any day after this. Medisa's expression is as if she's about to give me crap before walking away, so I continue talking with a softer tone. "I got us time off work today, you're welcome for that, now we have more time to…" What's that word she likes to use? "Chill."

"Bellamy let me have a late start and now he's giving me the day off?"

"Yup."

Medisa looks me up and down before finally deciding to let me in on her thoughts (another thing she does, but not all the time). "You sound off, like you're going to be ill. And you're already wearing layers so if that's not helping, maybe we should stay inside?"

"Nah, I'm good and we're not wasting time staying indoors, especially on a day off." There's a pub a few streets away, one that Maverick owns, the plan is to take her there.

After bickering back and forth because of her stupid solutions to non-existent problems, we both settle for doing a bit of what we both want. Medisa wants to spend time inside until the others get here and I said that I know a place that is close to our—their—meeting point.

I lied.

"I don't care, the next pub or shop we see, we're going inside." Medisa blows hot air into her hands.

I'd been making us walk dark streets for some time and now she's finally given up enough for her to be willing to get inside any building. Just to add a little salt to her small wounds, I look around the street that housed private buildings, pretending to be useful.

"We're in *central* London, there's supposed to be a pub on every corner." She blows some more air into her cupped hands before reaching into her pocket to dig out her phone.

She won't find it. I snatched it up fifteen minutes ago. "What you looking for De—?" I catch myself a little too late. If it weren't for her missing phone, I'm sure she would say something.

"My phone."

"When did you last use it?" Twenty minutes ago when she checked the time and I knew then that I had to swipe it before she receives a message from the real Kade.

"Forget it, I'll worry about it later let's just use yours for now." Her walk over to me is almost like polite stomps.

"I recognise that building in the distance, I'm pretty sure there's a street somewhere here that's lively and has a pub." I walk towards where I know for a fact Maverick's pub is, not giving her a chance to search me.

As we approach the pub, Medisa's face loses its slight joy for finding a building that's open to the public. As we get inside, Medisa's face is almost unreadable, but as I make use of context clues—a pub filled with men—I know that she's uncomfortable and will probably try to walk out.

Pinching the end of her sleeves, careful not to touch her skin, I guide her away from the door. Surprisingly none of these men have picked up a game of darts, so I drop her arm by the wall.

"Take the darts off the board, I'll be back, I've been dying to take a piss." A lie of course. What I really need to do is go through her phone then turn it off.

As soon as the door to the gents toilets closes, I whip out her phone. Getting into it is no problem, I saw her pin weeks ago when we were lined up for some food.

Kade and Amana's name are at the top of her messages. My thumb hovers over 'Kade', then quickly taps 'Amana WIFEY'.

I pace the toilets back and forth, thinking about what to say to her.

'Hey girly, might be late. See you later x'

I stare at the message then delete it before I accidentally send it.

'Hey wifey, might be late. Love.'

I add a peace sign at the end with its pre-chosen colour. Why is it three shades darker than Medisa's actual skin colour? I go through the rest of her hand emojis and all of them are different colours. I shake my head, realising I'm putting too much thought into this. Erasing what I had written, I try again, going for something much simpler.

'Might be late, something came up x'

I send the message then pace some more. How long do I have to wait? Will she reply now? I scroll through their old messages and see that Medisa and Iris never send an 'x' unless they were being sarcastic.

"Fuck." I can't delete the message, the stupid app won't allow me.

Turning her phone off out of frustration, I realise that she and Iris are definitely the type to share each other's location. So, I go back onto her phone and lo and behold, Medisa is sharing her location with both Iris and Kade. I could turn her phone off and be done with it, but if I wanted to make things interesting, I would keep her location hidden from him forever.

A message pops up at the top of her screen.

It's from Iris.

'What happened??'

I begin to sweat.

'I'll tell you when I see you.'

I send the message straight away.

'Cool. Let me know when you're out.' She replies.

I grin before switching her phone off. I can't be tempted to start a conversation. Not now.

Chapter 35
Kade
16/12/2021 (Thursday)

"Isn't she supposed to be out by now?" Bellamy asks as he scopes out the entrance, scanning to see if he could spot Medisa.

"Something must've come up. Her location did show that she was still here." I join him in looking around. We could get a pass into the University but it would be a waste of time considering she might be on her way down right now.

"Does she know that you track her?"

"Of course not."

"Do you track me?"

"Obviously."

He chuckles. "Well can you check if she's already left for the station. You know, our original meeting point?"

The meeting point changing was my idea. Medisa had taken time off work in the morning as her course became more demanding so, I convinced Bells to join me in grabbing her some hot food to surprise her with.

Today is the first time after a long time that we're doing something outside of work and it's only because Amana has agreed to join us. It's one of those instances where if you were to inform your past self of it, they wouldn't believe you. Things have been working out for us. Medisa tells Amana about what we get up to and in turn Amana slowly changes how she views me. It's what I planned for, what I hoped for. Soon I will be able to tell Amana the truth and make things right with Kassian. If not for me, then for the both of them.

I unlock my phone and go straight to her location.

"What's wrong?" Bellamy takes a step closer to me.

I stare at my screen, I even blink a few times to make sure that I'm not seeing things, then I finally turn it towards Bellamy.

"What am I supposed to be seeing?"

Turning the phone back to myself, I look to where her location is no longer showing.

"She's at his pub. Why would she be at his pub?" An unfamiliar feeling takes over me. My heartbeat becomes irregular and I feel as though my senses are zoning in and out.

There is no logical explanation to calm me down. She would never step foot in a pub and even if she did, why that one? Why would it be one that's nowhere near the station or the university? She wouldn't have found that exact one unless she was taken there.

"Call Amana!" I order Bellamy, then notice that he's already waiting for her to answer.

I call Medisa's phone, combing my hair away with my fingers then pinching the bridge of my nose.

Straight to voicemail.

I call again and the same thing happens.

Bellamy has better luck then me, Amana answers his call. "She's not with you?"

Taking the phone away from him, I try to keep my voice down. "Call her, locate her, find out who she was with. Whatever you find out, you tell me."

"Kade? What the hell is happening? She texted me a minute ago saying that something came up."

You know in movies when a character is too close to an explosion that they temporarily lose their hearing, all they could hear is some sort of ringing then the voices slowly fade in and grow to be loud with the surrounding noises all at once? I've never experienced something like that before today.

"What is going on?" Amana's voice holds panic and when my eyes flicker through the people on the ground floor, I see her rushing towards the entrance.

"Just see if you can get through to her, leave the rest to me." I keep my voice as close to still water as it can get. There's no need for all of us to be panicking. Once I hear the word '*okay*' leave her mouth, I hang up and turn to leave.

Chapter 36
Kassian
16/12/2021 (Thursday)

The smile on my face leaves as quickly as it had formed as soon as I see Medisa being groped by what I can only describe to be something that crawled out of a British horror movie.

She presses her hands onto her head after—I assume—headbutting him. Her efforts however are wasteful as he still has his grip on her. Without thinking I strip myself of my jacket and sprint across the floor.

"Medisa move!" I practically roar at her as I rip his hand off her back.

Once she's out the way, I swing at him. A man of his height and build should have some sort of strength or reflex, but his inability to take what I had landed says otherwise. He stumbles back into some chairs where he finally loses his footing and falls.

Medisa's breaths catch my attention and just as I'm about to turn to check her, she grabs onto a bottle by its neck and swings for the man to prevent him from getting up. I almost snort at the scene and how random it feels, but the rest of the group the man belonged to stand up and begin to approach.

The bottle in Medisa's hand shakes, giving away her lack of confidence. It's almost as if she's forgotten that I'm here and is being forced to defend herself.

Before one of them get too close to her, I pull her back and place her behind me.

"Why didn't you scream for me?" I'm almost annoyed. Our plan for Medisa and months of preparing could've gone down the drain if I had not come out when I did.

Still trying to process what's going on, she looks up to me as if I were in the wrong. Before I could say more, I catch the supposedly grown men carry away their friend, making room for a proper fight.

Deciding to do the same, I quickly gather Medisa in my arms and put her over the counter. "Stay. There."

Not getting time to stretch, I am forced into action. It's no secret that these men look as if they could eat me alive, but thanks to their lack of skill, I am able to still have fun with how I deal with them. I also have to remember that this is Maverick's pub and I cannot be indebted to him, so I must keep damages to a minimal, to both the building and the men.

One is frustrated enough to lift a stool.

"Now hold on, let's think about this." I hold up my hands. I may be able to afford to refurnish this place, but that doesn't mean that I want to.

He swings the chair by its legs and ends up hitting one of his own.

"That wasn't very smart now, was it?" I deal with him then turn to deal with those who have somehow ended up behind me.

So far, not one man has managed to land a hit and it's times like this where I *almost* understand why Maverick put us through what he did. I feel as if I should put my hands in my pocket to make things harder.

Suddenly, I remember why I'm in this mess and notice that she is dealing with two men on her own. I push away one last man then turn to her. It's funny watching her try to get out of this persons hold, should I let her do her thing or should I get involved?

I take a step towards them but my goal is interrupted when Medisa kicks herself and the man gripping her from behind backwards and onto the wall.

Oh *fuck* me.

I should've gotten involved before.

Things have taken a turn for sure but I can't deal with it right now, Maverick's just going to have to pull some strings. Medisa's on the floor backing away from the second man. Just as I'm about to help, she boots his ball sack, forcing him to bend over, allowing her to get a clean shot to his head with a full bottle. Unexpectedly the poor bastard is not knocked out, so she takes it upon herself to give him another kick. Seeing her in her own world in this way is a little enchanting, in a shocking way. Her eyes don't even notice mine on her until she moves past him, I doubt she's even noticed what she's done.

I should start calling her '*Watered-down Kade.*'

In the small-time frame it takes for me to witness Medisa and for her to notice me, two, maybe three of the men get their hits in. A few to the face, some to the ribs. I admit, all their shots held weight, but I also admit that it triggers me enough to forget about my audience and the owner of the building. She's already made a mess anyway.

I grab a man and flip him over me, putting him in an awkward position where I am able to break his arm. And I do. Another man tries to pull me off after the fact and is met with a similar fate. After that I see red, well, a slight tint of it. I'm aware of my actions but I'm also aware that I would never behave like this unless it is asked for. And I would say, a group of men on a power trip, *is* asking for it.

My eyes set on the man who started this all in the first

place. He's conscious again and I see no reason why he should escape harsh consequences.

As I'm about to land some sort of hit, I notice in our reflection, one of them behind me.

Turning too late, he sticks a knife into my side, just not deep enough for it to be worrying thanks to the grip I develop on his wrist.

Partially struggling against his strength, I turn the knife towards him, fighting to now push it into him. He hisses, I'm not sure why, but I do use it as an opportunity to plunge the knife into his neck. And the idiot pulls it out, so I stick it in again, this time making sure that it stays there.

Before his body falls towards me, I swipe him to the side, dismissing the damage I've done but also uncovering a stunned Medisa. Her hand held a broken but bloody bottle, solving the mystery as to why the man lost his strength, allowing me to push the knife into him.

I look her over again, realising I don't actually see her breathing and that the bottle she holds couldn't be kept still.

Gently is how I approach her, with my hands up, softening my look as much as I can before she sees me as a threat. As I slowly remove the bottle from her hand, I repeat the word's Kade said to me the first time I was forced to draw blood from someone.

"It's okay, it's okay, you're okay." My words are quiet as I rub the top of her arm, gently trying to shake her back.

And as if the timing could not have been more perfect, the man with the knife jammed in his neck begins to gurgle and cough up blood. I notice Medisa's tempted eyes about to look in his direction so I quickly become a shield, standing in between the already rotten man and Medisa.

Reinforcements make an appearance and it makes me

wonder if this were a coincidence. Not having too much time to get into my theory as they are now all equipped with some sort of weapon, I plan our way of escape. Medisa on the other hand, holds out her hand, asking for her broken bottle back, and I almost want to entertain the idea.

I loosely wrap my hand around her forearm and let out a chuckle. "Now-now, Medisa."

Before a move is made, I tighten my grasp and drag her out the fire exit.

Chapter 37
Kade
16/12/2021 (Thursday)

The state of the pub is concerning, but I don't make a move or allow myself to spiral until I am sure of what is going on. Bellamy was adamant on me being nowhere near the pub, he's worried that it may be a trap, so I have no choice but to find a coping mechanism on the side whilst he finds out what happened.

"Kade, let's go." Bellamy says as he approaches.

"Do you know where she is?"

"No."

"Hold on. What? What did they say?" I try my best not to get too temperamental.

"They recognise Medisa. Said that she was groped by a man, then the male she came in with saved her, made this mess, then ran away with her." He unlocks his phone to show me a picture he had taken of the man. "He's the one that got handsy. He's still in there, along with other bodies."

I look around, forcing myself to take deep breaths. Broken bones, bodies, a trashed pub, and yet there's no police cars, no ambulance, there's not one thing on the outside letting anyone who walks past know that something happened inside. It has to be Maverick. He snaked his way in and introduced himself. Hell, he must've staged this whole thing too, to make himself look like the hero.

Medisa's gone off somewhere with my brother. Her location and phone have been turned off. Two things which have already happened and are out of my control, for now. However, we do know one of the things that took place and I happen to know the perfect place to deal with it.

"Keep an eye on him." I walk away, occupied with strong emotions and awakening desires.

"Where you going?"

I briefly turn around to wave him off with a smile. "Don't worry. I just need to prepare something."

Chapter 38
Kassian
16/12/2021 (Thursday)

So far, my performance has been amazing. I could have been an A-lister if I weren't a River.

Right now, I'm busy barricading the doors to my own pub. Huffing and puffing as if I don't have the stamina of a horse.

"What if someone's in here?" Medisa whispers.

There are people here, upstairs specifically, but they've been clued in on the possibility of my arrival.

I grab her wrist to take her down to the basement, earning myself a few tugs and comments. When we finally get to where I want, I loosen my grip just as her final tug comes about. She's obviously going to bring up her not liking her wrist being held. Of course she is. Why wouldn't she? Now's the perfect time. We've just trashed a bar and now we're hiding in another one, so of course she should bring up her minuscule problem. Now *also* seems like the right time to give the battle wound some attention.

I hiss out in pain, slowly dropping to the floor.

Medisa tries to catch me to keep me up, but she ends up softening my landing instead. The urge to laugh is strong, but the moment she faces me, I wipe my smile off my face.

After her eyes search me to find what might be causing pain, her hand pulls my top up as if she were removing a wax strip. I almost worry my tattoos have been uncovered from the scrap back at Maverick's pub until I remember, todays the day she finds out.

"Easy girl, I haven't got the energy right now." I throw in some wheezes and slow blinks.

Medisa slowly stands up, her reactions are almost concerning, the cut isn't too deep but her reactions are making me reconsider how serious I'm taking it.

"Relax, it's just a deep graze." I may be speaking to the both of us.

Trying her best not to insult me, she goes back to pacing. Her hand raises to peel her lips but lowers as she tries to fight the urge. Then I see it. She's got her own cut across her palm. Parts of her blood have started to clot but it's either too big or too deep for it to have stopped dripping down completely.

I push myself to stand and Medisa notices and immediately comes to my aid.

"You don't just have my blood on you."

She follows my gaze until her eyes finally land on her hand, then she shoots her gaze elsewhere.

Using her unharmed hand, she grips onto her open wound, squeezing it whilst holding it away from her eyes. "For flips sake."

I look down at my already ruined shirt and think '*ah what the hell?*' There's already a slight rip, so I just continue it along until I have enough to tie around her hand. Medisa watches me rip into my top, I can feel her borderline-bug eyes on me, yet she idly stands by as if I am not doing this for her. I reach out and pull her close, examining her hand. There's dust and dirt and what not around her cut, making me back-track and question if we truly were in the same places.

I look around.

"Let's clean it." I don't say with what because I can practically hear the fuss she will make.

"No." Her firm answer confirms she's already got an idea.

"Do you want to lose your hand?"

"*Do you want to lose your hand?*" She mocks. "Relax, it's not that bad, just gimme your... that. Just gimme that." She holds her palm out for the ripped cloth.

"No." I so desperately want to clean her first. She deserves that stinging, burning feeling, especially after mocking.

"Why? What you gunna do? Sew it back on?"

"Yeah, I am. Do you have a problem with that?"

"Just give it to me." She tugs it away from me, though I wasn't exactly putting in effort to stop her from having it. "Idiot."

Her glares as she wraps her own hand, slowly turn into some sort of daze, something I truly have no time for. At this rate, she will know who I am tomorrow and I can't have that. It needs to be today.

Medisa randomly smacks her forehead after her eyes ogle me. "Oh my God! Kade where is your phone?"

Before wasting any more time, she teleports over and searches me, not caring for which parts of my body her hands run over.

After finding my phone—thankfully not her own—she rushes to call someone. This is it. This is how she finds out. There's no way she won't notice *something* out of the ordinary if not straight up different.

Medisa pauses, her eyes travel all over the screen and all I can think about is to make sure I don't get too excited.

She looks up to me, searching me with her eyes as I take off my hat and gloves. As her eyes does rounds on my body, I know for sure that she is trying to make sense of things as I peel away the 'skin' that hid the tattoos on my arms, neck and abdomen.

"You're not Kade." She's taking it well. No dramatics, just more alert.

The smile that grows on my face I imagine mimics the Cheshire cat.

I walk over and pop open a bottle to pour onto my 'deep graze.'

"No. I'm Kassian Koda River." I purposely introduce myself with Koda, the name I had given Iris. "Kade's gorgeous twin brother." Taking steps towards her, not caring for what part of me is exposed, I continue, "And you Medisa. You are my new friend."

I hold out her phone between two fingers and she hesitates before grabbing it back.

Watching her every move as she notices her new screen, I suck in air through gritted teeth. "Sorry about that. Got into a fight at the pub."

Once again, she ignores my comments. Her finger scroll through, revealing all missed calls and messages from those who she should be around.

"Oh my God." She moves her head closer, narrowing her eyes. "Oh my God." A hand is raised to her mouth. "You've been with me multiple times now, haven't you? The hair near your nape is shorter than the rest, which means you've had your hair cut to look like Kades, which means in the past you could've been with me or someone who knows Kade without having to wear a hat or hoodie."

She's not panicking.

Lucky for her, I'm not a complete psycho, so I'm not exactly bummed that it's something that I cannot rejoice. Her finally knowing and being able to connect some dots herself however, is something I must admit I am proud of.

"Question is, why have you gotten so lazy with it? Why go back to calling me Desmona?—And yes, I picked up on that—Why even call me Desmona in the first place?"

I want to correct her and say '*Desdemona*' but she's close enough and that's impressive considering I haven't called her that for months.

Remembering why I'm doing all this in the first place, I lower myself so that our eyes are level. "Because you were never going to get your happy ending." My voice is low but clear and once I'm done talking, I go back to standing at my normal level.

She doesn't say anything, which bothers me. I may not need her to scream or cry, but I do need more than she is giving.

I huff.

"I do have to say…I was worried that you were going to be all sizzle and no steak, but I think you've done enough to prove me wrong. You see, I didn't see the hype before, and I had to fight certain urges when I was with you, but you've finally figured it out." By certain urges, I mean I wanted so badly to knock her out and take her away, maybe even wrap her up for Maverick. "Not everything of course, but it's still something so…congratulations." I bow my head a little, then resume looking down at her.

I no longer care for her to react because I know she will tell Kade, and he, he will definitely give me the reaction i'm looking for.

"*Desmona*. I like it. It's short and has the same meaning." I speak to myself since Medisa decides to be mute.

"I didn't figure it out." She speaks as I'm about to turn away. "You *wanted* me to find out today." Her voice is somewhat serious, no hint of fear. "Why?" Now she seems to be the one talking to herself.

I let my head fall to one side as if I had a shoulder to lean on.

I suppose I could tell her more.

"It's about time you knew, especially when things are going to get exciting."

"What are you talking about?" Her tone is laced with an attitude.

No longer willing to tell her more, I stand and take it all in. There's no going back now. Eventually Kade and Iris will be informed and I will no longer have to hide.

"I need to find Kade—" She walks past me to get out of the basement.

No fear in putting her back to me.

A mistake, but I'll let it slide.

"And ask him some questions? Let me ask you this Desmona." I repeat my given name for her as a way of speaking her unfortunate events into existence. "What makes you think he'll tell you the truth?"

Now, not only will she doubt and question him, she will also fall down a rabbit hole.

Chapter 39
Kade
16/12/2021 (Thursday)

I breathe in the air of freshly laid out plastic. The room was already lined from years before, but there's just something about prepping that gets me going. What's that saying?

The process is art itself?

The tools I may need are out and I'm salivating at any thought of using them.

It's been a while so I'm not going to rush into this. I'm going to make sure I take my time and enjoy every part. I cannot allow myself to get carried away. Though today's events have implied otherwise, I doubt I would be able to do this again, so I need to make sure this lasts me months, perhaps even years before I feel the need to do it again.

Knowing how Bellamy would be opposed to this, I had gotten him to deal with Amana. She knew that something was happening and we couldn't afford for her to do something out of line, so I had sent Bellamy to ease her mind. Whilst Bellamy was away, I swooped in and took him and it was easy as taking away a child's sanity.

Speaking of, he is now beginning to wake, soon about to wonder why he cannot move or stretch the way he would like. I lean back into my chair and let him go through the process that leads to some sort of panic.

After his pathetic attempt of trying to free himself, he turns to me, where I'm already waiting with my most welcoming smile.

"Let's start with your name, shall we?" I say, too cheery for his liking I suppose.

His breath quickens. "Wait-wait I did as I was told! It's not my fault for the way things turned out!" He looks around more urgently than before, trying to spot some sort of window, door, crack in the wall, anything. Instead he spots the tools I have lined up. "Do you not see my face!? The state of me!? This has already not worked out in my favour! I should be asking for more money—but I *won't*!- I won't. I don't care about money, just, *please*, let me go—" He continues to waffle as I build on my theory that this *is* Maverick's doing.

"How much money were you offered?" My tone is curious and away from any sort of frustration.

He stops talking, his quick breaths are now taken through his nose and it takes a second for him to get himself together. "Five thousand."

I whistle. "Five *thousand*." I try to hold myself together but once some sand slides down, quickly does the rest. One single heavy breath escapes through my nose and I feel my charming smile turn to a sinister one. "Five thousand to get your grubby hands on a defenceless girl, that's easy."

Now he trembles with fear, coming to a realisation that this is not going to end well for him.

I laugh at my own thoughts.

"Would you say that you're defenceless? Right now? Tied down in this chair?" I look to him for a response but he's frozen. "I would say so." I bob my head.

"Wait-wait. Please, I was just doing as I was told! I would never do something like that otherwise."

'Lies.'

Without thinking—not that I would stop myself—I lunge towards him, landing several swings onto his face. I almost zone out from the lack of screams or grunts, so I take a step back, only to realise he's still awake.

I move away, there's not much I can do to him with my bare hands whilst he's tied down anyways.

My fingers glide over the tools until they land on a hammer. Picking it up, I throw it in the air and catch it like you would do a baby, if you were to throw and catch a baby with one hand.

The man whimpers. "Please." Tears fill his eyes as his expression highlights his wrinkles and the folds on his forehead. "I just needed the money."

Nodding as though I understood, I raise the hammer and bring it down on his knee, only when it's about to make contact, I pause. As soon as I see him release his deep breath, I do what I had originally intended.

I break his knee.

The constant screams quickly become screeches rather than music to my ears. Luckily for him, he passes out before I do anything about it.

Before I move on, or even prematurely take a break, I bandage him up. I can't have him bleeding out, or constantly passing out from shock after viewing his leg.

Several hours, a broken knee, strategic cuts, some missing teeth and bruises later and the man is still alive. Quiet now and unrecognisable, but alive. His breathing has calmed down, maybe because I took a little break? But I'm ready to get back into it.

"So, what hand was it?" I click my fingers in his face when he doesn't respond.

He opens his eyes mid-third or fourth click.

"Hmm?" I expect an answer.

"What?" He croaks, already tired of what's to come.

"What hand did you use to hold her in place and what hand made its way down her?"

His chest moving in and out is more noticeable now.

"Can't remember?" I click my tongue. "That's okay, I have an idea."

His hands grip the armrest tightly, nails marking where he's previously scratched.

"It has to be your right hand. There's no way you're one of the fuckers who is a lefty, or even an ambidextrous." I shake my head then come to an abrupt stop. "Well. Bite down onto this." I put a hand towel into his mouth.

The container has been sound proofed so I'm not worried about the rare occasion of someone walking by, it's just that his pleading and screams are starting to give me a headache. The first, in a *very* long time.

I start with his left hand. "Since you used this to grip her, I think it would be poetic to break it."

His pleading begins and shockingly, tears are still able to form and drop from his swollen eyes.

Paying no mind to his drama, I lift the hammer and get to work on his hand, starting with the fingers first. I should have a microphone to record the sounds created on impact, I'm sure a lot of people would enjoy them.

Once I am done, I check his pulse.

He can't leave me just yet.

"Okay Mr Doe are you ready for the grand finale?"

As if it were a good surprise, I bring the saw from around my back, even added a little gasp to get him excited.

This wasn't the original route I was going for, but it is

what's going to happen. I know exactly where to cut so this will be easy. Sunrise is approaching, if not already gone and Bellamy's just informed me that Medisa has texted Amana. So I need to be on standby. However, just because I am being rushed does not mean I will not complete what I originally set out to do; induce pain, create art.

I've cleaned his bones from his flesh and have the drill bits ready. Usually I would clean up first before I get down to things like this, but something about not getting to do this in years is making me create my designs now.

To finish things off, I put his rings back onto its assigned finger, then lean back to look at the final piece. Sighing, I look back to the man whose skin did not hold him together. If only he made it to see the final result.

He might have liked it.

Chapter 40
Kade
17/12/2021 (Friday)

"What did you do?" Bellamy's voice is stern, a sign he's done his check up on my latest victim and found nothing.

I hold the full glass of water in my hand, not bothering to bring it to my mouth, he's already done me the disfavour of spoiling it.

"Kade, an answer would be nice. *What* did you do?"

There's a slight pause—some would say hesitation—before I click my tongue. "I killed him."

I decide to take a sip anyway.

"Where is he? What did you do? What if you were seen!" His worries come through, though he still sounds like he could kill me himself.

"It wasn't my first rodeo. I've dealt with it accordingly."

He takes a deep breath that fails to keep his cool. "Dealt with it accordingly? What's that then? Dealing with what happened to Medisa? Because that's not dealing with it accordingly, no, that's straight up murder without proper cause." The annoyance in his voice becomes more and more apparent.

"Who's to say his next victim wouldn't have been a rape victim? I've done the world a favour."

"*Don't* act like you weren't happy to trick people into selling themselves before."

It would be a lie to say his words didn't bruise me.

"Wow... Okay." My head slowly wavers.

"I shouldn't have said that."

I let out what Medisa would call a '*bitchy laugh.*'

"You think I acted too quickly but what did you expect? Things have been too good to be true for weeks and my guards had been lowered, low enough for me to not have spotted something sooner. So yeah, *my bad* I killed the guy, but also my bad for letting things get this far in the first place." The victim in me makes an appearance and I know that it's mostly to guilt trip Bellamy into letting this go.

Things go quiet.

When I look to Bellamy to see if he's somehow slipped away, I see that he's stood there studying me.

"Kade." His voice is the audible version of him stepping on eggshells. "What is she to you? And don't you lie to me, I just need to know if you've realised that you're no longer acting. You haven't been for a while."

I hesitate.

"What is Medisa to you?"

I almost want to laugh at how ridiculous this is, but then it's ridiculous how I've not yet given an answer. Bellamy is about to say something, probably cuss me out, but I cut in. "She's trouble."

Melancholy eyes paired with a twitching smile appear on Bellamy's face before fully disappearing. Not in the sense that he wants to laugh, but in a bittersweet '*I feel sorry for you*' way.

"What you did was reckless, experience or not. As for Medisa, you need to think about whether or not she's good to have around. You won't say it out loud so I will, she triggers you to fall back into old habits. If it's not old habits, it's memories."

"She's not going anywhere." I act irrationally once and

all of a sudden, the solution is to get rid of her.

"Then you need to properly think about if keeping her from the truth is the best option." He begins to walk away. "I'm going to see if what happened yesterday is still being kept quiet."

Two whole floors, and yet I only find some sort of comfort in her office. It doesn't even have the best view, yet I'm staring out her window. Bellamy's words run through my mind, the whole conversation repeating again and again. I acted like a complete arse. His frustrations are understandable, but the immense stress I felt from the moment I saw her location at Maverick's pub could only be released by either physically seeing Medisa in front of me and away from my family, or that other thing I did.

As for telling her the truth, that can't be a decision I make by myself. There are layers to this and I'm afraid that after yesterday, after I agreed months back to do this, Medisa is already in too deep. If there's a chance—which there always is—to get her away from this without her knowing too much, I'm taking that route.

Footsteps stop at her door and I can already imagine all the things Bellamy has come back to say.

"Bell, please not now." I'm too tired to turn around.

"It's not Bellamy, it's me."

I instantly turn around. Her voice is like music to my ears. I didn't expect to see her so soon and those damn boots of hers give her the heaviest steps.

"Medisa." Walking up to her as though I haven't seen her in a while, I notice how she tries to act normal, how her eyes study me... it makes me regret how I approached her.

'*I wonder what she think she knows?*'

"What happened? We had plans and you never answered your phone." I put on a good act of not knowing where she had gone. "I asked Amana and at first, she was worried but now it feels like she's avoiding me." This part is true, something—most likely Medisa informing Amana of what she now knows—changed the way Amana is with me.

Medisa's eyes slightly enlarge as they begin to flutter between mine. Watching her make sense of her mind isn't exactly comforting, so I briefly look away, spotting her bandaged hand. That immense feeling I felt earlier begins to come back but with more anger than the fear of the unknown.

"What happened to your hand?" I fight the urge to grab and see for myself.

Not one of my questions have been answered, so far all I've got is a smile that didn't bother to reach her eyes and that was when I first greeted her.

Medisa continues to stare into my eyes, unsure which eye to focus on. I notice her grabbing her injured hand while trying not to bite her bottom lip. Her stiff, somewhat squashed-looking body seems as though she's fighting to keep her thoughts in.

After forever, she sighs and drops her shoulders.

"I met Kassian." Her eyes search for something on me, and it takes everything in me to stay calm. Kassian was never a suspect when it came to this. As far as I assumed, he was no longer in this country, let alone this close to us.

Medisa's not freaking out, or angry at me, so I can cross off him saying anything about Amana and Baronial.

I look down at her hand and then back up to her eyes. I want an explanation. I *need* an explanation before I 'overreact' again. If her silence continues, I may end up exposing more than what Kassian has. He's always been clever enough to come up with plans that made people self-sabotage, effectively doing his job for him.

I take a deep breath, but it does nothing.

I still need that explanation.

"He-he didn't do this." She begins to crumble.

Lowering my head so that it is somewhat level to hers, I inch myself towards her, pushing her to say more.

Medisa can be clumsy, but for her to have hurt the palm of her dominant hand the day she met Kassian is suspicious.

She slowly backs away from me, and I don't understand why she can't just be out with it? What is she trying to hide? Is she trying to protect Kassian? Has she always known about him? Is this a part of their plan?

"This was me." Medisa holds up her injured hand by its wrist. "I was trying to defend him—*us*."

I continue to get close until she stops moving away. How on earth were they put in a situation where Medisa was the one who had to defend the both of them? Kassian can take care of himself, so what game is he playing at? We were told that Medisa had been groped then saved, not Medisa had been groped and was forced to help herself and my apparent useless brother who allowed her to get injured.

Medisa shuts her eyes to avoid mine, then begins to pace her breaths. When she's ready, she looks back up to me. "I was trying to defend us and I didn't realise the spikey lid was halfway on, so when I hit the guy with it, it cut me."

'*Spikey lid?*'

The crown cork bottle caps?

How hard did she swing for it to have cut that deep? The thought of her contracting some sort of illness from the dirty cap rubs me the wrong way.

Regardless of how she got hurt, she shouldn't have been put into this situation in the first place. I understand Kassian may feel a certain way about mine and Medisa's friendship, but to take her to Maverick's pub, risk putting her under his radar...I'm going to kill him.

"Can you please sit or say something because I'm starting to feel myself shake and struggle to breathe." Her hand shakes over her throat, matching the rhythm of her voice.

I stop thinking about Kassian and realise that Medisa is genuinely breathing weirdly. I look at her hand once more, then at her eyes, and mentally kick myself for towering over her.

Luckily for the both of us, there's a chair for me to sit on, diminishing the height and in-her-face problem.

Despite sitting down, I continue to be tense and need more. She hasn't said anything of use yet. Yes, I now know how she got her injury, but the outcome of what I do about that was always going to be the same. What I now need is to know about anything and everything Kassian has said and done in her presence. He's no longer someone I know. He wasn't the night I left, and he sure as hell hasn't grown to be any different.

Medisa turns away so she doesn't have to face me. As she paces, she goes over everything, from the time she thinks she first met him to their most recent encounter.

Kassian, that cunt.

He's turned into me and he's good at it. Finding out about Medisa then deciding to wait until we grew close for him to reveal himself, slick, but to get involved when I finally felt different and was one hurdle away from earning Amana's forgiveness—what an idiot. I wonder how he will feel knowing that now *he's* the one that's messed things up.

Striding over to her when she is done, I study her face once more to ensure she has nothing further to add.

Her breaths are slow and heavy, she's clearly manually inhaling and exhaling.

Concerning, but a little amusing.

"Sit down."

Following behind her, I accompany her to the chair. Once she's seated, I rotate it so Medisa has no choice but to face me. This adjustment maintains a respectful distance while ensuring eye contact. I am not in her face like before; I've given her that distance.

Now I take a deep breath.

"I am Kade River." I pause, partly because I haven't introduced myself in a long time—it's like cracking ones stiff knuckles— another part because I really don't want to say this to her. "And I come from a long line of influential people."

I try to spot any reactions she gives off, a breath too short or long, the urge to peel her lips, twitching or enlarged eyes, shaking leg, but she does nothing, nothing but wait for me to go on.

"Things were supposed to be different for my brother and I, but things changed. I can't tell you everything, but just know me and Kassian aren't on good terms, we haven't been for years." I push the narrative of our troubled relationship to make any moves Kassian pulls against me barren. If Kassian did grow some and decides to make more idiotic moves by mentioning Amana, I might be able to convince Medisa that they are desperate lies and nothing to give attention to.

Her eyes wander off before she brings them back to mine. After licking her lips and scrunching her brows, she pauses.

Then, her lips part.

At first, nothing comes out, but then she just says it as it is. "Honestly... I'm so confused. From this interaction *alone*, I have so many questions. And I understand you not wanting to tell me everything, I do, but Kassian said that there's more to come. So, if there's anything that I should know, just tell me now so that I'm prepared."

Clever girl. She only wants to know the necessities, of course some would say the complicated relationship between the four of us is a necessity, but I'm willing to leave her in the dark for a little longer. Only to see if I could save the mess that Kassian's made.

'And to hide the one you made.'

"There's not another one of you is there? A triplet scenario?"

I look her dead in the eyes to see if she knows more. We're not triplets but we may as well be. Our genes are what people like to say '*copy and paste*' to.

I stop leaning on her wall and move towards her to see her out.

"Do not trust Kassian. I will find out his reason for being here. You just need to go home and rest. Stay away from work for a week—"

Her mouth opens to—I assume— ask how she's going to be allowed to take time off on such short notice.

"—I'll cover for you."

I move out her way for her to enter the elevator. Medisa gets in with no fuss, her mind on everything that's been revealed to her in the last thirty-six hours.

"Why would Kassian show up out of the blue to mess with me and you over something that you don't even know about? It doesn't make sense."

Her ability to question me, to imply that I'm not telling her the whole truth is admirable, but it's not something I need her to do. The curious cat thing is not needed.

Just as the doors are about to close, I jam my hands in and separate them, spotting Medisa jump at my last second decision. I search her eyes as she searches mine, contemplating if this is a good idea.

"The River's love games Medisa. If there's money involved, it's good. People involved? Better. Blood, twists and turns? Then it's great. The more the merrier. But it's only seen as a game because we know that we will win. So don't be fooled, the game is rigged." While it's true that we do love creating games and toying with people, I inform Medisa of it because once again, it is planting a seed in her mind to not be so trusting.

Letting go of the doors, allowing them to shut, I watch as Medisa's face transforms into one that is mentally questioning where I stand.

After a few seconds of processing the inability of changing the course of what has played out, I turn with full intentions of hunting down my younger brother.

Chapter 41
Kassian
17/12/2021 (Friday)

It's late. Close to midnight. Her parents should be home, but I don't see their car upfront.

That's okay, it's okay.

They can catch me leaving, or find me in her room—being in their house should be enough to disgust them into kicking her out. It's either this or Maverick stages an accident. And I don't agree with involving more people than necessary, so I'll be the one to extract Medisa from her household.

I repeatedly tap my finger on the steering wheel, observing the surrounding houses. She lives in a terraced house with a garage sticking out from the house three doors to her right. And since I can't exactly walk through her front door—*she* won't even let me do that—I will climb onto that garage roof and access the gardens from there.

Now that a plan has been made, I switch my car on and park it right in her parents' drive…it adds a little more to the nerve. Thankfully, the headlights don't grab the attention of anyone—if anyone is—in the front room. I even wait a minute to see if someone comes to the door.

No one does.

I walk over to the house with the garage and swiftly make my way into their garden. The original plan was to jump over the garden fences until I reached Medisa's garden, but things have been made easier. Each of these houses have a ground floor extension, so my new plan is to quietly walk across the roofs until I reach Medisa's house.

To my luck, which has obviously turned around recently, not only is a window cracked open a bit, but it's cracked open a little to a room which belongs to Medisa.

How do I know this? Well, she's asleep inside.

After my soft entrance, and before I approach her, I stand still. Not everyone in this house is asleep. Her siblings are awake and clearly express their animus towards Medisa. Their voices travel up the stairs and into this room, and judging by how peacefully she sleeps, I think it's safe to say she's used to their gossip.

I crouch down beside Medisa, so that we're eye-level. Here she is, sound asleep, unaware of her friends lives. She's probably the only one that actually gets to sleep while they're out there not only going through their own horrors, but also worrying about her.

What is it about Medisa that makes her so special?

The same brand of lipstick Iris wears for a few clients, in the same shade, is in my pocket and I can't think of a better look for Medisa to get into trouble in than that.

It's almost poetic.

It doesn't take long for Medisa to begin to wake. I did leave the window wide open, letting the cold in. And since her room door was close to being shut, the cold air only circulated in this room, avoiding her relatives downstairs.

My eyes were on her, but my ears were on those below. They're talking about a package Medisa received today. My attention peaked when her brother had mentioned Amana's name, but it quickly disappeared when her sister changed the topic to something completely unrelated.

Medisa, now awake, has somehow managed to drop her phone off the bed, retrieve it without getting out of bed, and is now searching the room through squinted eyes.

"Whatchu looking for?" I decide to make my presence known.

Her head snaps in my direction.

She wastes no time in getting out of bed and marching towards me.

"What the hell are you doing here!? You can't be in here! If you're caught, we're literally going to die!" Though she is whispering, desperation and anger peak through. I'm almost surprised a vein isn't bulging. It's also comedic how she said '*we're*.' Her words and her clown lips really do go well together.

"How's the hand?" I ask. She's now wearing a cleaner, better wrapped bandage. I wonder if she got professional help?

"You need to get out *now*. I'm not joking if they—"

"I'm going to assume you told Kade about me."

She better have.

Oh well, I guess after today, she definitely will.

Before she can confirm or deny, or perhaps even carry on trying to get me to leave, the rooms light is switched on and her sister walks in.

Finally, some fun.

Medisa's body slowly swivels to follow her sisters casual steps to the bed. Just as her sibling, who I now have a proper look at and have some doubt on their relation, make's it to their bed, she too freezes. Her eyes can't decide if she wants to look at the handsome man or her spoilt sister.

No one says nothing, no one moves and when I look to Medisa, I see that she's noticed her face in the mirror above the bed. In confusion and anger she turns to face me, only for her eyes to grow in shock. Yes, I put lipstick on Medisa like a drunk girl, but I also smudged some on myself.

Quickly, she turns back to her sister. I would've thought she would sing the truth by now, but nothing comes out her mouth. Her sister however, wastes no time in running downstairs. You would think a fire was in here with the way she ran. I almost feel for Medisa when I myself realise her own sister wouldn't hear her out.

The girls take themselves downstairs as I opt to stay here. There's no point in moving, her brother is bound to hear what the commotion is about and will investigate for himself.

"Medisa was in our room kissing a grown arse boy in the dark! Look at her face! She's wearing lipstick and everything! It's all over their faces!"

I scrunch my brows, my fingers close to blocking my ears. I did not expect her to sound like that at all.

Someone's footsteps sound close, not quite to the stairs, but approaching them.

"Shut up Ataya! That's not what happened! We weren't kissing! He—"

I tilt my head to the side so that my good ear faced the floor. What will Medisa say? What can she say that they would believe?

There's some sort of stomping then scuffle?

I move to the stairs landing.

"She's lying, none of that happened!"

"Then why is there lipstick on your face! *Why* does what you look like match what she's saying!" Her brother's voice is already filled with anger and he's directing it towards her? He didn't even come to check, even if there is a chance of me being gone.

"You're acting like I couldn't have put it on before I went to sleep!" Medisa's voice wavered.

I take a step down.

"You. Don't. Wear. Lipstick."

A thud happens straight after his words.

I take more steps down.

Medisa mutters a few words, but I can't hear her. My mind is simply too busy thinking about how different this all turned out to be.

"An interest in something can happen randomly. Why the *hell* would I have to announce that I'm suddenly experimenting with some lipstick?" There's a slight pause before Medisa lets out a scoff like laugh. "You stupid, *stupid* bitch."

I shut my eyes because I know that would be enough.

A few heavy steps and two loud thuds later and Medisa is on the floor of the entrance to the room her siblings are in. I didn't even realise I had made it downstairs and was this close to her.

"He's there look!"

Ataya, is it? Yeah, she needs to do everyone a favour and not talk again.

Medisa latches herself onto my leg, blocking my way into the room. Ignoring the '*don't fight*' message, her brother advances towards me, but Medisa is quick to intervene, halting his approach while simultaneously bracing herself, anticipating a potential impact in the same second.

I quickly move her out the way before she feels his weight. And not being able to brace for her brothers weighty barge myself, I find myself in their small hallway and almost instantly shove him back into the room for more space, and away from Medisa.

He fights with his face in mine. His swings are heavy, his defence is good and he makes use of footwork, but he can't expect me to take him seriously when I just discovered that he's okay with using his advantages on someone with Medisa's build, not to mention, a girl.

People like him really do piss me off.

I bring two fingers to the new cut on my lip. "Can't say that felt as good as her lips. Wait. My mistake. I should've waited for an attack on my dick."

There's a slight pause in him before he goes completely ape-shit. I don't do much damage back, that's not what I came here to do. The more bruises he gives me the more I can stick on him and this family, keeping them away from Medisa and anything that she will be forced into.

His stamina does not decrease, and he seems to have gained more strength.

I stop fighting completely. There's something about the buzzing feeling that comes with each hit that is reminiscent, and sometimes I can't help but indulge. I grin as I stare up at his face, maybe I should stage an accident? Just not with her parents.

Before he delivers what I assume would be one of his final punches, I notice the stupid girl foolishly get in the middle of things.

Her brother is too blind by the rage I provoked, but that's no excuse for his elbow connecting with her face.

Medisa falls to the ground, her eyes slowly close as she dissociates.

Her brother doesn't even notice. Surely, he felt his elbow connect and heard her fall? but no, there's no reaction.

Before he gets in another hit, I stun him by going straight for his nose—several times—which releases me from the weight that held me down. I don't allow him to recover, he doesn't deserve to, so I give heavy hits into his sides. Usually, that's enough to take an ordinary person down, but he's just not dropping. My options are to hit him across the head with the salt lamp I've just spotted, or I can restrict his breathing until he gives up. I go with restricting his breathing since I could say to the authorities (if they do get involved) that I restrained him after he beat the shit out of me and his sister.

Ataya tries to escape to God knows where, but I grab her, staining her top with her brother's blood.

"Let me tell you something." I lazily lower my head. "She was telling the truth." I grin. "Your *sister*, was telling the truth. And you, you spiteful bitch, couldn't *wait* to run off and sell a lie."

She attempts to tug her arm away but that just makes me tighten my grip.

I lead her to the sofa and almost fling her onto it.

"I'm taking Medisa with me. Feel free to call the police but know that it won't do anything. Medisa will testify that she let me in and that your bull of a brother started this." My finger swirls around, pointing out the blood we got everywhere, then I pull on Medisa so that she sat up. Once I gathered her in my arms, I make Ataya see us out and unlock my car.

I smile.

I knew it would do me well to park the car this close.

Chapter 42
Kade
18/12/2021 (Saturday)

I may have to sell this place after this is all done.

Standing in this elevator, taking it up to any of the floors used to bring me a sense of joy as it served as a reminder of my successes. But now, I feel that joy deteriorate, like this place and entire situation has been polluted.

Maybe it's always been polluted? From the moment Kassian's brain conjured up the idea of befriending Amana, that moment is truly what has connected every event that's played out since. Everything goes back to his mistake…or mine. I guess it's a matter of perspective?

One thing's for sure, I'm losing my soft spot for him. I think seeing Medisa's bandaged hand started it. I won't allow myself to lose it completely, as his feelings are somewhat valid. I know that if our positions were reversed and the girls switched, the likelihood of me killing Amana would be high. That being said, did he really have to be a child about this? He couldn't have just approached me? He *had* to risk her chances, waving her around in Maverick's pub. What was he thinking? —Rhetorical.

Things have been taken too far, even for Kassian. It's going to take time and effort to get things back on track. Fixing this won't be easy for anyone. All parties are stubborn and having one in the dark and conflicted with curiosity does not help either.

The elevator doors let me out.

My attention is quickly drawn to the light in my office. I don't need to be in there for me to know that it is coming from Medisa's gift. The thought of whether or not I had turned it on before I left did not exist, I would stake my life on the fact that I did not use it.

Someone had made their way into my office, and with the state I'm in, I'm not sure if I want to be civil for Bellamy's sake or once again, line a room with plastic.

I may even let them go for another time as I am in no mood for whatever part of the game this is.

The closer I get to the room, the clearer the figure sitting in my chair becomes, reassuring me that my imagination had not conjured up an entity. They aren't facing me and I don't know if it's stupidity or bravery—two which often go hand in hand—but I find myself admiring it.

The stranger is either busy looking out the window or at something in his hands; I can't tell from here.

Letting myself in, I wait for whoever thought that this was smart, to make a move.

"Name: Medisa Menaal. Age: Twenty. Date of birth: May 25th 2001. Height: 5ft3. Eye colour: Brown. Hair colour: Black. Ethnicity—"

"Get up." The words come out a little more casual than intended, almost as though it were muscle memory to be addressing Kassian in this manner, like I—in Medisa's words—can't be arsed.

"Ethnicity…" Kassian swivels the chair around. "Pakistani. Physical appearance—"

"Get. Up." I speak through gritted teeth.

His smug look is accessorised with fresh cuts and bruises. The muppet obviously crawled under someone else's skin before he got to Aros.

Before things get physical, he stands and moves towards the drinks that have not touched my lips for weeks.

"She's got stubby thumbs, plump *juicy* lips—more so for the bottom lip, and her bra size—"

He knows not to go on. I'm in his face, forcing myself not to give in to any one of our satisfactions of ripping into him. Kassian's face holds no remorse or fear like it used to, and it's this that makes me think he's finally acting the part of a proper River man.

He grabs one of the drinks, then drinks in front of me as though I am not here. After two large gulps, he sucks in air through his teeth like he were thinking of the next thing to say.

"I met her by chance—or was it fate? Anyway, I was going to ignore her, but then I figured out what you had done." He laughs to himself. "Then I thought, '*hmm what would be the best way to screw Kade over?*' You know, to make things fun? So, I got a whole makeover to look like you, then I spent time with her, learning what I could and my, oh, my, did I learn."

Taking a hidden deep breath, I hold it. Kassian has the upper hand in this, anything said and done now against him would only concrete his petty plans.

"Turns out she knows nothing about what you did and used to do. And I *was* going to keep it that way until I realised, she's your friend. Not someone like that dog you got working for you, no, an *actual* friend. Someone you genuinely care for and surprisingly, she cares for you too in her own weird way. So…brother, imagine how fun this is going to be when she finds out what's been going on behind her back, what her fate has been tied to and who it was that secured that knot." He downs whatever remained in the glass. "I'm going to return tenfold what you did to me."

Reacting would not be the best way to go about this. I know I have done some damage that I cannot take back, but shit, to harbour all this hate, to let it marinate and to come back to take revenge over a relationship that barely begun—give me a break. This just adds more to the list of reasons on why I regret meeting Amana the way I did, and I know exactly how I would write it: 'A PATHETIC KASSIAN IS BORN.'

I don't allow myself to say anything, my mind is running on too many thoughts, arguments, and my tongue would not choose the best one to communicate with.

Kassian now stands near the window with another drink. I'm sure the old him is still present, faded, but still there. I just need to check myself before I try communicating with him.

"You should've never gotten involved." Kassian speaks as though we were shoulder to shoulder. He continues to stare out the window—thankfully, otherwise he would've seen me half roll my eyes—then turns to face me. "You would've been better off if you had just let her sign the contract."

'*Sign the contract.*' Oh, so he's not talking about Amana.

"That was never going to happen." Even if I hadn't gotten involved, Amana would have come out and told Medisa the truth about Baronial. Medisa may have been on their radar, but she would never be in their grasp.

"She's in the ideal circumstance! Poor family—wealth and health wise. Desperate and in need of rescuing. Innocent, attractive *and* she would've gotten a wish!"

I see what this is. He wants Medisa to sign herself into Baronial, wants to make her go through what Amana did so that I can be the way he is. Idiot. Doesn't he understand that our separation was enough for me to fall down in the slump he's in?

"It would've been against another wish." I try my best to keep calm, to have my voice at one level. How this interaction goes will affect what Kassian decides to do next.

"She is no one's wish."

'Careful Kassian, your delusion is showing.'

"Written down or not. She's her wish and you know it." I don't say Amana's name, not when it's still on thin ice.

Kassian's emotions becoming heightened does not stop him from grabbing another drink. In attempts to prevent him from becoming a drunk emotional mess, I take a step towards him.

"Kassian, doing this will change nothing, if you could just see that and drop it—"

"If you had minded your own business everything would've been normal!"

Now I know that he's talking about me recruiting Amana. I hold back on telling him the reality of his own (recent) actions and scoff at the irony of him saying those words. "*Nothing* about what we did is normal."

"No. Just because it isn't right does not mean that it isn't normal." The sound of his glass being put down gently strongly indicates that he, too, is done with this interaction.

Kassian walks over to the door, leaving without giving me a chance to explain, without allowing this to settle and for us to repair things together. As he leaves like I'm just some whore Maverick told him to fuck, my anger builds up inside and suddenly I no longer want to be mature about this.

"I thought you would've grown, would've become stronger, but you're still a fucking pussy with no brain. You try and ruin her, I *dare* you, I just wonder how Amana will take it when she finds out."

Kassian's sigh mimicked a laugh that'd been cut off.

He turns to face me once again, shrugging. "I don't care."

There's no hint of a lie that I can pick up on.

"And since your relations with Medisa are clear, it will hurt even more when you watch as we slowly break her, and turn her into something so ugly, that not even you would care for what we do with her lifeless body."

'*We.*'

That's what stuck with me as Kassian walks away. There's no mistake, he did say it, twice in fact.

As soon as the elevator doors shut, and Kassian was no longer in sight, I threw the first bottle I managed to grab, against the far wall, knowing that I was losing control over what was originally an *innocent* rescue plan.

Chapter 43
Kassian
18/12/2021 (Saturday)

When she said her family did not get along with her, I did not think that she meant they're abusers. How could I think that when she acts so…

'Normal' is not the word.

I want to be furious and, in a way, I am, it's just not the way that I want. I want to use it to fuel what's to come, and to use it as a way to be okay with what will happen. But I'm frustrated and it's overpowering everything else. I can try to deny it all I want, but Medisa tried to help me tonight, twice. And both times got her into trouble. Now she's here, unconscious in my car and instead of dropping her at Aros—the original plan—I'm taking her to be caged.

Medisa's role in Kade's punishment is vital, without her there's nothing. How she's lived under her own roof shouldn't affect this, it can't. This is all Kade's fault. He asked for this, he could've fixed this when he had the chance but he didn't, so now my hand is forced.

Regardless, whatever happens will be on him.

Chapter 44
Kade
18/12/2021 (Saturday)

Despite how late it is, Bellamy wastes no time in making his way into the kitchen, where I'm busy pouring the last bottles of drink down the sink. I can imagine it—and the broken glass scattered across one side of the office—raising more concerns for him than me wishing him over did.

"Before I pour the last bottle down the drain, would you like some?" I hold the bottle out towards him but he turns it down.

He takes notice of the display I have on top of the kitchen countertop; the microphones and cameras from Medisa's office.

"Kassian had tapes cut and looped, it's how we never noticed. I've searched the offices for any additional items and found nothing. Tomorrow we'll start searching the floor for anything that's not ours." I rub my forehead, staring down at the tech I ripped from the walls and hidden compartments.

When Bellamy doesn't say anything, I realise his guilt is taking over.

"It's not your fault. I asked for one man to go up against a team." I lean against the cooker. "This isn't even why I called you here, so you can stop pouting." He was in fact not pouting, but exaggerating his expression did help him move on to a curious one.

We stare at each other for a few seconds before I finally let out a scoff. I don't understand why I haven't been out with it yet, it's not a big deal.

"I don't love her. *If* that's what you were getting at. It's not love." My head shakes in disagreement. "I don't know what it is." My voice quivers, like I'm afraid. "I don't know what's changed but I find myself caring, and right now it's the only emotion I can make sense of because it's what I felt for Kassian."

He doesn't say anything. Not verbally anyway. His brows are harshly pulled together but they calm down once a pitiful smile—barely—grows.

"Okay?" He says as though I've randomly spouted out information. "Where is she now?"

"I've given her the week off so that I can thoroughly search this place. And you, if you don't mind—" My words earn another face, but this one lasts a second. "—will be posted outside her house. After things are checked here, I'll move on to finding my brother."

"What will you do when you find him?"

"I don't know."

There are only two moves that make sense. Hold him captive in my container or, kill him.

'They're the only two moves that make sense for Medisa as well.'

Chapter 45
Kade
24/12/2021 (Friday)

Medisa has been avoiding me all week. I told her to stay away from Aros, I did *not* tell her to stop texting me. After our last interaction, I thought that it would take a day or two before she finally encourages/enrages herself to text, or even call me with all sorts of questions and demands. But there's been nothing. Even when I texted her, letting her know she's got another week off due to whatever business reason I could think of, she didn't reply. Yet when I got Bellamy to deliver the same exact message, she replied with a ':)'. She's being a brat, and I want so badly to storm into her house and find out why—I know why, I just want her to talk to me. Can her dissertation that's due today not wait? Can she not spare me a second?

Anyway, other than her juvenile behaviour, the activities of this past week have contributed to my mood. There's nothing on Kassian. Never has been, never will be. I shouldn't be surprised; information about us has always been a word-of-mouth thing, never something documented. I've never even seen a birth certificate. There were also no additional cameras or microphones in Aros, which means the time I spent thoroughly searching for one was a waste. Yes, it gave me a peace of mind, but not before making me paranoid. I also had Bellamy erase my access into the elevator, to make it so it never existed. Not only will it prevent Medisa from wandering into this mess, but it'll also deter Kassian and any other party he's invited.

I must confess, a huge part of my paranoia was influenced by Maverick's involvement. The word '*we*' hasn't slipped my mind. I do not doubt that Kassian has gone low enough to team up with our brother.

Maverick has eyes and ears everywhere, it's almost impossible to move around without him knowing about it. But that's the thing isn't it, it's *almost* impossible, it's not *entirely* impossible.

Chapter 46
Kassian
24/12/2021 (Friday)

The state of this place isn't as bad as I thought. A few smashed-in windows and a broken roof… that's a decent ventilation system with the mould it comes with.

I would not say this out loud, but I have been working out some more because of the slight difference in mine and Kades appearance. It's almost a kick to the gut that he is first in almost every aspect in life, but no matter, I will match him if not surpass. How else will this all be fair?

Medisa has been alone in that hotel for a week now. There's not been any concerning complaints about her so I haven't bothered to go back to put her in her place. I did tell her something along the lines of her only staying there for a few days, but in the end, I realised that I'm still in some sort of conundrum. To put it simply, Medisa is a growing guilt, and I don't understand why I'm not just handing her over to Maverick. Let him deal with it.

The loud voice in me is siding with Medisa, pleading to give it another week to think things over. But I can't get past the fact that letting go of Medisa, means letting go of what I have over Kade.

Despite my need for revenge, I am leaning towards giving it another week. They say '*absence makes the heart grow fonder*,' perhaps in this case it makes me come up with a creative way of using Medisa without completely letting her go? Not to mention, another week and it's New Years, it'll line up perfectly with the changes.

Chapter 47
Kassian
01/01/2022 (Saturday)

My phone doesn't have to ring more than once for me to answer. If it's this early in the morning, something has transpired.

"What's happened?" I get straight to it knowing that it's one of the girls keeping an eye on Medisa.

"Medisa just received a package. She tried to go after whoever delivered it, but they got away."

I immediately grab my keys.

"Did you get a look at them? Or at the package?" I don't know why I'm asking. Kade wouldn't send *Medisa* a package.

"I didn't see them, but the package is gift-wrapped."

My blood simmers. This is Maverick's doing.

"Has she left?" I raise my voice.

"No, she's still here." Despite my volume and the urgency, she kept herself calm, professional.

"Good. Tell me when she leaves."

She will leave, I know it, especially if the package is something that is supposed to make its way back to Kade.

Swiping whatever busied his table to the ground, I slam my hands down. "What the hell are you playing at?"

Maverick casually leans back onto his chairs arm.

"You're taking your time. It's been weeks since the 16th and yet nothing has happened on either end. Why?"

I should've known he wouldn't keep out of it until it was his time to get involved. One minute of nothing happening and he is able to sniff out doubts, regrets and any thoughts of backtracking.

"I've been thinking of what to do with her. The *best* thing to do to her." I say, like my motive is obvious and not ridiculous.

"Are you sure you don't mean the best thing to do for her?" Now his head is held up by his left hand. He's tired of seeing through me. When I don't speak, he brings his lips in, creating a frown. "Okay. Let's help her out."

Automatically, I slow my breaths so that all my attention is on his words. I don't even blink for the sole purpose of taking in all his micro movements.

"You're right, why should her luck run out now? She's managed to live in a bubble, why pop it and allow her to see what her friends truly go through on a day-to-day basis, what your brother has put people through, including you and thousands of others." Maverick's voice does not hold a sarcastic tone, it's understanding and matter-of-fact. "If you think Medisa should be shielded from the things closest to her, I will stand with you. You are the one who has witnessed Amana—her closest friend—put on a mask and pretend everything is okay. If you think that's fine and should continue, then I will look away too."

My eyes feel a little more moist than usual. They must give the impression that I am considering it, when in reality, I want to laugh.

It doesn't matter what decision I came to after two weeks, because in the end Maverick has made it for me.

Chapter 48
Kade
01/01/2022 (Saturday)

My hair is growing. Cutting it is surprisingly not a priority these days, finding Kassian is.

There are no crumbs leading to him, nothing. The camera's at and around Aros could only lead me so far, and it was not far enough.

I haven't been texting, calling or camping outside of Medisa's house either, I'm not allowing myself to until I've secured my brother someplace away from her.

Avoiding every reflection, I walk through the kitchen and into my office.

"Medisa?"

I'm *not* imagining her, not this time. Why would I imagine her on her knees behind my desk, wide-eyed and with the cabinet open?

'Yes, why would you imagine that?'

We both stay where we are, guaranteed a thousand questions run through her mind, whilst two repeat in mine; Why is she here? And how did she get in?

When I remember that Bellamy is also here, one question disappears and the other becomes louder, more concerned. I take steps towards her as she stands up. Before the distance is somewhat comfortable and less awkward, she tosses a gold bar across the table towards me. The name 'KADEN ARRIO RIVER' printed across.

Medisa's a smart girl. She's seen this office, she's seen me casually come in here with wet hair (it is not raining outside) and now she's pulled out my name from a desk she believed to be Bellamy's. Medisa knows, or at least has a strong idea of who I am, therefore suspects me to be lying to her about other things. I just can't figure out if I want her to brand me as a liar.

Her eyes burn into mine as she slams her hand onto the desk. It's not until I glance down that I see the cards beneath her palm. And I recognise them. I wish that I didn't, but I do.

Medisa looks as though she herself doesn't know what to say or do, but I don't have it in me to talk. I don't want to tell her why Kassian and Maverick are toying with her.

"Are you playing me?" Her voice is fragile. Not in a whiny, teary way, but with exhaustion, as though she's on the brink of giving up, that, or I'm moments away from her blowing up.

My lips part, but nothing comes out. How can I tell her that I've been hiding things from her? How do I make things better by telling her that?

"Are you and your brother messing with my head? For entertainment?"

"No." My response is automatic. "No, Medisa I would never do that." Another lie. That is something I would do, probably have done, just not to Medisa. Do I tell her that?

She no longer looks into my eyes, no longer wants to take in the expressions I make. Does she believe me? Do I have a tell?

Her eyes concentrate on the cards, then she singles one out. "I got the first card with a note after I spoke to you at the office, a boy delivered it to my house." She makes sure I listened. "It came in a box, a gift box. With a hand. A real, human, *skeleton* hand."

I don't react, not externally anyway, I don't allow myself to. I can't afford to. Prematurely reacting would bring no good. We both don't know who the hand belongs to.

'Liar.'

"It's the man who grabbed me at the pub, I recognised the rings"

For fucks sake.

"I *know* it's him." Her emphasis dares me to convince her that it's someone else.

Other than the sudden urge to check the container, I am impressed at Medisa's ability to remember something that she saw for what, a minute? His rings must've left an impression. I should've melted them and poured the molten onto his hand. Or made her a new ring, she would've liked that.

She gives an upward nod to the next card. "That came today at the hotel Kassian took me to."

I take a deep breath and straighten myself out. I've been everywhere searching for that prick and she's telling me that he's been with her, in a hotel?

I pause.

Why did he take her to a hotel? What hotel? When? For how long?

"It came in an identical box, this time with three white roses, no written message. I thought that it was Kassian sending me notes, but that doesn't make any sense."

Medisa may not understand, but the three white roses was a message, and she doesn't need to describe what the box looks like. I know that it was wrapped, with a bow, probably with some sort of decorative filling. One brother—or both—thinks it's funny to use an old cruel joke of mine. And the three white roses? I want to laugh. I know what they mean, I just want to know if Medisa has made that connection to the design on my body. And it better be my body that she makes that connection to, I don't even want to think about how she would know to bridge it to Kassian's.

Her eyes stay on mine after previously staring at the cards. "I'm not leaving until you tell me the truth, all of it. I don't care how dangerous, upsetting or gory it is, I want the truth or I swear to God I will make your life hell—"

"Okay."

Medisa stops talking and waits for me to carry on. And if I've learnt anything from the past, it's that I should sit down.

So I do.

I let her have the option of my seat while I sit on one of the guest chairs in front of the desk.

First things first. "My name is Kade River. I don't go by Kaden anymore. And I have a middle name; Arrio. I just don't really use it. My mum—"

"*Oh*, but you want to name a whole business after it."

Arrio and Aros aren't exactly the same, but correcting her is not the best thing to do right now. Also, I may be allowing her to have this attitude, but its only because—other than the fact that it's understandable—I'm going to be the same when it comes to finding out about what her and Kassian got up to.

"Before you continue, as it is fresh in my head, why *did* you take me off the system?"

"You were never on the system, it was too risky, so we only gave you what you needed to get into the elevator. My pin."

She thinks it over for a second. "Continue."

"You've already met Kassian, my twin—"

"I have."

It takes little for me not to react. Her behaviour continues to be amusing, therefore she's allowed a pass, or two, maybe more.

"Who you don't know and haven't met is our older brother, Maverick."

"Oh great! There's more." Her sarcasm isn't shy. In fact, she sounds so joyous, if I didn't know the context, I may believe her.

How do I explain our relationship with Maverick to Medisa?

"When me and Kassian were eight, our parents died, leaving us with him. And Maverick, he er, he." What's a polite way to say that he was most definitely born a cunt? "He had problems, we didn't know then what had caused them and we don't know now, but whatever's wrong with him meant that we had to suffer too. If we rebelled and refused to listen to him, he found new ways to make us, and he *always* got what he wanted, one way or another."

I get up as my mind starts to have some sort of claustrophobic effect on me. Maverick being able to create and pull on our strings and how he's done so in the past plays in my head. I still can't seem to pin point when the exact moment I actually started to enjoy some of the things he originally forced.

I now stand near the empty bottles of what used to be expensive drinks. A shot or two would be nice, make things a little easier.

When I turn to Medisa, I notice her expression missing its attitude.

"Maverick owns Baronial Medisa." I get straight to it. It's her way of doing things, but now I need to explain. "No one is given the opportunity to join by chance, they're checked then scouted, and if they have the right circumstances, are given a contract." I try not to approach her, to urgently shake things through. "Signing the contract means signing your life away. You become a company slave. Whatever they ask of you, you do it. No questions asked." I try to summarise. "The higher the level of intensity you are put through, the more money you make. The pay they offered you, that money is given to those who are made to sell themselves." My hand shakes out in front of me, showing the desperation for her to understand in a way that my stable voice does not.

"How is that even possible? I would've seen it in the contract."

"It's possible. Through loopholes, through threats—blackmails, tracing your signature, edited conversations, fingerprints—there are many ways."

All of which I have used.

Her hand raises to peel her lips, a bad habit Medisa has for when she gets lost in thought.

"Those cards may not have been directly from Kassian but they may as well be. He stands with Maverick. He would stand anywhere if it were against me." I look into the hallway where Kassian made his threat.

My mind goes over the several things I am missing out, like why this is all happening in the first place? Why is it happening to Medisa?

"That day at the University, the first time we met. Amana had mentioned how you applied at Baronial." Finally, some truth that would hit closer to home. Amana will confirm my story and Medisa will trust me again. "I couldn't help people before, but since I no longer was under Maverick's roof, I wasn't going to sit back and let things play out the way that I know they would. So, I told her that I could get you a job, here, at Aros."

"Okay, but I didn't sign a contract. So what does he want?"

"I left my brothers to live my own life. My guess? They want me back but not without a few scars."

Medisa's brows twitch up as though she were—in her words—'*gassed*' at what this meant.

So I have to humble her.

"No."

"What?" She's quick to act dumb and offended.

"I saw the look that just glitched across your face. You won't be a scar, my brothers just *think* that you will be."

She cannot know how much influence she has. Even if it is a little bit.

"Yeah, you keep telling yourself that. I've been told that I'm magnetic and that people actually feel my lack of presence."

"Yeah 'cause of the lack of headache." The words pour out of my mouth in a way Medisa usually delivers her jokey insults.

Her jaw drops as three breathy '*ha*' escape.

"I'm joking." I smile, but it quickly fades as my words become serious. "You'll be a scar, Medisa." Though I am certain of what I say, my voice is low, almost shy. I hate it. "I value our friendship and because I do, I've made you a target. Maverick will rinse what he can from you to get to me, it's his idea of fun whilst teaching me a lesson."

Medisa looks to the ground, chewing the inside of her mouth instead of peeling her lips. Her lack of animosity towards me, or even words, lets me know that she no longer sees me as someone on an opposing side.

To my surprise, she walks over to me and doesn't stop until she's stood directly in front of me. Her eyes search mine and I'm worried that they are more windows than walls right now.

"The truth is, I don't know if I could protect you Medisa, but I'd rather go through what Maverick had put me through again than to not try with everything I've got."

She stops a laugh from escaping, I thought it was a compressed hiccup until I saw her expression.

"Thanks? But I'd rather you not go through that again. Can't have you beating my traumatic life."

I allow myself to smile, being glad that she is taking this well, but, *'traumatic life'* and *'hotel Kassian took me to,'* ring throughout my head, so my smile drops.

Straightening myself out, I peer down at Medisa, closing the gap she left between us. Yes, there are other things that need to be discussed but I don't care, it's my turn to receive information.

"Now." I say as she takes slow steps away from me, quickly hitting her back against the shelf.

Medisa's disappointment in herself is visible, but I couldn't care less, she's not escaping this. Leaning down with my arms resting on the shelf above her, I cave over, thinking about how dumb she is for skipping around with Kassian, and following him into a hotel room *after* I warned her about us.

Medisa doesn't have to raise her head as much as she usually does because of how much I've lowered mine.

"Tell me." I search her eyes, her lips, everything. "Why did you go to a hotel with Kassian?" It takes a lot for me to not ask that important question with the word *'fuck.'*

I must remember to celebrate this medium-size achievement.

Her eyebrows turn from cautious slopes to ones that look a lot like the brows she forms when she's about to *'take the piss.*'

Letting out a scoff, she finally responds while playing limbo with my arm, freeing herself in advance. "Does it matter? Figured if you guys have the same genes, the experience would be the same too."

My grip on the shelf tightens. I know she is joking, but that doesn't mean I want to hear or vividly see what she is blatantly insinuating.

I back away from the shelf and turn to face her. "Be grateful I'm respecting your faith Love. I could be proving that to be wrong right now." I realise how that sounds and quickly come up with words to fix it. "With your permission of course."

Medisa doesn't say anything.

No snarky comment, no arguing for the sake of arguing. I've obviously overstepped a few boundaries. I shouldn't have trapped her and said what I said. I should apologise, though I still want to know why she went to a hotel with him.

"We got into some trouble at my house." She begins to explain as though she can hear my thoughts. "Long story short he made it look like me and him were up to no good—*physically*—" Her hands circle each other with the word.

My lungs are momentarily put on hold, and I—with extreme amounts of force—hold onto all questions and reactions until she is done.

"—then we got caught together…alone, resulting in a physical fight. I lost consciousness then Kassian somehow got me out and gave me a place to stay. I don't know the details of what he did when I got knocked out but yeah…I basically can't go back. Not right now anyways."

"Knocked out?" I know what it means, I just want to know how it happened. How did it get to that? Was it necessary to get to that or was it him once again failing to protect her? And so help him God if I find out that he's been purposely making her get hurt.

"If it makes you feel any better, it wasn't Kassian that done it, it was my brother."

"It doesn't."

"Hmm?"

"It doesn't make me feel better. Why would it?" How did I not know what her environment is like at home? How did I not pick up on it?

Medisa looks to her feet, not knowing what to say and I realise that it's my fault. I'm being a shithead and it's making her feel uncomfortable.

"I'd much rather it was Kassian so that I could beat the shit out of him myself and let you watch, but 'cause it's your brother I'm guessing you wouldn't want that." I mentally take note of the time and date so that I know how long it takes for me to pay her brother a visit.

"I wouldn't want you to do that even if it was Kassian…I think." She scrunches her face as she mentally goes over her words, meanwhile, I'm struggling to understand her relationship with my brother.

"What is it with you and Kassian?" I want a genuine answer, but I don't demand for it, yet.

"I don't know. I don't want to say that I feel sorry for him, but I do. There's something he's hiding and if we could help him with whatever it is, he might join us in whatever we're going to do about Maverick."

With her thinking like this, there's only a matter of time before what I put Amana through comes to light. My days with Medisa have always been limited, but it's only now that it's actually starting to feel like it. Truthfully, I'm bothered by its presence and constant reminders.

"There is some sort of good in him." She attempts to convince me. "He let me stay at an expensive hotel for two weeks when he could've left me at the house."

"*Two weeks?*" My frustration comes back. "He's the reason you had to leave in the first place." I try not to shout.

"Oh yeah, I forgot to mention when it all went down."

'Conveniently so.'

"And I was planning on leaving anyways, he just sped up the process."

Of course she's found a way to be in a position where she's the one who has to be grateful.

I scoff. "Do you always give people a chance?"

"Always."

Her answer induces hope.

"Not everyone has good in them."

"I know. But sometimes I like to know why they are, the way they are before I pass judgement."

I search her to see if she's just saying that to have an argument against me or if she truly goes by that, because when the time comes, I'm going to need her words to be true.

Walking past her, I head straight for the door that led me into this interaction. "Follow me."

Almost as soon as we enter the kitchen, Medisa takes her shoes off, so I tell her to wait before carrying on myself.

After finding a pair of slippers and opening all doors, I come back to her and notice her compare the size of my slippers with her foot. I want to make a joke about comparing the size of other things, but vote against it as I need her to be comfortable for this next reveal.

Once she wears my slippers, she waits for me to lead the way again, so I do.

Since all the doors are open for her to see what room is what, I wait for her to be done with her observation before I interfere. "What d'you think?"

"I like it, it's not too crowded, not too empty. I just find it a little weird how you liv—"

"Great. This is where you will be staying from now on. Make a list of everything you need, I'm not hearing any excuses, especially after you stayed at a hotel at my brothers expense."

"Technically, I didn't willingly go in. He carried me while I slept or whatever you call it when you're too exhausted to move."

I practically feel my eyes darken. She had to have known mentioning that would hit a nerve.

"But this is cool." Medisa backtracks. "I love it. I would willingly stay here. Yep. Love. It." She gives one single clap as her eyes look around trying to avoid mine.

They fail.

"A list. *Today*." I demand.

"Has a dog been in here?"

I want to say that this is a poor pivot attempt but the way she delivered her question makes it seem genuine, so I stop walking away and turn around. "No, why?"

Medisa goes on to saying something about angels and not being able to pray, but I can't help but think about how she is going to be staying here. Does this make things easier or harder?

She finally sits down on the sofa, not exactly comfortable, but not exactly proper either, and busies herself with the tv. I myself, move through the kitchen then freeze as I need to say one more thing before I go.

I stop at the living room door.

"By the way, the bedroom is yours now too. I'll be on the sofa, or downstairs, if being outside your room makes you uncomfortable. I'll have the keys to the main door, but tomorrow I'm going to put a lock on the inside of each door to make you feel more comfortable. You get to choose who comes in whilst you're here." That should make her feel safe.

"Oh no, it's okay really. I'll stay downstairs." She attempts to stand up, but I raise my hand and shut that notion down before she sees it through. "I sat down because I thought we were going to chill here for a bit." She continues.

"I actually have to go somewhere, so get comfortable." I'm not worried about her leaving without me knowing. I've installed new cameras in the floor below, the elevator and the car park, not to mention, Bellamy is still here.

"Okay, cool. I might steal a pillow and take a nap."

This is ridiculous.

"If you're asleep on the sofa when I get back, I'll carry you to the bed."

If Kassian gets to carry her to a hotel room, I get to carry her to her new bed.

"Oh my days Kade. The sofa is *fine*, seriously."

Stubborn little shit.

"Don't force me to sin Medisa." I leave before she can argue. There's nothing that she can say or do that will change my mind anyway.

I've already made it up.

Chapter 49
Kade
02/01/2022 (Sunday)

Shopping took some time, but I'd rather get most of it done now than go out again and again, wasting time that could've been spent with her, or on looking for my cockroach brothers.

As I've come back later than I had intended, I quietly put away the things that go into the fridge/freezer. Medisa hasn't said anything yet, so I'm assuming she's asleep. For her sake, I hope she's fallen asleep on the bed and not on the sofa or somewhere downstairs.

Quietly entering the living room, I quickly notice her sleeping body. A podcast she frequently watches continues to play as I search for the remote.

After carefully removing the remote from between her and the pillow like some sort of surgeon, I switch it off and crouch down beside her.

How annoying can one be?

Medisa must've fallen asleep ages ago. Her lips look more plump than usual and her skin has a certain fresh look to it. 'Soft' is the word that comes to mind and somehow, I feel more protective of the unconscious version of her. It's also hard to ignore her relaxed cage around a pillow. It's like her sad version of a childhood blanket. And to top it all off, I know that Medisa is not big on physical contact—Amana excluded, obviously—which just makes things sadder.

After seconds of close inspection, I notice a change in her

breaths, specifically it's pace. Her breaths seem to be taken manually, as though she is holding them in for seconds longer to make use of her other senses. And though her eyes are closed and she is in the exact same position she was in when I first entered, she looks more aware.

She's awake.

"I thought I told you not to make me sin?"

Medisa scrunches her brows as her eyes open to squints, then she blinks a few times until they are able to be kept open. She's a good actress, I'll give her that, but it doesn't work on someone like me. I may not bring it up, but I definitely notice.

She sits herself up and yawns. "We'll take turns, one day me, one day you."

"This isn't up for debate Medisa. Let me look after you properly." I don't know why I bother to give her the illusion of choice.

She looks around, either for the remote or her phone. I can tell she'll use one of them to move on to something else. I should've just picked her up like I said I would.

"You are living here, and I'm going to get comfortable downstairs." I can live without the comfortability of a bed, I've done it many times before, one of the things I can—but would not—thank Maverick for.

"Do you wanna watch a movie?"

I mentally question whether or not she's hearing me, then engage with her attempts of pivoting regardless of the answer. "This late? Are you sure you can stay up for it?"

Medisa looks around again through squinted eyes, with the addition of a yawn. "What time is it?"

"2 AM." I waste no time in responding, and I can see it in her face that she regrets her suggestion and doesn't have any more ideas. "How about we talk?" I suggest. "The first one to shut their eyes for longer than five seconds has to go sleep on the bed."

Medisa will lose either way, I on the other hand will win. My night would turn out how they usually go, lonely, or, I would have Medisa's company because I have no doubt her stubborn arse would keep her awake.

Without saying anything, Medisa gets up and walks towards the bathroom. A minute later and she comes out all wet, and I can't help but smile. Water can only keep her awake for so long.

"Before I forget." She speaks through a yawn. "When I slept at the hotel, two or three people came in to check up on me at night. And I don't think that they were the usual girls."

'She didn't think to bring this up before?'

"Would you be able to recognise their voices?"

Medisa shakes her head. "For a while I thought I was having one of those realistic dreams, but then after certain events and one or two things being moved, I thought otherwise. And I don't think—"

'She can say that again.'

"—That they were there on Kassian's behalf. The workers that I know have a direct link with Kassian, checked up on me during the day. Whoever those people were, they came at night when I was asleep and left once they saw me."

Maverick. He must not trust Kassian as much as my twin thinks he does, which means he has ulterior motives that Kassian may not approve of.

"Truth? Or do you want me to lie to a degree?"

"Truth, obviously."

"They're girls who work at Baronial, and you're right, they don't work in Kassian's favour. Which means Maverick has another plan for us that Kassian might not know of, or agree with."

"Yeah." She stretches out the words then hisses. "I figured as much—You know that you don't have to lie to me?" Her voice jumps and quickens with her question. "Or keep things from me by not telling me everything? I can handle it. I'm not a glass doll and I'm actually really level-headed. So, from now on, I want truths...please."

"I know, I know." But I don't want to tell you everything. "What I don't know is if your level-headedness is bottled insanity." I suppose how calm she is makes sense. She's already been exposed to certain traits and behaviours in her own family, so another person's family feud shouldn't be as big of an effect on her. *If* we ignore the severed hand, the home intrusion and whatever else we've put her through.

"Ah, to-may-toe to-mah-toe." She swats her hand, pushing the idea away. "How does Baronial work? How does it make sense that they have a 'slave contract' but are also expected to live normally around those that know them?" Medisa curls up against the sofa, waiting for a response. She's more awake now and though I wouldn't mind staying awake all night with her, I can't risk even one of her questions, or my answers, allowing her to connect the dots to Amana.

I go into my old bedroom and grab her a fluffy blanket.

"You have this weird habit of walking away with the intention of coming back with something useful, but because you don't let a girl know that you're coming back, it makes her think that she's said something wrong and that you're done with the conversation."

Do I do that?

"Sorry, I'll work on it." I get comfortable at least three seats away from her. "Does a boy have to talk like this now?"

Medisa quickly grabs and throws a pillow at me with the

biggest smile on her face.

"Tell me more about Baronial. How does it work?" She yawns out the question.

Sleep calls her, so I hold up a finger, pausing the conversation once again in attempts to help it some more.

I rummage around the kitchen as though I don't know exactly where I put her cookies, then finally grab them and a glass of milk. Medisa's told me in the past about her battles of trying to stay awake after eating. If I remember correctly, she loses almost every time.

I hand the cookies over to her. "Like Aros, Baronial has different sectors, it just swaps the people around." I sit back in my seat. "It would be obvious if people's lives changed or if people went missing. So, they are given a 'faux' job—where people with close relations would see them—and they are given the job at Baronial, their real job."

Medisa continues to give no reaction, but she is starting to look a little drowsy.

"Baronial has rich clients, the type of money that would drive people crazy for, and delirious with. Since we give those clients what they want—Males/Females for pleasure, sport, or any other sick thing that they could think of, or even something as normal as a server—they provide 'faux' jobs for said workers. And since the workers are under Maverick, he uses them to get information on his clients for his own sick uses."

Her eyes are no longer on me, so she's either not paying attention or she's following along with her mental commentary. I almost want to say something unhinged and unrelated to test my theories.

"Each worker is granted a wish."

Her brows pull together as she looks towards me.

"Sounds childish, I know. But whatever is written for their wish must be seen through and cannot be changed or ignored. For some, a wish is a certain amount of holiday time, or something they think is beneficial. Some others use it on their friends or family." I watch to see if she's following. "For example, Baronial wouldn't be allowed to approach friends or family, or Baronial would have to pay their friends or family a certain amount—to pay off debts, medical bills or just straight set them up for life. However, a person cannot choose to save both friend and family. They can only choose one group."

"Another one of your brother's games?" She doesn't seem impressed. "It's sick, but not that sick. Only a bad or fake friend would hate on the decision of someone trying to save their family instead of them—assuming that they are aware of it. And besides, the Baronial person doesn't even have to save anyone, they could've wished for something for themselves, so they can't even be called selfish in the first place."

I guess that's one thing solved. When Medisa finds out about Amana, she won't be angry or sad about not being a part of her written wish. Even if she does get pissed, as soon as she finds out who got Amana into Baronial, her anger would be diverted towards me.

"How many people did you get to sign the contract?"

I don't outwardly react.

"I can't remember, I was practically a slave myself." It's the truth. I stopped counting when I realised there was no benefit to it.

"I would have never brought people on knowing what they would go through." Medisa's eyes slightly enlarge as though a thought was said out loud.

"I said and thought the same, but I had Kassian. Maverick deemed him the weaker one then quickly found out I would fight for him. So, whenever I didn't do what I was told, sometimes Kassian was the one who suffered the consequences."

Memories race through my mind, but so do Bellamy's words. '*It may have stopped feeling like you were kids at some point, but that was what you were, kids. And though it felt like you made choices, you didn't, so the consequences were never truly your fault.*'

"You did what you had to do. I get that. If someone threatened me with Amana, I would do whatever they wanted regardless of what it was. I shouldn't have spoken so impulsively, I'm sorry." Her brows were like slopes and she leaned a little forward, like she needed me to see how bad she felt.

This is my chance.

"If you're really sorry, you'll sleep on the bed."

"And just like that, I take my words back."

I dramatically grab onto my heart as though I were experiencing pain, then drop back onto the cushioned sofa. The whole act is rewarded with her giggles and a scrunched-up blanket being thrown at me.

"I'll sleep on the bed, *if* you consider—and when I mean consider, I mean that you're going to do it—bringing Kassian onto our side, okay?"

And the reward almost instantly comes to an end with her words. I balance my weight onto my elbows and adjust the lower half of my body.

"Medisa. Love, it's not just up to us. He needs to *want* to be on our side." And that may not happen since my plan is to kidnap him.

"How hard can it be to convince him?"

I can't tell if it's her stubbornness or her naivety that's

showing.

"I don't know, you should go sleep on it." I quickly turn as I throw the blanket over myself. My eyes are forced shut and I almost want to snore to really add to the act.

Medisa sighs then finally walks into the bedroom.

"Goodnight." I quietly say, my face all smug.

Chapter 50
Kade
05/01/2022 (Wednesday)

Her brother, Ayaan. I can't kill him. I can't even maim him. He just so happens to be the breadwinner of her immediate family, ergo, anything happening to him makes things shittier for the rest of them. I couldn't care less as Medisa won't suffer the absence of that fool because she'll be with me. But I don't want her to feel guilt, or the need to help them, which is where the predicament comes in. If I turn him into someone who is unable to earn money, One: Medisa will know my part and Two: she knows I have enough money to support her family a stupid amount over and yet, will not, despite my involvement in pushing them to struggle. Simply put, I don't want to chip in and waste money on people who, in my eyes, deserve some sort of punishment.

'Because taking away their son is not enough.'

But then I want to do what Medisa wants (ignoring her request to not harm her brother) which means I would have to help her family out in some way—ridding them of that dastardly being does not count—some way being providing money. And I really, *really* don't want to be doing that. So, I found where he works, found out about everyone above him, and decided to make his work-life hell. If he chooses to leave and join elsewhere, I will find him again and do the same. I would say that's fair, except, it's not just his work life I'm infiltrating, it's every other aspect in his sad life. He has a seat booked at a restaurant? Not anymore. He's picking up food under his name? Already done and eaten. He's booked a holiday? No he hasn't. I'd rather invest in making sure that disgrace never has a moment of peace in his life than pay her family to make up for his absence. I may even pay extra for someone to break into their home to replace all groceries with ones that have expired. And since they would already be there, they should take things further and plant rotten fish in places that would take weeks to find. While he suffers, Medisa will be enjoying her life, even more so after I deal with this Kassian-Maverick situation.

Now that she knows Aros is mine, she's been messing around much more, not that I'm making her work, in fact, she's now being paid to stay where I can protect her. For some time now she has abandoned—or rather, lessened—mentioning Amana. No more '*Oh, me and Amana done this,*' '*Amana would like this,*' '*Amana says this is good.*' Her words now form questions and remarks about me. And dare I say, I enjoy it.

Our hands are currently busy painting. We have a large canvas leaned against a wall, the goal being to paint a scene within clouds. Medisa really, and I mean really enjoys looking at the sky, especially the nights sky, so it's no surprise that the theme is sky-cloud related. While she is going for a sunset look, I've decided to go for a pre-sunrise look. We were supposed to take turns in adding to the canvas, but now we're painting together.

"I give up. It's not coming out the way I see it in my head." She leans back so that her weight balanced in her hands.

I stare at her side of the canvas, trying to come up with a compliment. "Aren't you a design student? Why do you not have a basic understanding of colours?"

She throws a paint-stained tissue at me. "I draw and colour on a tablet, it's different. You don't need to mix colours."

"Show me what colours you're trying to achieve." I put down my paint brush and palette.

Medisa has her inspiration pictures ready, and to be fair, she's not far off from achieving the colours she wants. I motion for her to pass me her palette with two fingers then suddenly feel like my age is catching up to me.

I demonstrate how to get three of her colours and how to create their shadow and highlight. When I'm done, I pass the palette back thinking that she would ask more questions or even try to create another colour, but she goes back to painting with the colours I created.

She used me.

'And pathetically you liked it.'

Switching between balancing the palette on her crossed legs and holding it up with one hand, she finally settles with holding it up.

I stop myself from going back to painting, to instead take her in. Only a part of her hair is held back with a clip and even then, her short layers and fringe have escaped it's hold. Before I realise it, I've already reached out to move one side of her hair out of her eyes and behind her ears. She turns to face me, first to see what I am doing, then to question my actions with an expression.

"What? It's hair, not skin." My voice does *not* give away the sudden vulnerability I feel.

Medisa jolts back. "*Boy*, you're not even supposed to be seeing my hair."

She gives little energy towards a laugh, takes a sip of her drink then quickly goes back to painting as though we were in a timed competition. Meanwhile, I don't even have the words to counter her, or *any* of my thoughts because I'm too busy staring at her like she's a damn sunrise.

It's quite late, but something doesn't feel right so I have to wake her up. I don't know what it is, but I feel like something's happened, or will happen.

I quietly rush into her room. The lack of light plays tricks on my mind, her hair looks longer and a little more defined, her body even looks slightly different. For a second, I think I hear my name being called but as I move around the bed, I see that she is still asleep.

Just as I'm about to wake her up, I see something coming out of her mouth. She's not drooling, that wouldn't be so dark.

I've already come to a conclusion as to what it is, but before I give into what my minds constructed, I gently touch her face. The liquid latches on to the tip of my fingers allowing me to see more of its dark red glow.

Quickly dropping my hands to urgently get her to wake, I hear my name being called again. Ignoring my caller, I try to move her, try to pick her up but it feels impossible.

She's heavy.

The blood continues to drip off her chin and all I can do is grip onto her.

A hand is put onto my arm and my name is called again.

"What's happening? What's wrong with her?"

My arm is shaken. "Kade."

I swing my arm to free myself from the hands gentle hold.

"*Ow*." Medisa grips onto her face with both hands as I start to feel the knuckles and fingers that made contact with her.

I quickly move to be crouched down beside her, my hand hovering over her covered face.

"What are you doing awake?"

"I was thirsty. Are you okay? I think you were having a nightmare." Her voice is muffled due to her covering both her nose and mouth. "Do you want me to keep the door open so that I can—"

"No, no it's okay. Don't do that. I'm okay. How are you? Are you bleeding?"

Her eyes subtly study me. "No, it just felt like a weird amount of pressure. I'm okay now."

"You sure?"

"Yeah." She lowers her hands while her eyes continue to watch me.

"I'm sorry for hitting you." I don't know what came over me. I barely even remember anything now.

"It's okay. Don't worry. I'm going to go back to bed unless you want to stay awake?"

I grab her water bottle and stand up. "Nah. I'll fill this up for you then go back to having sweet dreams." I smile with all my teeth but somehow, I don't think it helped lighten the mood.

Chapter 51
Kade
06/01/2022 (Thursday)

Another night with the same dream and somehow, the fact that I am actually falling asleep seems to be more shocking. I remember more of the dream tonight and there's a simple explanation behind it. I spent the whole day today with it at the back of my mind so of course I would dream about it again. One thing's for sure, the girl is Medisa. I could see her face more clearly this time, even if the rest of her is different.

Despite trying to play it off, I am not okay. I am bothered to the point where I need to, where I *have* to check on Medisa. I pinch the bridge of my nose and try to think of something else but nothing is stopping the strong want to go into her room.

I scoff. This is stupid, but still, I walk towards her door and try my best to be as quiet as possible on my way in. She hadn't properly shut the door and I hadn't put a lock on it yet, which is currently serving to be a good thing. With the way I'm feeling, I would've broken it down to make sure that blood hasn't pooled where her head rests.

Just like my dream, I move around the bed to face her. The dim light from the living room makes things easier to see in here, and as soon as I see that there is no blood exiting her mouth, I allow myself to breathe. But here's the thing, that's not enough. I need to check her pulse to make sure.

I lift my hand to do the job, then bring it back down and turn away. This is stupid.

But I need to check.

I force my eyes shut and go from pinching the bridge of my nose to using my finger to repeatedly tap my forehead. I am *not* going to cross a boundary because of a stupid dream.

Medisa adjusts a pillow in between her legs and arms whilst I stand like I am meant to be in here. When it's clear that she won't be moving again, I realise how odd she sleeps. Her head is barely on a pillow and the pillow that is touching her, is one that she continues to hold hostage. Seriously, does she need to hold it like that?

"Did he have them before?" She asks, her voice cautious.

I don't say anything. My eyes travel from the door to her face again and again. If she wakes and sees me in here, she'll leave.

"Kade?"

I don't panic, instead my mind runs through excuses, explanations, her sleep talking being one of them.

"Did he have nightmares when you guys were kids?"

The hair on my arms stand. She must be talking to Kassian in her dream, their conversation is just slipping into my reality.

"He did." I keep my voice calm and low. I don't want to shock her into waking.

Medisa lazily smacks her lips together as though she were parched. "Do you know what they're about?"

My eyes become a little dry, or wet? Something that happens when I don't blink. "I don't."

I never told Kassian.

She scoffs, or is it a dry cough? I look over to her near-empty water bottle and pick it up.

"How do we help him?" Soon as the question leaves her lips, it's as though all thoughts of mine are hidden from me.

And since I now know that she is alive and well, I don't waste another second in leaving her room.

Chapter 52
Kassian
07/01/2022 (Friday)

Things have proved to be harder than expected. Medisa is protected in her tower and hasn't left in days. I don't know why I ignored her spontaneous tendencies and relied on her curiosity and moral compass to keep her at the hotel. Maybe a part of me wanted to give her a chance to get to Kade?

I eye my phone.

It's been ringing for the past ten minutes with breaks in between every three calls. As I don't recognise the number, I refuse to answer, but this pattern has raised my curiosity. They clearly are determined to reach me, so I might as well entertain it. For all I know, it could be another sneaky woman who got a hold of my number during one of our late rendezvous, and honestly, I could do with a bit of distraction.

After answering, I wait for whoever it is to speak first. And to my disappointment, it's a man who seems to be talking to someone in the room with him.

"Your lucks not so bad after all, he answered."

I furrow my brows. It may not be the distraction I want, but it's something.

"Kassian! Don't come! They're going to—" The voice is muffled.

"We know that you were the one with her at the pub so—"

Oh it's Medisa. They've got Medisa. She continues to shout in the background, but they've obviously stuffed her mouth with something because no words are clear. But honestly, are her words ever clear?

"—there's a construction site in her area, can't miss it. Get here before ten. I don't have to tell you what happens if you don't." It's clear that he's about to hang up but I refuse to let Medisa meet her ill fate early.

"Do you know the amount of construction sites in her area? Give me an address, let's make this quick."

He takes his sweet time thinking about it.

For the love of God, come to a decision.

"You know what? Just text me the address." I hang up before he refuses, or adds conditions.

Viewing my lock-screen, I work out how long I've got until ten.

Three hours.

Hmm. It would take about an hour to get to her, which means I have time to rest and leave at my own pace. There's no need to rush.

The plan to take my time diminishes as quickly as it was conjured as soon as my mind reminds me that Medisa had tried to help me multiple times, one being when I had framed her in her own home.

You know what? It's good that this has happened. Now I can get even with her before things truly are the worst of the worst, then I can fully enjoy where she ends up.

Call Kassian Koda anything, but do not say I am not fair.

Chapter 53
Kade
07/01/2022 (Friday)

Admittedly, there is a part of me that does not trust Medisa. I questioned whether or not she were putting on an act, so I was ready to deal with any uninvited guests or even her escaping. Now, I am putting it down to her truly being oblivious to what may come, and personally, out of the two, I can't put my finger on which one is worse. There's no win-win situation to either explanation for her behaviour.

For the first time in a while, it is completely silent in Medisa's space. Usually I would hear something, like her moving around, or a podcast or movie, but there's nothing. From previous experiences I've learnt that when things are this quiet, it's usually because she's taking one of her hibernation naps, or she's praying.

Though I have an idea of what she may be doing, I still have an itch, so I walk into the living room, see that she's not there, then walk up to her bedroom door and knock twice.

No response.

I am about to grab onto the handle but stop when I remember one of her rules. *'Don't walk in front of me while I'm praying, in fact don't even be in the room, other eyes make me uncomfortable and distract me. If you need me and it's important, just talk through the door with a summary, I'll come out and respond when I'm done.'*

"I got some groceries on the way back. I'll cook something up." If my observations are correct, she should be done with this particular prayer within ten-to-fifteen minutes.

Ten minutes pass. I stop moving and look towards her bedroom door, but it doesn't open. She must be praying for a lot this time.

Fifteen minutes pass. The office phone starts to ring and ignoring it does nothing for me. It continues to ring until eventually it gets under my skin enough for me to finally give in to personally turn it off.

As soon as I reach for the phone, it stops ringing, so I turn back around to head into the kitchen. I don't make two steps in before it starts to ring again, and before they hang up just to call *again*, I rip the phone off its stand.

"Brother." Kassian stretched out the relation, a bit too jolly for my liking.

"Kassian. What do you want?" I hold the phone away for a second to see if I could hear Medisa exit the room.

"I take it I'm calling before you've realised that Medisa isn't actually with you."

I can feel his stupid smirk.

"Please do tell me you are wearing something fitting for her collection. Your little friend is currently a damsel in distress thanks to a third party."

"Where?"

"Ugh, don't be boring, we'll go together. Meet me on her road. You do know where that is don't you? Or am I the only one that's actually been inside her house?"

Chapter 54
Kassian
07/01/2022 (Friday)

It's no coincidence that our dear friend Medisa has been taken. Her captors only demand my presence, not money, which means that they've already been paid out, but before I jump to that conclusion, I have to confirm.

I've rung Maverick three times now and neither him or one of his little assistants have bothered to answer. And if that's not suspicious enough, then the text message that just appeared on my screen is.

'Do not fight back.'

Huh, now what does he mean by that?

Chapter 55
Kade
07/01/2022 (Friday)

Standing outside while Kassian is literally taking a piss on the side as though Medisa isn't being held captive by sad, sorry excuse for men, is a position I would much rather pass on. But here I am.

The only reason I am waiting for my brother is because I know that this whole thing is his fault, and letting him get away with this would be to my discomfort. So, at a risk, I am waiting for Kassian to be done with his business so that I can drag his arse inside to deliver him myself. The thought alone tickles satisfaction.

"Did I tell you that we have a time limit?" Kassian approaches, adjusting his jeans. "Good thing we're here five minutes early." He shakes off bottled water from his hands.

Any thoughts of sparing him from whatever the sad men have planned disappear. He quite literally took the piss on how we go about this. I mentally thank whoever gave me the talent of having a good poker face because I want to deal with Kassian myself right now.

"Let's go."

We move deeper into the structure and only begin to make our presence known as we walk into the tinted lights.

The scene has been lit up for us.

Medisa is smack bang in the middle, surrounded by men almost double her age. Her arms are tied behind her, her legs tied to the chair and she isn't moving. It's not that she's tired, no, she's unconscious. Her head is dropped forward and it's pulling the rest of her body off the back of the chair.

I keep my eyes on her whilst coming in to a brighter shade of dimness.

"There's two of you?" A bald muscular man speaks up. "Which one of you was with her at the pub?"

I glare at him. My mind not shy of hiding away any gory thoughts.

"Him." I lazily tilt my head towards Kassian, then I move in Medisa's direction. "I'm taking her."

"You see, the thing is, now that I know there's two of you. I think it would be better justice if we punished the lot of you." He sits down and rests his feet on a chair in front of him.

In the few seconds that we have stood exposed, I have grown bored of the entire situation.

I sigh to outwardly show how I feel.

"You wanted Kassian and here he is. I don't know what you think he's done but I assure you, she's got nothing to do with it so…before I snap, I suggest letting me take her out of this place and the dumb equation that you so quickly came up with."

Someone from the side, equipped with a metal pole, walks up to the bald-headed man. He tries to lower his voice so that it was close to a whisper, but I hear him with ease.

"Dave, you weren't there that day, him alone—" He looks to Kassian. "—Took out a bunch of us with ease. We should just deal with him and let the girl go with this new one. We've already done her some damage. This doesn't need to get messier than it already is."

'*Dave*,' takes a deep breath, looking between me and Kassian, and then Medisa. Once he's gone through his options, he keeps his eyes on me.

"You're okay with your brother not walking out of here?" He's intrigued, but also in need of assurance.

"As I alluded to before, I don't care."

I walk over to Medisa.

Crouching down, I free her legs from the chair first—tactically leaving them bound to each other—then free her body, leaving her wrists.

She smells like salt.

Her hair somewhat damp.

Gently, I lift her head and before I can get a rough idea of what's been done, she begins to wake. The men twatting Kassian in the back does not help what was supposed to be Medisa taking her time in waking up. Her brows tense in response to the unintentional pain I cause by holding up her head, and before she's able to make sense of the situation, I quickly scoop her up and leave.

Throwing her over my shoulder would've been more ideal, but I don't want more blood to rush towards her head, so I've just got to deal with cautiously carrying her over to the car.

I could tell from her sluggishness that she's trying to figure out whether or not I am a figment of her imagination, but that quickly went to shit when some bastard in the back cried out.

Moving away from the commotion, which Medisa is now aware of, is difficult as she starts to fight me whilst I try to grip onto her without inflicting more pain.

"I don't care if this is haram, I'm taking you to the car." My grip tightens as I adjust her so that she's in a position where she can't fight as much. She continues to whine about something and since I have a clue as to what, I ignore.

When I pull out my knife, she stops moving. I do have an itch to scratch, but it's not towards her. Right now my mind is mainly on freeing her wrists from the zip ties.

"I don't want to hurt you by taking that off."

Medisa's eyes look as though they are saying '*seriously*,' then she holds them shut as she peels the duct tape off and pulls out a scrunched cloth from her mouth. She speaks and though I can hear her, my attention lies elsewhere as she moves her hair away from her face. Her cheek is mixed with all sorts of pinks and reds, I can imagine it feels like its burning with waves of pins and needles. She has cuts and scratches all over, the worst one being on her lip and her hair has clearly been pulled.

I study all of her marks and picture how they appeared, the more I see, the more I mentally thank her for giving me a reason, an opportunity, to blow off some steam.

Before she can make a move to get out, I throw my jacket at her and shut the door. I'm not worried about her escaping because once I lock my car, nothing is getting in or out.

As I walk away, Medisa calls for me whilst banging on the window, and with each step I take away, I block more of her voice out.

Kassian's groans and the men's grunts as they took turns beating him with fists, kicks and poles are things that could be heard before they even came into view. Returning to the scene with heavy steps instead of quiet ones makes no difference as the majority of men focus on Kassian.

Coming into the light and being welcomed by Kassian at my feet, spitting out blood like he had been collecting it, is something that would've made me somewhat happy. But my mind is currently occupied with something else.

"Ah, I knew you would come back for me." Kassian

grins, showing off his bloody teeth.

"<u>Go fuck yourself</u>." I throw him the car keys. "<u>Get her out of here</u>."

Kassian chuckles, needing no more convincing to leave, he's practically out the place as soon as the keys touch his useless hands.

Despite my emotions, I do take in the sight of my brother, his blood and the men who made him look like that. The circumstance almost mirrored our past.

Once it clicked in their slow minds that Kassian is in fact leaving, they waste no time in attacking. None of them are co-ordinated and almost all hits were as though they're taken in the dark. If I hadn't just seen the state of Kassian, I would think that they were all talk, with absolutely nothing to show.

I take a deep breath as I convince myself that I won't snap. I'm better than that now. I have more control. Just injure them and leave.

"Did you get a good look at her?" Dave is still sat in the same spot, unknowingly digging all their graves a little deeper. "I'm pretty sure she took a few hits to her body too." He scratches his scruffy beard then sighs as though he knew how this would play out. "Look, she was there at the pub and got herself some male attention. The bitch was practically asking for—"

Pulling the closest man towards me with the weapon he beat Kassian with, I force his head down onto my knee before he, or anyone could react. Allowing him to fall onto my body instead of the ground, I hold him up, offering support with one hand while I gut him with the other. His body drops soon after I let go, revealing the site of me whipping my wrist to get rid of excess blood.

I step over his body.

Adrenaline makes its way over me. I feel the shakes in my bones and crave more. The sensation feels as though I have been starving myself from some sort of release, and I have, I have been starving myself for *weeks*.

I place the knife upside down in between my fist, almost guaranteeing that every man will bleed.

None of the men outwardly react to what they had just witnessed. It's not until I move closer that they all snap out of their thoughts and simultaneously circle me.

"*Finally*. Some coordination." I hold my hands out to my side as though I have something on them for people to see.

Three come into the middle, and it's now that my brain decides to make vivid connections to the past.

'*Remember to think of Kassian and how he's practically starving to death. Oh, and remember to take a few hits too, need them to think you're going to lose, makes it more fun don't you think?*' Maverick's voice runs through my head.

And I no longer see the men that took Medisa.

I see opponents in the ring.

We can only get out of this—we can only survive and move on *if* I take a few lives. I can't hold back. I can't take on too much damage either. I'm going to win. It's okay to do this, they know what they got themselves into. I'm already ruined, the rest don't need to be, it's the only way that I can save Kassian—Medisa!

Medisa's name and all the thought's that come with her snap me back to the reality of things. Dave is on the ground, pleading while I'm crouched over him with a bloody knife to his throat. Everyone else is either dead or on their way to be.

"Please! *Please!*" He holds out a damaged hand and speaks through quick breaths.

"How did you know where she was?" I grab his hand so

that it is positioned in between our faces, then hold the knife at the start of his finger, ready to cut through like it's an apple.

Dave's eyes grow. "We-we got an envelope with pictures of your brother with Mikes body, a number was at the back of one of them."

I cut into his finger, pushing him to talk faster but instead of useful information, I am given screams until I stop sawing into his finger.

"We got-we got a call from that number today! He told us where she was! I swear! I swear!"

I drop his hand then hold out my palm, indicating for him to hand over his phone. Dave gives back his mutilated hand instead.

Dumb-ass.

"Your phone. Give it to me. If it's locked, unlock it."

Amusing as it is to see Dave cower and struggle to enter his pin multiple times, I have grown bored and am set on putting him out of both our miseries once I have the number.

As the call goes through, I continue to stay crouched over him, displaying a set of knife tricks over his chest. Dave cowers some more, itching parts of my brain that needed to be itched from when I first saw him. So, I continue to taunt him until someone answers.

Someone picks up.

I stop playing with the knife and stay quiet. Quickly putting it on speaker, I motion for Dave to talk.

"We-we have them."

Idiot can't act even when his life depends on it.

"Excellent. Show me." Mavericks voice is like smelling something familiar and your brain putting together all the times you've smelt it.

I smile at Dave, then shove the knife up his throat, letting Maverick hear him struggle against me as he gurgles and coughs up his own blood for a few seconds.

"Construction site. You have till dawn to find and clean up the mess before our faces are planted everywhere, making whatever you want, much more difficult to achieve."

I can see exactly how Maverick is reacting to my voice, a vivid image is in front of me. I know he hung up the phone to hysterically laugh as the game he desperately wants to play, now has active players.

Chapter 56
Kassian
07/01/2022 (Friday)

Driving towards any main road leading into the city is pointless. We need to be far enough to be away from the drama but close enough to go back in case we are needed.

Medisa has been talking non-stop, demanding that we go back, that we *have* to do something. Thankfully Kade chucked her in the back, not back enough, but she's away from the steering wheel so that's something.

I thought the noise in the background—Medisa—would eventually die down, but she's adapted to hitting the back of my chair *and* using her voice. Her kicks eventually lack power and that's when I see her reflection. Almost immediately I turn around to see how bad she actually is. I've been ignoring her since I got into the car, I hadn't considered the damages she'd attained.

Parking up on the side of this dark road is a risk I'm willing to take. If she dies now, on my watch and because I pissed off a bunch of men at a pub, I'm sure to die next. What is wrong with her? Why beg to turn back to Kade, instead of mentioning that something is not right? I swing open the back door and notice she's moved to the opposite end, like a cat avoiding bathwater.

I haven't got time for this, *she* doesn't even look like she has much time.

Though she has her back to the door, she's not quick enough to get her legs away from me. So, I do what anyone with no time or shits does, I grab a hold of her and pull her towards me until I've got enough of her to throw over my shoulder. We have supplies in the back, I can do what I can until she gets proper help.

First, she tried to get herself off me, now she holds on.

"No-no *wait*, I won't say anything anymore! Don't put me in there I'm claustrophobic!" Medisa grips onto the clothes on my back.

I stop moving.

She thinks I'm going to shove her in the boot?

Wait. Should I?

Maybe after I see what's wrong with her.

I put her on her feet and watch how she struggles to find balance.

"You're hurt, I can't tend to your wounds in the back of the car, so you'll sit comfortably in the boot *with* the hood up as I take a look at what they did to you."

She half limps her arse to the boot and takes a seat. Her leg is the first thing I see, it's difficult not to, her blue jeans give away the blood.

"Don't even think about it."

"What?" I act as if I have no clue as to what she insinuates.

"You're not allowed to see my legs and I can't—"

I rip into her jeans from where she's been cut. And I'm not a complete prick so I only expose what needs to be exposed.

"Sorry, you were saying?" I wait for her to say something—though I would ignore—but instead she throws her hands over her exposed thigh.

Great.

So not only has she been cut, but she's now shoving her

dirty hands on top.

I grab onto her hands then force them down to her sides, my face closer to hers than needs be.

"We haven't got time for this act. You're bleeding all over the place. What kind of man would I be to let that continue?" It's a rhetorical question but she still opens her mouth to answer. "Ah-ah I haven't got the energy for this, as you can see, I'm hurt too. Now, *sit quietly*, before I find something to restrain you, clean you up, then leave you in the boot."

She stops trying to get out of my grip, so I go back to having my attention on her thigh.

It needs stitches. It could be worse, but leaving it for any longer may be just as damaging.

"I always said that I would have a first aid kit with some blankets and food in my car." She—annoyingly—tries to make conversation.

"Don't think that you both share great minds, I brought this on the way here knowing that someone would need it."

That someone being me.

Cleaning her thigh is satisfying. The way both dry and wet blood, along with any dirt from her hands, run from her exposed skin, *ugh*.

I press down with some cotton, not only to dry her, but to slow down/stop her from bleeding.

"Now for the fun bit."

I saw her try to hold in her pain, or rather, her annoyance when I used more pressure than needed to dry her, but this bad boy will definitely make hiding her pain difficult.

Medisa doesn't even wait for the antiseptic solution to be opened, she jumps straight to covering her thigh, this time, her dirty hands hover over.

I want to laugh.

"Hold onto something, it'll be over quick. Just breathe in when I say." I try a soft approach.

She grips the top of her injured thigh, bracing for the inevitable burn. "Do it."

"Take a deep breath and hold it."

Not wanting to waste her breath, I pour—more than I need—the liquid.

Red face Medisa pushes down as much weight as she can at the top of her thigh, holding on like her life depends on it.

"It'll be over quick." The breaks I take in between each pour are unnecessary but contribute towards my entertainment. To make up for it, I bandage her up really well.

"Your turn." She hops off the boot and circles me as I don't allow my back to be to her. So now, the boot is behind me.

I sit down. What else is there to do anyway?

"It was Maverick you know." Her voice is low, like someone may be eavesdropping and she continues to clean my brow despite me no longer being amused.

Her statement, her timing...too rash.

"He knew enough about the pub incident to send me gifts and any other sort of message, like how he has eyes on me. I even got a message at the hotel which is why I left—"

Maverick sent her more than one package? What else has he done that I don't know about?

"—And today...How did they know where I was? And how did they know to call you?"

She's right. At the pub, Medisa called me Kade, so unless she's mixed up our numbers, how would they know to call me? Why would they call me? Maverick also avoided my calls today and told me not to fight back. What the heck is he up to?

Medisa stops cleaning my brow. "Your current revenge plan is making you blind—"

So Kade has told her something.

"—'An eye for an eye would make the whole world blind.'"

"Did you just quote Gandhi?"

"Did I? Ew. Anyways, what I was trying to get at, was that you don't see Maverick doing you over because you're so distracted by wanting revenge on Kade."

Medisa reaching this conclusion with little information is triggering. Have I really been that blind? That naïve?

I stand up and take the antiseptic cream away from her.

"They wanted to kill you back there and if you think otherwise, you're dumber than I thought!—*Sit back down* I'm cleaning you—" She stomps in front of me and snatches back the cream.

I do as she says, but only to get this over and done with.

"I don't know why you're siding with him—I don't even know why you have a problem with *me*! But you have to realise, Maverick is not your friend in this."

This isn't as big of a shock, he hasn't been much of a brother so why did I expect him to let me do this?

I say nothing.

Medisa continues to do what she can for my face, no longer trying to talk some sense into me.

She sighs as she takes a step back, the back of my hands being her new focus point. "I wanted to be close to my siblings *so* bad when I was younger, but they constantly took me for an idiot and abused me whenever they felt like it, and there was *never* a good reason for it."

Oh, spare me the forced common ground.

"And since I knew what they were like, I stopped being a

beg. I didn't need their attention, or praise… Later on in life, I met my best friend and she was everything that I wanted in a friend, everything that I *needed* from my family. And even when the abuse continued, it didn't sting as much 'cause I knew that I had one person in my corner. One person who would be with me no matter what, who saw and actually respected me."

Amana. She's talking about Amana.

And I don't want to hear about having a person in my corner. It's a stupid thought.

Medisa angles her head so that she can catch my gaze.

I hadn't even realised that I was no longer trying to burn her with my eyes.

"Maverick isn't in your corner Kassian, but you'll find someone who is, me and Kade are—"

This is outrageous.

I get off the boot, this time more aggressively. "Kade?" How dare she try to say he's in my corner. "Kade—he—"

My phone rings.

'Kade'

I scoff at the timing of this guy.

"Speak of the Devil." Without much thought, I answer.

"Bring my car back to me. I'm at the big Tesco near her house."

I hang up, but something tells me we both hit the button at the same time.

"Let's go get him."

Medisa stays in place, frustrated with the crumbs I've thrown her. "*No*. Tell me what happened! Tell me what he did that was so bad that you're taking it out on me!"

I can't hear this. I don't want to hear the voice of reason, it's unfair.

"What did he do?" She continues, her voice louder, emotional, anger? "What did I do?" Her arms, her hands all help convey her emotions, her words.

Nothing. She's done absolutely nothing wrong. But I still try to block her out as I walk to the front of the car.

Medisa follows me. "I know what you do at Baronial—"

Butterflies take flight in my stomach. What has Kade told her? Has he refrained from telling her about himself, did he just expose me?

"—with people you don't know, but you've spent time with me and you're still okay with what could happen? How much of a shitty person are you pretending to be? How far are you willing to take this?"

I don't know what I'm doing.

"I *know* that you have a heart, you're just pretending that you don't."

Why does everyone think I can't be the bad guy? Do they want to see where I take this?

"How big of a heartbreak was it that you're letting it blind you from the truth! Maverick doesn't care about you! He wouldn't—"

I *know* that he doesn't care for me.

I yank the passenger door open then turn to her. "Get in the car Medisa, or I'll put you in the boot."

Her eyes give away every single emotion she felt, including fear, yet she still has the nerve to go against me. She takes a seat in the back, the one place that wasn't an option. I have too much on my mind to actually put her in her place, so I slam the passenger door shut and make way to the driver's seat. When my door opens, I'm half surprised she didn't attempt to lock me out.

Kade leaning against a wall with bags filled with food and some sort of tropical juice in his hand, waiting for me to pull up beside him, is not how I thought this would all end.

While he put things into the boot, I get out and move into the passenger seat. I think I deserve a ride after all this and he better be thinking that too.

Kade quietly gets into the driver's seat. Nothing is said between the two of us and we both look like shit, difference is, the blood on him isn't his, rarely is.

"How is she?" He asks.

I bitterly smile.

"Her thigh's been cut. I've done what I can, but you should still get it checked."

Kade's hand on the wheel tenses and I want so bad to do something irrational. Can't he see that I'm hurt too? Damn.

I turn on the radio, refusing to drive in silence.

Kade turns it off.

He probably doesn't want to risk waking Medisa up, but I don't care so I turn it back on.

He turns it off again.

I turn to give him a '*really*?' look and see that he's already looking at me with a deadpan expression. I ignore and turn the radio on once again, tempted to put the volume up but instead lower it.

Kade allows it to stay on.

Prick.

Chapter 57
Kade
08/01/2022 (Saturday)

I open Medisa's door having every intention to carry her to bed, only to see that she is now awake.

"I know what you're going to say, but I'm still going to offer."

She supresses a yawn.

"Would you like me to carry you upstairs?" The light is to my back so I must look terrifying—and this is without it highlighting the blood—but it does show off Medisa's leg and face. I act as though she looks normal to not make her feel uncomfortable when in reality, though I feel as though he had no idea about this, I want to take things out on Kassian.

"It's okay, it's not that bad and we have the elevator so I'll be alright. Thank you though."

I step aside to give her space but remain nearby, ready to catch her if she stumbles or needs support. Her pace is nowhere near the speed she usually moves at, a clear sign she's in some sort of pain.

Kassian and I wait for her to get into the lift, then we walk in right after.

"<u>Just say you don't like her, why make her walk?</u>" Kassian keeps his head straight, almost convincing me that I'm hearing things.

"<u>Just say you don't have a home, friends, why stick around?</u>"

It's been a while since we've conversated with other languages, almost feels as nice as dissing him. And it makes the actual lessons Maverick forced us to take to learn our mother's languages worth it.

Medisa says nothing. She doesn't even turn to inquire or make animated expressions.

Is she reaching her breaking point?

We are let out into the hallway where Medisa wastes no time in leading us to where she currently stays. I couldn't care less about Kassian knowing where we live because I am not planning on letting him leave.

Things are made difficult when Medisa decides to stay in the kitchen with us, and that's when I realise, she's probably not eaten all day. Thankfully Kassian's used his half-brain to put the groceries on the countertop, so I can get right to it. I know exactly what to make, it'll soften Kassian up and fill Medisa.

After I set water to boil and put the pasta ready on the side, along with the spices, Kassian immediately put together what I am making. He's goes from being a child in the kitchen to a pest, pulling out and adding more ingredients, thinking I won't deliver the consequences (Medisa just needs to look away).

I peek over at Medisa now; she's watching us through her cuts and bruises. She might be feeling a little left out, or is disconnected mentally, and I don't think her clothes are helping the situation. Perhaps I should help her out of them, get the dirt, their prints and any other current thing that may be upsetting her away. It could give her some relief until she's ready to talk about it.

"I'll be right back." I tell her, not Kassian. I couldn't give a shit about him being upset or confused about me getting up and leaving.

Medisa has a new wardrobe, it's not exactly everything, but it is everything she needs. She's got the basics, the casuals, the formals, the backups, the outerwear's, lingerie, and yet I still want to hand her clothes from my wardrobe.

I come back into the room to see Kassian stare at Medisa like a fucking perv, and Medisa's own eyes flicker between me and him as though something scandalous transpired.

'Don't think about it. Don't think about it.'

Medisa takes the clothes as she mutely thanks me. And even though she is moving at a decent pace, my mind seems to think that she's rushing to get away.

As soon as she locks the bathroom door, I narrow my eyes at Kassian who continues to interfere with my cooking.

"You touch her and I'll make you wish for death."

"And if she touches me? Does she get the same treatment?" Kassian's coy smile is enough to provoke.

I give him a *gentle* push away from the stove, checking if there's any need for damage control. I don't need to worry about poison, not even this idiot would ruin this meal.

"Are you hurt?" I pull on a heartstring.

He doesn't answer.

I can't even get a good look at the expression he wears. I catch my own reflection while trying to get a glimpse of his, and the only question that crosses my mind is, '*how the hell was I not stopped and detained in Tesco?*'

I damp a hand towel to wipe what I can. "I'm just asking so I know how much damage I can inflict without killing you."

Kassian chuckles. "It's been a few years. What makes you think that you'll win our next fight?"

Our hostile stare breaks when Kassian decides to speak... pussy. "She's either animated or she's not. There's no in between."

"Or maybe you can't read her as well as you think?"

"And you can?"

"I'm getting better."

"I'm sure you are."

Before things are heightened, Medisa unlocks the bathroom door, pushing us to busy our hands rather than push the other to make an aggressive move.

Medisa, now clean and in her new clothes, momentarily freezes a step outside the door. Her eyes travel between mine and Kassian's, just as ours do to her and each other. Something happened between the two of them, and as much as Kassian tries to play it off, I can feel how tense he gets when she is present.

"So, which one of you is going to tell me what I missed?" I keep my eyes on Medisa.

"You first brother dearest, we all know that's not your blood on you. What did me and sweet Medisa miss?"

Oh would you look at that, the *one* time Kassian saves Medisa.

I shrug. "Nothing worth mentioning."

Kassian does me the honour of moving on by opening the oven door to check up on the garlic bread. I busy myself by grating some cheese and stirring the pasta pot.

"You're not making it right." He complains.

"You're not made right." I joke and am momentarily granted amnesia, forgetting the last five years.

Kassian dumps some more cayenne pepper, allowing me to realise that he doesn't need poison, he just needs too much of the right ingredient/s.

"Don't do that, don't do that." I hold my finger out and wave it between him and the pot. "Deal with the garlic bread."

Distracting him with the oven, I grab what I know will balance out the pasta with his added measurements.

When he sees me grabbing a bowl for myself and Medisa, he does the same. We practically race to place her bowl in front of her, then wait like puppies for some sort of praise.

She giggles—music to my ears—looks between us then drops her smile when she grasps how serious we are in her presence, waiting for her to decide.

Medisa being Medisa, tries to get up and get her own bowl but is quickly put back into her seat. She will eat from the bowl I chose and that's it, this is not serious enough for her to walk around on an injured leg. I place my bowl on top of Kassian's, fill it with pasta, top it off with garlic bread, then hand it over to Medisa.

We all get comfortable in different parts of the kitchen. Medisa faces me and Kassian, Kassian faces her and I face the both of them. There isn't much conversation once we all start to eat, just the sound of us attacking our bowls.

"The right way or not, it still tastes the same."

All thanks to me.

"I won't argue with you on that." Kassian stuffs his mouth as though each fork gave him more time with his memory.

I enjoy the pasta, not really caring for memories because they were on the way to becoming words from a time that is currently recalled as a blur.

Medisa's eyes observe us. I can practically read the questions in her mind.

I should answer at least one of them.

"Our parents used to make this every now and then, we would beg them too and then—"

"Then we begged Maverick to, or to at least tell us how to make it."

I try my best not to blow up in front of Medisa.

"You should see, or at least hear about the conditions he gave us for it—"

"Enough." I almost throw my bowl in the sink. "She doesn't need to know all that."

"I'd beg to differ. If I'm going to be on your side, I should have a say and I say…" His eyes travel and set on Medisa. "She needs to know as much as she can to be able to defend herself."

On our side? Don't make me laugh. This is a trick.

"Don't all jump with excitement." He leans over the stove and fills his bowl with more pasta. "I'm no idiot, I knew that he specifically wanted me there today, not caring about the outcome. And I would've been blind or in denial rather than come to my senses. It would've taken me ages to accept it without Medisa. She just helped speed up the process."

The wink he gives her makes my eye twitch.

And what did Medisa do tonight that convinced him to join us? What was different about that and how she's been with him every other time?

"I'm not buying it." I keep my eyes on him, worried that looking at Medisa will give away a part of their relationship I don't want to confirm.

"Suit yourself."

Ha. If he thinks that that will make me overthink and accept him onto our side, he's wrong. There's no way he doesn't have a trick or two up his sleeve.

"Kade." Medisa gently calls out to me and as though she were a siren, I feel my body listening to her words. "Just give him one chance."

Repositioning myself, I'm able to look at the both of them with ease. "What about your revenge? Am I supposed to buy that you've dropped it?"

"No." His tone is matter-of-fact. "Because I haven't dropped it. I'm simply postponing it."

My eyes narrow in on his.

I don't believe this. All these years of harbouring hate and now all of a sudden, he can put it on pause…for what? Because as far as I'm concerned, Medisa is the only one in any real danger.

I heavily sigh. "Leave whatever happened in the past *in* the past, Medisa doesn't need to know everything. Other than that, I agree." I turn to face her. "Medisa, we'll teach you whatever we can, as soon as we can." I look back to Kassian. "And you, if you're still playing games—"

"I'm not. But we will be. With Maverick. I'll be your insider." All of a sudden Kassian's a bundle of joy…great.

"He would find out and plan something malicious for us." I only say what Kassian knows.

"For me, you mean. In his sick head, I'm the one that would be betraying him in this scenario, and I'm ready to risk it if it gives us a chance." He faces me with a look I haven't seen in a long time.

Kassian wants me to be okay with this. With him. Even if it is temporary.

I give in. "If this is going to work, you need to leave now. Talk to him in person, convince him that his little test failed in making you turn away from him—"

"Okay, but if any of that really works, how would we communicate? Maverick made it seem like he knew about every step I took. How would you guys train me if he watches all of us?"

"Leave that to me sweet Medisa. Leave that to me."

He's no longer 'weird' around her, in fact, this is the most comfortable I've seen him in all of our recent interactions.

"Speaking of training and communication, do I have to learn the languages you guys were speaking too?"

"We haven't got *that* much time." Kassian responds before I do.

"And there's no point." I add to make her feel better. "Maverick understands every language we speak."

"We're just accustomed to speaking to one another in those languages when there's a third-party present."

'She could think that she's a third-party... *She is.*'

"Like those who work for Maverick." I clear his words.

"But he could just hire someone who also understands you?" Her face gives away how dumb she thinks Maverick is.

"Yes well, he won't. At least he didn't when we all lived together. He wanted us to try him, not to teach us to grow some, but so that he had the opportunity to demonstrate what happens when we do." Kassian feeds her more insight.

"He sounds like a prick." Medisa casually delivers her insult.

"Aren't we all?" Kassian's eyes stay on mine. His eagerness to do something beaming through them as he sits as though his knuckles aren't aching to latch and detach from my face.

"Alright, get out, we'll discuss the details later. We need to rest and you need to do some acting, which I have no faith in." I tilt my head towards the tv room, calling Medisa over.

"No faith? I fooled Medisa for days pretending to be you."

Medisa risks whiplash with the speed she uses in turning her head towards Kassian. "I didn't know that he was, slash is a twin, but Maverick does."

"Fair." He says to her point, but smiles at me.

I don't think too much into it, but I do feel satisfied as I hold up my middle finger towards him as Medisa comes to my side.

Do I trust Kassian? Not at all. Am I doing this for Medisa? Yes. Do I like it? I'm not sure, yet.

Chapter 58
Kassian
09/01/2022 (Sunday)

It's late, but it's not been a full hour in the new day so I don't reschedule. Maverick will see me, 'fresh' from the scene. I could let myself into the room, but I think it's more dramatic if I knock a few times and wait to be invited in.

A woman opens the door, of course. She's barely dressed so I feel a little sorry for her when I lock her out. I don't care who she is, or how much he trusts her, she is not going to hear this conversation.

Maverick sits at the table in his robe, waiting for me to complain about him screwing me over.

"Have I not been feeding you information about Kade and Medisa? Have I not been letting you know of my plans?" I strip out of my top, One: to show him the bruises I attained because of his order, and Two: to swap my dirty top for one of his clean ones, I don't care for the size difference. "Why did you not tell me about what you had arranged?" Am I annoyed? Yes. Hurt? Slightly, but I am able to keep my cool.

"There was a small window to further escalate the situation and I did you the favour of handling it myself."

Of course, silly me. How could I be so ungrateful?

"I hope you aren't too injured. It would make today regretful."

I move around the room to avoid him seeing any expression I can't hide. "I'm good. In fact your plan has bettered our outcome."

Maverick's brows twitch.

"Getting my arse handed to me allowed for some vulnerable time with Medisa. And she thinks that she's gotten through to me. Kade's not fully on board yet, but he's willing to give me a chance." I pick up a fat grape and pop it into my mouth. "It's going to take some time to convince him that I'm willing to drop things for the sake of dealing with you, but, other than that, you, Maverick Rhodes River, have got yourself a double agent."

Maverick's lips lift from one side. It's a devilish sort of smile, one where I don't know if I've successfully won him over.

"If you are going to do something to our brother and that girl, tell me in advance. That way I can *really* sell my story."

Maverick's brows raise and I'm reading '*oh really?*'

He gets up and heads towards the door to let the woman in. "You continue to surprise me, Kassian. Well done."

Somewhere along this interaction—no—somewhere along any of our interactions from the moment I informed him of Kade to now, I wondered when this turned into Maverick's way of doing things instead of mine.

Chapter 59
Kade
09/01/2022 (Sunday)

Medisa's habit of pacing has rubbed off on me. I don't know when it happened but it *has* happened.

Bellamy's older sister Ava and her husband Charlie have agreed to come to examine and patch up Medisa. Problem is, Medisa hasn't come out of her room yet, and I don't want to wake her up after what she's been through.

I notice her bottle in the kitchen and decide to use that as an excuse to approach her door.

I knock twice.

"It's not locked, you can come in."

After passing her water bottle, I lean on her doorframe. This should be enough distance between us.

"How you feeling? I called for my doctor to get you checked. I would do it myself but I googled and it said something along the lines of needing to be a doctor or it needing to be an emergency or something."

She gives me one of her 'lazy laughs.'

"Thank you, although I'm pretty sure your doctor brother got me covered."

Unknowingly, I was blessed by distraction. Now, I am reminded, Kassian saw her thigh.

"As dumb as he is, he's actually good when it comes to stuff like that. We all are."

Medisa's brows are pulled together. "What, does every River have a failed medical degree?"

Her humour is still here so that's a good sign.

"Something like that."

Her lips part, indicating she did not expect that response. "What does that even mean?"

"It means that if we wanted the degree, we would have it. We don't know *everything* that there is to know, but we do know en—"

"Yeah-yeah, I got it. You guys aren't just all looks." She circles her hand in the air around where I assume my face is.

"No." I feel my lips stretch a little. "Definitely not." Rivers, well, my brothers and I are blessed with a remarkable retention ability. It's come in handy throughout my life, except for the part where I can no longer recall what my parents look like.

"What's your favourite module in this '*degree*'?"

"Anatomy." My mind races through all the different sounds made yesterday, the squelches, the clicks, the cracks.

"What do you like about it?"

I don't mention the fact that she's woken up with questions today, more than usual, because I already know that she's probably distracting herself, or is easing her way into a conversation she actually wants to have.

"The colours, the layers, the intricacies…" The textures, the placement. "I like drawing or painting, or even sculpting parts of the body."

"After graduation—"

Her graduation…somehow, I've dismissed the day all together.

"—or after this is over, can I see your drawings and sculptures?"

I become some sort of statue. I would love to show Medisa my work, to teach her, but it's not going to happen. Not when Maverick's alive or with Kassian wanting her to know the truth.

"Yeah." The word barely comes out. "Of course."

"Anyways." She gently shakes her head after smiling. "When do we have to go see him?"

"Hmm?" Why would she think that I would be okay with her having to travel? "Oh no you're not going anywhere, he's coming here." I turn to leave as I assume this is where this conversation will end, but then refuse to allow myself to walk away without giving her the chance to talk about yesterday. She was kidnapped, she was hurt, probably still is, and she saw the blood on me. I need to know if she's okay or if she's uncomfortable around me.

I raise my brow after seeing her expression.

Medisa has more to say, I know it.

"Can we talk about what happened yesterday?" She cautiously asks.

"We can. I didn't want to make you uncomfortable by saying something first, or too early." I give her some truth as to why I have not yet said anything.

"No, I want to." Medisa almost seems as desperate as me. "I just don't know how to go about it."

"Okay." I come back inside the room. "That's okay, just say it how it is in your mind and I'll listen."

Her eyes fill with appreciation with sad undertones, and somehow it makes me feel comfortable. It's as though her eyes confirmed her being okay with me, okay with being around me.

Medisa tells me about how she ended up back in her area, how she was taken and how she felt with those hydrophobic men. She's not exactly afraid of what happened to her, that's not what this conversation is about. It's about how she unintentionally put me and Kassian at risk. I don't show how I feel, but I am *irritated* that she isn't exactly focussing on herself even when she was physically attacked. Her mind is on us, and what '*she put us through*,' she's even pitying the apparent incels who took her, and is putting herself down. Ridiculous. I mean, I'm surprised they even lived that long with their combined braincells of…three?

"Can I come sit at the end of the bed?"

"Yeah." She nods as she pats the space in front of her.

Though I face the window, I turn so that she can see my face. "I'm sorry you felt so cooped up in here that you felt the need to sneak off to do something normal whilst I was away." I say '*away*' and not '*gone*' because that would imply that I would never come back. "We'll go out more often now I promise, *together*, if that's what you want. Or you could go with Bellamy instead." I smile at the thought of Bellamy's face when he gets given that task. "The men yesterday were weak enough for Maverick to manipulate. Anything that they had done to you was because of him, not because of a phantom fault they forced on you. You're strong Medisa, look at everything you've been through, how you handle things. Most people would freeze or scream, but you think logically. And I need you to think logically right now, on this silk bed I *deeply* miss, and see that you didn't put us in danger, Maverick did. You were in a bad situation and by the end of the day you made it better, by still having some fight in you and forcing Kassian to see the truth. As for getting yourself out of these types of situations, we'll teach you. *I'll* teach you and then you won't need us, you'll be more of a badass." As I speak, I see Medisa's smile make an appearance.

"With a fat ass." She raises her hip and one leg whilst awkwardly pointing at her bottom.

I clear my throat.

"Yeah er... We'll work on that too." I joke and before I can make up for my words to prevent Medisa from developing body dysmorphia, she whacks me with her pillow.

"Can I vent about something else?"

I slowly drop any cheerful expression.

"Of course." I say when I am fully expecting her to bring up the state of me yesterday and how I got to it.

Medisa instead speaks about her worries. Apparently, her mind is not too kind to her and it tends to blame her (and sometimes who she allows herself to be around) for what she goes through. It also presents tempting solutions that go against her faith, convincing her to '*give in and have fun,*' since she hasn't got the best hand dealt to her. The situation itself may not have a big effect on Medisa, it's the thoughts after that do. Her mind almost forces her to mentally spiral and she's worried that one day she'll give in and stay disconnected.

After expressing herself some more, I realise she worries about me not grasping how serious this is for her and how it may not be something I can fully imagine because of how different our lifestyles are.

"I understand you. You make perfect sense to me, so don't feel odd. I don't want to say that your thoughts are normal or natural because I don't want to invalidate them, but I do want to let you know that it is something that you'll be able to get through. I know because I did and I continue to. And if you ever get to a place where you can't pull yourself out the dark, you don't need to worry for too long because you have people like Amana and me to pull you out." My heart aches a little knowing that this is all set up for her to find out soon, and it'll be a time where she needs to be helped but she won't want it to be me. "And maybe Kassian." I say to bring out her smile and maybe to give myself that hope.

I am about to get up and encourage her to join me, but I sense that she wants to say something else.

"What happened to you yesterday?" Medisa asks.

My vision blurs before becoming clear again.

Just because she's going to find out about what I did to Amana eventually, does not mean that I should come clean with everything else I've done.

"You had no open wounds but you had blood on you. What happened?"

I take a deep breath then slowly exhale. Her face can give away too much and right now, I see that she just needs confirmation to her thoughts. I'll grant her it, but I'll spare the details.

"I think you know what happened. You act as if you're unaware of things, like you're the ditsy-witty friend, but I know you—" I've been watching. "—And you're more than that, more than you yourself could possibly imagine." She may think that her mind is fragile, but I think she does it to herself, to keep herself at bay because if she doesn't, she too would be unhinged. I keep my hands planted on either side of me to prevent myself from getting too close. "And you know that yesterday, we had a problem, so I fixed it."

Medisa continues to stare deep into my eyes like they painted vivid images of what I refuse to give away. I'm impressed, she continues to break eye-contact records.

"Alright c'mon then, let's get you to the office, he'll be here soon." I stand up, ready to get her checked so that we can plan accordingly.

"What?" Medisa is clearly confused by the jump in conversation and shift in mood. "This early?" She recovers quickly. "What if I was still sleeping?"

"Then I would wrap and drag you by the covers to the office...no skin-ship." Time and time again I find a loophole. I'm just too good.

"Nice. Sounds like a plan." Wasting no time, she grabs a hold of the covers, gets comfortable, then attempts to hide herself under. However, with my speed, she's unable to tuck and be hidden for longer than a second.

"Training starts today." I say as soon as she looks confused as to how I was able to strip her of her cover. I grab a hold of her bedsheet and pillows then walk into the living room. "Today's lesson is self-discipline."

Self-discipline should be her thing as a Muslim, but considering she bends and snaps rules, I'm going to go ahead and say that she needs to work on it.

I check my phone then turn to Medisa. "They've arrived downstairs. I'm gonna go get them. Get your arse to the office."

I leave before she can say anything.

They already know about what happened to Medisa and pretty much everything else that they would need to know in order to make her feel comfortable. So far, everything seems to be good, Medisa is cooperating and Charlie and Ava are doing what they can to not seem intimidating.

I know what Medisa's fears are, and needles are one of them, so I, with the help of the good doctors, have moved on to a topic that would definitely distract her, mostly because she's never experienced it.

Ava is on her third story. "It's been about ten years and I

still refuse to sleep with Charlie on silk bedsheets."

Charlie snorts. "You've got to tell them why, otherwise they're going to want to find out for themselves."

I freeze, which is silly because I know that he doesn't necessarily mean with each other.

"You don't have enough grip that's why. I ended up falling off the bed and landing awkwardly on my wrist. Some view that must've been."

Charlie tries to hold in his laugh. "It wasn't that much different from before you fell off." He mutters.

Someone is whacked and it's definitely Charlie.

"Kade." Medisa calls out to me and I almost turn around forgetting that she's got her thigh on show.

I hum instead.

"What's the worst injury you got or gave?"

A broad question, but since the topic is 'sexual injuries', it narrows it down.

"I've never unintentionally physically hurt a girl and intentionally would be another story." I doubt someone with my upbringing would have any normal, loving stories.

Medisa does not verbally react. Perhaps her leg is no longer feeling numb and she is starting to feel her stitches?

As Ava does whatever there is to do left—I don't know as I still have not turned around—Charlie faces me.

"Any deeper and it would've been critical." He whispers.

I would have a drive to do something, but I've already dealt with the men who done this.

"You said she fell unconscious due to a hit to the head before this?"

I raise and drop my brows to confirm. As far as I know, the last person to do that to her is her brother. And we don't know how many times he's done that to her before.

"Well unless your goal is to damage her brain in the near future, I suggest you pull her from the trouble she's in, *today*." Before he can say more, Ava approaches and says something about me being able to turn around.

"Keep her away from any demanding physical activities for at least two weeks, if not three. And Medisa, I will be checking up on you, if I feel as though you're not looking after yourself, I *will* bring you in so that I can personally monitor you." Her soft but strict tone is almost like Bellamy's.

Medisa better not make that connection.

Chapter 60
Kassian
24/01/2022 (Monday)

I met Kade once over the last two weeks and that was for him to see this place for himself before he risks bringing Medisa.

No one else but me comes near this building so when I hear people inside, I know that it's them.

"I knew you'd be here early." I look between the two then approach. "How'd you like it?"

"How d'you know that Maverick won't find us?"

Damn, no hello, nothing.

"I don't." The truth and nothing but the truth.

"We've taken all the precautions we can, so we should be good for a while." Kade attempts to save the day.

"Care to fill me in on said precautions." Medisa questions me when it is Kade who mentioned them.

Is it just me, or has she grown to be more of a bundle of joy?

"You both left Aros through doors every other person that's not you, uses." I explain as Kade undressed, not bothering to take over. "You wore a wig, glasses etc. You took a vehicle that's not too showy in someone else's name—"

"I know what we've done. What precautions did you take?"

Oh, how I can't wait *to teach her.*

"This building's been under my name for a while now, so it won't look suspicious when I come here every now and then, since I *have* been coming here. And I've been giving Maverick little bits of information about you to keep him happy and away from what's actually going on."

Did I need to tell her that? No. Do I regret telling her that? Yes.

"What kind of information?"

"Information that seem like they could be beneficial and lead to something, but in the end are nothing."

Medisa starts to undress herself, revealing the clothes she will train in. "Yes. But like what?"

For the love of God. This is what interacting with no one but Kade does to someone.

"Does it matter? It won't affect anyone." At least not anyone she truly cares about.

"If it don't matter, why can't you just tell me? Let me be the judge of how valuable it is." She tries to get in my face but Kade stands in her way.

I move to the side to arrange what we will be working with while Kade handles her.

"Your university timetable, those on your course, the journeys you make while at Uni or after, your life at school etc."

"Are you kidding me? How is any of that not beneficial?"

I approach the two of them with a pair of knives and though Medisa sees them in my hand, she does not see me as a threat.

"Next time you need to give information, ask me, I'll think of better, *safer* things to tell him."

"Safer for who?" I lower my head to get a good look at her eyes. "Do you think he won't see past the information you'll magically come up with?"

Medisa's breaths become heavy, her facial feature subtly

scrunch and I bet she just needs one more push before she attacks me.

Is this the right day to train? And I hate to be that guy, but is she on her period?

"Give me a knife." She demands.

I place a knife in her hand as Kade explains a few things to her.

"Kassian is going to be teaching you today." He doesn't bother to stop leaning on the table which makes me question whether or not we are going through with our plan. "The knives are blunt and close in on themselves, so that you are protected from being sliced or stabbed."

Just in case her heads still a little fuzzy from two weeks ago, I demonstrate with my own knife, pushing it in on itself.

"But not bruised." I add.

"At the end of the day." Kade continued. "You can fight Kassian as though it were real, this is of course, *after* we've taught you a few things."

"I thought that you were good with knives and… everything else?" She asks Kade.

"I am." Kade speaks with such confidence and humour. "But then what use would Kassian be? We need to make him feel like he's doing *something* useful."

Ha-ha.

Medisa's brows raise and her smile slowly falls when she sees me place the knife upside down in my fist. I am so psyched for this.

I raise my fists up. "You ready Desmona?"

She boredly rotates her finger in the air. "Cue the training sequence."

Kade wastes no time in going at her with a suitable amount of force as I step to the side to analyse how they both move. By some miracle, Medisa is able to miss Kade's swing at her, which she may be happy about but that just means he's going to increase his speed until she reaches a level she can't miss.

"What the heck, I thought Kassian's teaching me?"

"You need to learn to expect the unexpected. We're not just going to lay everything out for you." Kade swings at her again, with the same speed as his initial move, probably to make sure that her dodging wasn't a fluke.

Medisa doesn't dodge in time, finding herself to be trapped in Kade's grip, giving him the chance to slice her throat or stab her until he gets bored. He holds her in place, giving her the chance to somehow escape and when she doesn't, he let's go.

"Medisa you could have easily ducked to the side and got his back. Or you could've gone even lower and got his thigh, his calves. And when you were trapped in his arm, did you forget that you still had a weapon? Why did you not stab his face? Or the arm that held the knife?"

Kade pulls the exact same move on me so that I can demonstrate how to get out of it. She takes it all in and is no longer holding an attitude, or her confidence.

"It's okay." I say because for some reason I feel a little bad.

"No, it's not." Kade butts in with his bullet-point advice. "Medisa, protect your head. No matter what. Only use it as a weapon if it's your last move to pull."

Medisa's bug eyes look between us and I'm just as confused.

"Again." Kade's impatient arse gets ready to put Medisa in another position she needs to learn to avoid or get out off. This time he doesn't give Medisa a chance, he goes straight for her braid, pulling her into him and sliding the knife across her throat.

He really isn't playing any games.

Chapter 61
Kade
31/01/2022 (Monday)

Medisa has strength in her, I feel it sometimes, but it's nowhere near where it needs to be in order for her to do some real damage to stall and get away.

She's probably picked up on it by now, but we are trying to focus on her defence. We don't have much time and we know this, which is why we are cramming everything into these hours. Medisa is only excused when she has to pray, use the toilet or eat, all other hours are used up to better her physically (stretches, running, weights, shooting, going up against one of us etc.). Her meals and drinks are different to what she's used to, but it's so that she can get some weight on her. I don't think it's an exaggeration to say that a young teen could easily lift her.

Her stamina and reaction time has improved which only means that we need to up the difficulty. And though this last week we have been using knives, I have been trying to drill it into her to protect her head (which then of course messes her up as she leaves her body open to take shots).

This week we're going to work with our fists, legs, knives, maybe even real knives and whatever the hell else we feel she needs to learn her way around.

We started off with knives first because they are an extension, and if she can dodge an extension, she can bloody well dodge a punch.

Then there's Kassian.

He confuses me, sometimes more than Medisa. He was okay with screwing her over before, but now he doesn't agree with how I am with her. I ignore it most of the time because of this good-cop bad-cop strategy, but when he interferes with one of my lessons, I do get pissed.

I'm not sorry for being so harsh on her, it's all for her own benefit, but I have made a mental promise to make it up to her when she finally reaches a level that I'm comfortable with.

Chapter 62
Kade
07/02/2022 (Monday)

Medisa's ability to take in her surroundings and those around her, and see a threat or the risk of something happening before it does, is above average, and so is her hearing. So when I am standing directly behind her in this creaky chapel and she doesn't automatically turn around to check me, I admit, it simultaneously toots my horn and disappoints me.

I bring down the bag on her head, cutting off her vision and clean air. She drops her body while her hands rush to try and take it off, but they only make it easier for me to grab onto, pull behind her back and cuff her.

I shove her into the room then continue to nudge her until she reaches the stool and is forced down.

She's made no attempts in preventing all this from happening which just fuels how aggressive I am in taking the bag off her head.

Despite now seeing me, she continues to hold a perplexed expression.

When I am comfortable leaning against the table, I show her my phone with a timer ready.

"Would be nice if you escaped today." I start the timer.

I don't expect her to dislocate her thumb to break free from the handcuffs—although that is an option to make things easier—I expect—too much really—her to somehow make it past me and out the chapel. There are going to be times where Medisa can't make use of her hands, feet or legs, hell, there might even be times where she could be cut off from food or water, so she needs to learn to adapt.

"How the hell do you expect me to get out of these cuffs with no key, pin, stick—"

"Tik-tok."

Medisa looks around to find something that will benefit her, but before she is able to make a move, Kassian swiftly barges in and gets her up. There must be a reason for him to suddenly be so bold, so I wait until he brings whatever he's discovered to light.

"Whatever kinky lesson this is can wait till later, someone was followed." He speaks close to a whisper as he pushes us further into the small room next door.

Without thinking, I aid him in opening up a random cupboard, and when we see that it's big enough, Kassian puts Medisa in, then himself.

We all stand quietly to avoid making any noise, but to also try and hear whoever had followed Kassian (yes, I am blaming him. A part of me even believes he brought the bastards).

Medisa tries to adjust herself in this small space and I blame myself for her lack of comfortability.

"Easy girl, there's no time for that now." He whispers above her.

The whites of Medisa's eye grow as she moves away from him and I make a mental note to sort him out after the intruders leave.

The chapels door (that needs to be replaced or oiled) lets us know they have now made their way inside. Kassian pulls Medisa back into him with his hand over her mouth, which would've been fine as he is keeping her from getting caught, but then, he winks at me.

As Medisa is not someone who screams or shouts, Kassian's hand being over her mouth for longer than it needs to be, annoys her to the point where she risks us all getting caught by burrowing her heel into his toes. Kassian gives in and removes his hand from her mouth, stopping me from reflecting Medisa's lack of attempt in the morning to instead think of this.

The followers sound as though they are no longer near this room, so I push the door open on Kassian's side and give him no choice but to leave.

He brought them here. He can deal with them.

Chapter 63
Kassian
07/02/2022 (Monday)

It's funny watching Kade get all heated and throw me out. If it wasn't for Medisa being at risk, I think I would've stayed in the cupboard, or I would pull Kade out with me.

"Care to tell me why you're following fellas?" I try not to make it seem as if I just came out of the one room they walked past.

"Boss wanted to check where you've been running off to these days."

Dragging the stool we left in the middle of the room to the single table on the side, I get comfortable on it.

"What? Can't a boy let off some steam in peace?"

I forgot his bloody name—*do I even know his name?*—but he's stares me down like I'm lying.

"You wouldn't mind us joining you today, would you?"

If he were as observant as he thinks he is, he would have seen my eyes give away how tedious I find this.

"Not at all."

Kade and Medisa have the simple task of staying still and they can't even do that. The cupboard creaks loud enough for us to hear, and I mentally curse out the timing. If it had creaked when I spoke, they would not have heard it.

"Anyone we should know about?" The other one speaks.

"It's an old building you git." I put too much venom in the word. "Why would I bring your sister here when I have access to the best suites in London?"

No reaction.

These guys are good, they aren't getting offended and turning their attention towards taking out their emotions on me. Instead, the second one moves to explore the room with the cupboard that holds Kade and Medisa.

Without thinking, I move towards the punching bag and use it. Maybe if they see how nonchalant I am, they will leave the cupboard alone?

"If Maverick wants to see me more often, he should've told me on one of our little dates. In fact, let me call him now while you search the place. Hopefully he doesn't get annoyed when I find another place to run off to, since you guys weren't exactly discreet in finding out what I'm up to in this one."

The man walks away from the small room, obviously not wanting me to call my brother.

"Put the phone down Kassian, we're leaving." Just as he is about to be out of sight, he stops at the doorway, then turns his head back. "Tell your girl I like her perfume, it's... all over this place." His eyes and finger move around the room to really exaggerate Medisa's scent.

Shit.

Chapter 64
Kade
07/02/2022 (Monday)

"You can come out now." Kassian calls out to us.

We walk into the 'gym' and find my brother near the door as though he had just come in.

"They're gone, I saw them out. They both got into a car and drove off. And I doubt they will be coming back anytime soon."

'Yes, because they've got what they need, so when they do come back, it'll be to take us. Bloody idiot.'

I try not to let my blood boil, but it's difficult when it's already been heated by his behaviour.

"He knows. They know. Which means Maverick basically knows." Medisa also sees the truth of the situation.

"They don't know that it's you. It could be any girl." Kassian tries to reassure her.

"But *I'm* the girl that you're supposed to be tricking, it would make more sense if it were me. Why would you bring a sneaky link here when they obviously know that you would take them to a hotel?"

"Medisa," I softly call out to her. "We're okay. We'll stay here until I know the coast is clear, then we'll train back at Aros. Kassian will continue to come here to stick to his story and then maybe we'll be nice enough to let him join us."

A stupid plan really, Maverick would've known about the three of us prior to this invasion, but we need her to let us—me—take care of the situation, not let it distract her.

"So, what? We're going to camp here for a bit?"

"Precisely." Kassian sounds and looks too glee for my liking while Medisa looks to me for some sort of confirmation.

"Only for a little bit." If more people are sent here, or the man who stayed behind approaches, we could use them for Medisa's practice.

I place the handcuffs on the table, knowing that this idiot would say something triggering.

"Aw, we're done with them so soon?" Kassian's head rolls in Medisa's direction. "Let me know if the taste in there wasn't enough, will you?"

There's been a development in the way I react to things. Instead of tensing up, I become more relaxed. Something that hasn't changed, is my habit of pinching my nose.

"Stand up." I address Kassian.

"Kade—"

"Don't worry sweet Medisa, just sit that pretty arse down somewhere."

Medisa is about to take steps to get in between us, but I don't want to put this on hold for any longer. I need to do something to not only release the tension between us boys, but to also get rid of any added stress from being caught today.

"Get comfortable Medisa, let us show you how things could play out." I watch as Kassian's eyes turn from playful to eager.

Why bother to wait for him to make the first hit when he's waited years to do something about emotions he felt five years ago?

I don't hold back on my punches and land two of them. Kassian takes them but doesn't messily come at me like I suspected he would.

"Use this opportunity because we haven't got time for this bullshit. Using Medisa to piss me off will no longer be ignored."

Kassian listens to my words then finally tries to land a hit, his speed has improved, I'll give him that, but I won't allow him—just yet—to make contact. Quickly after dodging, I knee him, forcing him to lower himself onto me where I 'gently' hold him in place by his nape.

"C'mon Kassian. What was that? Hit me like the man you want everyone to believe you are."

And that is it.

Apparently, these words are enough to tip him over the edge I thought he had already fallen from. The last time Kassian attacked me like this, he was drunk and I defended myself. But this time, I allow for his attacks—with hardly any breaks in between—to hit me, because as annoyed as I am at him, it is my fault that he is this way. And I'm going to be the one that gets his frustration out of him so that we can all move on.

When your head and body is being battered, the majority of the time it feels as though you are beyond time and space itself, so when Kassian stopped, I actually have no idea how long it took for him to feel as though he had done enough.

We are both somehow on the floor now.

I had my back on the ground when I first zoned back in, but now I am sitting up with Kassian parallel to me.

He's on his knees, staring at our blood on his hands.

"Better?" I say in attempts to pull him out of whatever state he's in.

"A whole day." He says, almost to himself.

"What?" My lips sting.

"You spent a whole day apologising to Medisa, probably over something trivial, to someone who at the time you considered to be insignificant. Yet you didn't bother to put a pinch of that effort towards me, your *brother*." He finally lifts his head up to look me in the eyes. "I waited. I was still outraged, but I waited. Days, weeks, months, I waited. I waited for your stubborn arse to force me to see your point of view, for you to even beat me into seeing or hearing your explanation."

My eyes become moist, my blinks more frequent.

"But you didn't. You ran away and left me with Maverick. So when I heard you spent an entire day apologising to Medisa—*Iris's* friend, Medisa— I wanted to ruin your friendship by getting him involved because then, even if I had changed my mind or died, I knew that Maverick would still do something."

I don't have a right to defend myself, I don't, but I don't want Kassian continuing to believe that I found it easy to stay away, and had no problem with what I had done.

"As much as you think that this is all your fault, it's not. It's mine." He lowers his head. His hands now rest on his lap. "I was naïve and delusional in all my thoughts about my relationship with Iris, which then led to all four of us suffering the consequences. But you have to understand. You had your art, your studio, your container, to deal with the things we went through and I barely had you. So, I made her my escape and blindly traded that illusion for you."

"It wasn't an illusion." I speak before he carries on. "She was your escape. She *did* make you forget and feel better, that wasn't something you convinced yourself of. She was your friend, and in the small amount of time you had spent with her, she did a better job at helping you breathe than I ever did. You grew with Iris and you may have had delusional thoughts about the future with her, but if I hadn't messed it up, it could've worked out exactly the way you had pictured it."

Kassian gives a melancholic smile, then his eyes search the room which moves on to him urgently looking around. "Where's Medisa?"

I get on my feet, slightly dizzy, but I push through it.

"Medisa?" I call out.

"Yeah?" She sounds a little distant.

"Come back inside." I won't lecture her, but damn she should know better.

I turn to Kassian.

I need to say something before Medisa gets close. "Thank you for being the reason why I know who Medisa is. You were right—at least on the 'friend' aspect of things. You're the reason why we'll all have stories to tell—" I peek to see if Medisa was close enough to hear us. She was not. "And I can't wait to reintroduce you to Amana."

A conversation that's long overdue needs to be had, but we can't have it with Medisa around the corner. I will tell Kassian the truth, my side of things—just not now.

"You know they left a man behind." He says after appreciating my words.

I did know that, which makes Medisa being wherever she is much worse.

"I do." I say and appreciate the look on his face. He was obviously expecting me to cuss him out or rush towards Medisa.

Medisa enters the room and her face says it all: She doesn't know if tensions are still high.

"Change of plans. We're not training today." I pack our

things.

"What are we doing instead?" Now she is a different type of confused.

"Right now? We're going back to Aros." I throw Kassian's car keys at his chest. He reacts slowly, making him catch the keys when they reach the lower part of his abdomen.

"I don't think leaving right after we almost got caught is a smart idea." Medisa vocalises her thoughts.

"Medisa. Honestly. Just trust me on this." We've already been caught together so I don't care about the abundance of evidence we're about to supply. A stupid high, yes, but again, I don't care. We are going to have at least one day of genuine happy memories together.

None of them make a move until I do. I suppose they are both still processing different things. No matter, when they see what I have in store for them, they'll be fine.

Chapter 65
Kade
07/02/2022 (Monday)

I make the two of them face the bookshelf, but I don't remember telling them to stand and look like they are out of place, tired, and like I am a child they are entertaining.

"I wanted to keep this a secret, especially from someone like Kassian—"

Kassian has enough energy to put his middle finger up.

"—But I figured we all need this." And I trust Kassian now, so I don't care about him seeing a spot where I could hide Medisa if anything were to happen. "Anyways, we all get to choose one thing to do today, one thing that we all have to experience together. And my thing is…" I pull on a handle hidden behind a few books, revealing part of the shelf actually being a door.

They both enter the room, curious and cautious.

"I know that you got issues, but a rage room? Seriously?"

I actually haven't used it as a rage room in a long time—it is not fun to clean up—but I doubt they would believe me, not when it looks like this.

"Part time gym, part time rage room… I had Bellamy add some things for us to break."

'*Some*' is me being humble. They have plenty.

I turn off the main lights and turn on the best decision we ever made for this room, LED lights.

Medisa doesn't give enough time to take in the new vibe of the room; she goes straight for a bat, so I quickly move to give her a welding helmet and jumpsuit. She puts on her protective gear with no fuss, then turns to me to see if she has my stamp of approval, obviously not wanting to be interrupted again.

I pull her close via her helmet and inspect her. Her eyes follow me as I double check and I have the neediest feeling to take the piss and keep her in place to see how long it takes for her to speak. I won't, but maybe I should give her some gloves too?

As she half-trudged her way to her target, me and Kassian share an expression with each other. Somehow, Medisa makes the baggy jumpsuit look as if it has weights installed inside.

Medisa looks at the chunky screen that's almost double her size and definitely double her weight. Lowering her eyes to her feet, she adjusts her stance before swinging at the screen. It falls to the ground in one hit, but that doesn't stop her. She continues to bash it again and again, taking the bat back as far as she can before bringing it down, full power.

"Oh shit." Kassian lets out as he gives a clap or two.

When Medisa is done, she walks back to us like she's been summoned.

"Does the wittle baby want to take a nap now?" Kassian teased, putting on a baby voice and his own helmet. Medisa chuckles, whacking his arm as he moves to his target.

A shelf filled with glass containers which either hold some sort of glow in the dark paint or marbles, is the next victim.

Kassian decides to dismantle the shelf by picking up each glass jar and using them to knock other items out, either by throwing them or hitting them with his bat.

"Medisa come here and try this." He holds out a jar filled

with marbles. "You ready?" He holds out the jar so that it is at the level of her eyeline then drops it when she nods her head.

The sound of the metal baseball bat connecting with the glass, followed by the marbles scattering across the floor, is probably one of the best sounds this room has ever produced.

'One of the best.'

Revealing a target on the wall and some axes, I tempt them into a game where we all have a few rounds before the two of them decide to go off and destroy whatever they can.

I keep my eyes on Medisa to make sure she doesn't hurt herself or get too close to a raging Kassian. And I keep an eye on Kassian to make sure he doesn't suddenly switch.

When everything is destroyed and all we can hear is the sound of each other's heavy breaths, I turn the main lights back on and open the door for us to go to the games room.

Though they seem to be out of breath, they both still have energy for a little competition. We start with the arcade punching bag. I go first, then Medisa, then Kassian. Both of them surprise me, with Medisa's punch reaching 710—on her third attempt—and Kassian's punch beating mine. I am tempted to try again but I know that it will start a cycle of us beating each other and I don't want Medisa to get bored, especially when the plan is to try all the games in this room.

Kassian's choice is a pub he owns in London. It's not like other pubs, it has a twist, obviously.

Medisa enters first, fiddling with her camera to make sure it's on a setting she likes. We enter right after her, and as soon as we are surrounded by all sorts of sounds, Kassian turns to me.

"I bet this entire building Medisa doesn't remember this place."

"Same." I agree, knowing he wanted me to oppose and bet one of my properties. But it's true, she may feel like it is familiar but I don't think she will know why, especially since it's one of those buildings that look completely different in the dark compared to what it looks like now, with all the lights and decorations.

Kassian disappears almost immediately after I ruin his chance of getting some extra pocket money, so I take Medisa to a free table where she decides now's the best time to take pictures. After a few shots, she puts her camera down and watches everyone on the dancefloor as well as the band, looking as though she wants to join but can't. Just as I'm about to tell her that it's okay to want to get involved, Kassian slams a tray that holds our drinks down. He only got his own and Medisa's order right because mine is not some sort of fizzy or water.

Removing a piece of clothing draped over his arm, he hands Medisa a historic dress. Then, he removes the cowboy hat that was layered on top of his head and places it on mine. I am about to say something but am distracted by Kassian chugging his drink, and then by his confidence in going onto the dancefloor.

Medisa continues to watch rather than participate, and that's when I remember the mother I noticed when we first sat down; she tried to calm one child while her other attempted to drag her onto the dancefloor, so I doubt she would mind if Medisa dances with him instead. This way, Medisa has an excuse to get up, and the mother can catch a break.

I sit by the woman and her active son, close enough for him to see me. He stops tugging at her clothes.

"What happened to your face?"

His mum gasps and is quick to apologise for his behaviour.

"That's alright." I say to her, then lower my gaze to him. "I keep bad guys away from this place." Selling myself as one of the security guards to the mum who I know is overhearing our conversation, is the best way to go about this. She won't let her son go with me otherwise. "I actually saved that girl over there." I point out Medisa and spot Kassian holding his hand out to her. "She needs a dance partner too." The mother, who is surprisingly good at handling a child crying, loud music, people chattering and a stranger talking to her child, looks to Medisa and sees what Kassian is trying to do.

"Charlie, go ask that girl for a dance."

Thankfully she can't see that Kassian and I share the same face and is assuming that Medisa is younger than she really is.

Her son, Charlie, rushes over to Medisa.

"I'll keep an eye on him and bring him back." I make sure she hears me so that her night isn't completely overrun by paranoia.

Getting back to our table, I watch how both Kassian and Medisa are distracted on the dance floor, allowing me to finally unlock my phone and do what's been at the back of my mind all day. Text Amana.

'Hey. You busy?'

I know that it's not wise to rekindle Amana and Kassian's friendship before we've handled our brother. But if I could get him a few minutes with her after all these years, I am going to do it.

I wait for a response or even a 'read' but nothing changes from my message being delivered.

When I look up, I see that Medisa is now with a group of women and Kassian is dancing with a bunch of kids. I make sure to document it all with Medisa's camera but it is slightly lowered when I realise the song has changed and Medisa is a partner away from dancing with Kassian. Kassian, who like her, has the biggest grin on his face which forces mine to mirror it.

I stand up to approach her.

After days of being harsh with training, I want to be in front of Medisa when she's having fun and smiling, but I also need to put a stop to this because we are ruining her personal goals. So, I'm going to interrupt, *not* because I'm jealous, but for Medisa.

Something happens on her end, which makes her bump into someone and fall backwards. It's almost like ice skating all over again, except this time, I am stood behind her and am able to catch her a little more appropriately.

A man who would have been dancing with her right now, had she not fallen, asks if she's okay.

"Yeah sorry, I just got a little dizzy." She stays where I placed her as if she were thinking about joining in again.

I don't say anything. She may be thinking of sitting out herself which means I don't have to be the party pooper.

Medisa's shoulders raise like she were cold, then, she slowly turns around to face me. Her expression is as though she were waiting for me to raise my voice at her, but then her shoulders drop once she realises it is me and not an angry stranger.

I lower myself to talk close to her ear. "You can take a break you know?"

Cocking my head a little to the side, I try to read her reaction.

"I'm okay, I just didn't want to dance with a man."

"Oh, so Kassian doesn't count as a man?" He may have my face but she does not see him as a potential.

"Ah, no." She exaggerates her response then looks around to—I'm assuming—find him.

As we move to go back to our table, Medisa swats at my arm.

"You're supposed to dance too, you cow. You're dancing to the next song." She holds her finger out, waiting for me to protest.

"I didn't want to scare the kids."

Her eyes travel over my face, looking over whatever Kassian had done to me. "Oh please, you look fine. And besides Charlie wasn't scared of you—that's the boy who you got to approach me—and yes, I did realise you had influenced him."

Of course she knows. How could I think there was a chance it would go unnoticed?

Another song starts to play, bringing me and Medisa out of our minds. Medisa moves in the direction of the table and I follow after, not wanting her to be alone.

We do not make it to the table.

We are both surrounded by a bunch of ecstatic kids and tipsy/ high-on-emotion adults who give us no choice but to join in. I look to see if I need to get an uncomfortable Medisa out, but she's found a child partner and seems to be more than happy to join in with the crowd. I have a few kids around me and a toddler who wants uppies.

'Ah, what the heck?'

I lift her up and join in on the nonsensical dance.

Chapter 66
Kassian
07/02/2022 (Monday)

Taking a break from holding multiple kids at once, I take myself to the side of the 'stage' where I notice a bimbo press herself against my brother with a drunk sensual dance.

Ugh. My body shivers as I cringe.

There are kids around and besides, she is not Kade's type. There are times (rarities) where Kade may ignore his standards for a certain type of fun—which I can tell he's in no mood for—but even then, I doubt he would entertain her. My eyes then bring an unfocused Medisa in the background into focus, and she does not care for looking away.

I slowly move to approach her so that I can get her eyes away from him, but I also have no doubt that my brother will not disappoint.

And he does not.

Kade spins the girl around, lets go, then gives her a gentle push in the direction away from him. Before she is able to process the offence and turn around, Kade moves towards Medisa, who does not bother to hide the expression her face made at his moves. I want to let out a laugh, but I join them at the table instead.

"Let's go to the back rooms."

"What's there?" Medisa asks.

"You'll see."

"No, no, Medisa's turn's next."

"Oh, come on." I plead. "It's right there and besides you

took us to two places."

I'm right. He knows I'm right. Medisa knows I'm right. It's why none of them say anything…ignoring Kade's loud expression.

"Great!" I stand. "Follow me."

No word of a lie, I did not expect Kade to choose a song and deliver. He must've snuck a shot or two before he went ahead and sang 'Shower' and despite his deliverance, I *know* he meant those lyrics. We—me and Medisa—cringed, we laughed, we joined and then it ended.

It's Medisa's turn now and I catch a glimpse of *something* run across her eyes, so I get ready to be entertained further.

She chooses to have the original track play in the back, and instantly, and I mean instantly, I know what song it is. My brows freeze in their raised positions as my grin sets a new record for how wide it can be.

This is bold.

The first verse starts without her as her cheeky arse adjusts the autotune on her mic.

I glance to Kade who seems to have processed the lyrics and song now. He leans forward. His hand wipes down his face as if he has a beard and then he finally settles its grip on his chin.

Medisa goes *in*, she doesn't care for the lewd, provocative lyrics. Her shame? Not with us in this room. She left it at the door, and when she harmonises and confidently talks about tattoos on peoples skin and being turned on, I hold my breath and quickly side-eye Kade to see if he's picking up on all of this.

We must be past her bedtime.

I join in, in the back, moving to the beat, ad-libbing, wanting to pick up the second mic.

Kade jumps up and went for her. At first, I thought the room was about to get steamy, but he went for the mic in her hands. And if it wasn't for me, he would've got it.

Chapter 67
Kade
08/02/2022 (Tuesday)

Medisa the terror wants to choose another song. And that's fine if she chooses something appropriate and not… not… not whatever that was.

Despite being in recovery from her first performance, I monitor her new choices and give her no choice but to have my approval first.

She does not listen of course, but that's okay, I'll just have to use my quick thinking to both save and entertain her.

The door bursts open, making her jump and 'accidently' choose a song. Her song of choice—again, one that I would rather we listened and did whatever to without an audience—blasts through the speakers as three large men enter and shut the door behind them.

As soon as the door is locked in place, both me and Kassian do what we can to keep them away from Medisa.

These men, they've specifically been chosen to batter us, maybe even take us. They're not the average man, these are what I would say are mine and Kassian's level, if not higher, and a large reason as to why that is, is their weight and height.

In the past, Maverick would get these types of men to fetch us when he couldn't be arsed to, or when we didn't listen. They can handle most of our attacks, but if it were switched and Kassian and I had to take on men who were okay with killing us, we would be in some serious conditions.

One of the larger men ram me into the wall and hold me

in place, his weight crushing me against the wall.

I'm about to make another attempt to free myself when I hear someone struggle next to me.

Medisa is on her back on the table beside me, held in place by sausage fingers and is about to be stabbed through. I can't get out of my own man in time to save her, so once again I am left with no choice. Grabbing a hold of whatever I can on her body, I drag the top half of her towards me, just about making her miss the attack.

Elbowing the back of the man who assigned himself to me, I partly release myself from his grip. With Medisa busy and out the way, I grab the knife meant for her (left jammed in the table) and use it on him. Not to kill him, but to clip his wings.

"I was wondering when someone was going to show up." I sit in front of the man who looks most awake while his companions relied on their restraints to keep them up.

A lighter clicks a few times behind me and I suspect Kassian is about to start his new method of extracting information. When he doesn't come close, and smoke fills the air, I turn to see him inhaling the contents of a cigarette.

"Since when did you smoke?" Disappointing really. Alcohol I understand (somewhat). Drugs I understand (somewhat). But cigars and cigarettes? Fuck off. And he better not have smoked that shit in front of Medisa.

On cue, Medisa walks in and takes in the new sight of the three bulky men, beaten and tied. She shouldn't be too surprised. She should actually be proud, one of them looks that way because of her.

Back to the man.

"What did you expect was going to happen? Your plan, at best, is banal."

"Is it?" The mammoth sized man sounds as though he's smoked for the world.

I click my tongue and lower my voice. "You know I think I remember you from before."

He continues to show no fear.

"For your sake," I continue. "You should pray that's not the case. Before I do to you what another man is owed."

"Yes, do tell us you weren't expecting to win here?" Kassian cuts in, probably doing me a favour. "What was the plan anyway? To distract? To hurt? Or to kill?"

The elephantine doesn't say anything, but I suspect the answer is all three.

"How fatuous." I take Kassian's cigarette and for a moment, I am close to drawing a design across the man's face until the heat dies. But Medisa's here, so I flick it at him instead.

"*Yeah*, you silly fatuous cow." Medisa joins in out of the blue, coming across as someone trying to embody a mean girl.

"Medisa." Kassian calls out to her, no doubt to point out her mistake. A part of him probably wants to take the mickey too, so I glare at him. He doesn't need to ridicule her now, not in front of this specimen, even if he isn't going to make it through the night.

She turns to me after Kassian's somewhat abrupt pause. "What?"

From what I can gather from her expression, she already feels embarrassed, so I give in. "'*Silly*' is basically the definition of '*fatuous*'."

She gives each of my eyeballs exactly two seconds of attention before responding. "Oh... I don't understand how you guys didn't go to a normal school, didn't have a normal childhood, spent most of your lives doing Maverick's bidding—" She gives each point an assigned finger. "—and yet you have a better vocabulary than me."

Jumbo snickers, getting all eyes on him.

I'm going to kill him.

Putting on a friendly mask, I turn to face Medisa. "Why don't you get yourself a drink and think about what your two things are?"

"Okay." She—shockingly—complies, which makes me want to leave this hefty sack of meat to see if there's anything that she would like to say.

I don't...but I do consider it.

As soon as she is out the door and, I assume, steps away from the room, I knock the voluminous man out and turn to Kassian. "Change of plans."

He stops prepping.

"We're just going to leave them here." I continue.

"For Maverick to find?"

"He's already found us." I use my hand to present the three cyclopean men.

"Why the sudden change?" He looks down his nose.

"We can't waste time here and cut into what Medisa wants to do. Also, I don't want her thinking the worst. The less time we spend in here, the more I can prove the worst version she has of me in her head wrong."

"Okay." Kassian nods. "Let's tie them in place and lock the doors."

"I'll do that." I grab materials from his hands. "You call brother dearest and summon whatever believable bullshit you can, to buy us some time."

Kassian dramatically gasps.

He's about to say something, but thinks it over.

I raise a brow. "What?"

"Is now the right time to let you know that Maverick's always known about the chapel, the training, the—"

'One hit won't kill him.'

Chapter 68
Kade
08/02/2022 (Tuesday)

Exploring the streets of Central London. That is what Medisa wanted to do, so we did it. Kassian was a little drunk and Medisa was… Medisa, so they matched each other's energies perfectly well. We walked, ran, played tag everywhere without care. We even made sure to document it all with Medisa's camera, and now, after buying some burger meals, we are finally resting at Southbank Skate.

Comfortable on a slope with Medisa sandwiched—with gaps—in between, Kassian breaks the silence. "What would you say is the weirdest thing about you?"

"Where do I begin?" Medisa breathes out the words. "Oh, oh, sometimes when I sleep, I wake up and move around or engage in conversations, and then I'll fall asleep and not remember any of it. And if I do, it's like a blur. And I only know that I do that because Amana told me."

I make sure Kassian doesn't say anything that would make her feel insecure while recalling the few times she's had one of those interactions with me.

"And not to make things depressing or anything, but I realised that I have conversations in my head as if someone else were with me. Like I would pretend that I'm being interviewed about my life or that I'm in some sort of therapy session *or* that I have a friend that's constantly with me. And I would narrate, or we would discuss my life and do deep dives into things and make jokes and they would say comforting things or call me out on certain things and blah blah blah... I don't know. I think I do it to comfort myself. To make it seem like someone's listening and understands why I am, the way that I am... *Oh* and sometimes I view things that are happening in real time as though they are already in the past. I think that I do that so it's easier for me to move on. But don't worry, I'm working on that one." Medisa is so casual with how she delivers her words that if I were not blessed with the ability to actually use my brain, I would think she is normal.

Me and Kassian slowly and quietly turn our heads to exchange the same expression—we did not know how to react or what to say—then we face forward before Medisa looks up to one of us.

"What about you guys?" She turns to each side to question the both of us.

"I do something similar, except I imagine how life would look if our parents hadn't died—"

I hold my breath mid taking one in.

"—Or when I do something or meet someone new, I would think about how my parents would react. If they would be proud, or guide me a certain way."

Am I a bad son for not having those thoughts?

Medisa looks up to Kassian's face. "I don't think that's weird. I think that's normal. Someone *not* having those thoughts might be a little weird."

I stay frozen, not knowing what to think or say. I've never really had time to think of my parents when my mind was filled with me and Kassian, and whatever Maverick wanted. And when I did think of them, I came to some sort of thick haze or void.

I feel myself zone out, hearing a blurred version of the conversation Kassian and Medisa have, while also trying to force my brain to remember *something* about my parents.

"If you guys could meet and be with your younger selves for a small period of time, what would you say or do?" Medisa's question pulls me back to where they are.

Kassian sucks in air through his mouth, then blows it all back out. "I'm gonna need some time to think on that one. Brother? Care to answer while I think? Before Medisa goes back to having conversations in her head."

Medisa looks to me, her curious eyes in my peripheral.

"I would tell him to spill the drink." Out of all the memories, this is the one to rise to the surface, this is the one my cruel brain uncovers a glimpse off. Had I given myself a second to think it over, I would not have said my thoughts out loud. Not with Kassian here.

I don't get to hear all of Medisa's answer to her own question because of how quickly enraged I became, but I do hear her say she would struggle not to tell her younger self about her having someone there for her eventually.

"Three someone's." Kassian corrects.

"Hmm?"

"You have Amana, Kassian and me." I add on to Kassian's response, facing Medisa so she knows that I mean it.

I don't care if she wants me to stay away from her after she finds out the truth, I'm not making the same mistake again, I'm going to force her to hear my words, keep myself accessible to her at all times, and eventually, she'll let me in.

Chapter 69
Kassian
08/02/2022 (Tuesday)

The Sherlock in me is saying '*something's not right.*' First the random inspection in the morning, then the obese basketball players showing up at the pub. Now on top of that, it's Maverick's lack of communication after the matters. He hadn't even bothered to do or say anything when the three of us were prancing around the empty streets of London last night.

Telling him about the chapel; fine. Telling him what we were doing in the chapel; fine. Not getting information about the two of them and Aros; not fine. I am running out of useless information to give. There's only so much a person wouldn't mind having out there.

I want to say '*sooner or later*,' but I think the time Maverick notices and decides to bring them in has already come. And if that's true, then bloody hell, him and Kade really are on the same wavelength in terms of giving us all one last day.

I let myself into the room I had put Medisa in all those weeks ago. I've been staying here for the past two weeks, but after yesterday's events, I would rather stay with them at the skate park or even sleep on the floor at Aros than in a luxury room like this.

Getting comfortable on the armchair with a drink in hand, I massage my forehead. I don't feel anger towards Kade anymore, well, not as much as I used to, and I definitely do not want Medisa to be further dragged into this. I'm such an idiot for even getting her involved in the first place. She said she forgives me, but the worst hasn't even happened yet, so I won't hold that against her or hope for the best.

I'm not Kade.

Finishing what's in the glass, I put it down for a refill. Only, I had not put it down on the side table; I somehow missed it completely. Not bothered enough to clean the mess, my hand moves to pick up the bottle.

The next sip or two are both thirst quenching and extraordinary, and my vision begins to blur a little more than a lot.

My brain works faster than my body, I have the option to call and warn, but that would expose more than I would like and it's benefit is less significant when up against its detrimental effects.

I throw my phone as hard as I can to get it under a piece of furniture before I no longer have control of my limbs. He'll find it, no doubt, but at least I tried to take away his ability to impersonate me.

I should've thrown it out the bloody window.

Chapter 70
Kade
11/02/2022 (Friday)

I should return before Medisa decides to do anything stupid, but as a fail-safe, I have instructed Bellamy to come and keep an eye on her. He's to entertain and inform her that I have not disappeared like Kassian; I will be coming back.

Sitting in my car with no destination is as infuriating as things constantly going wrong. Why the *hell* did he get himself caught? Has his brain not developed? Is this a trap?

I call Kassian's phone—the most stupid, incriminating thing to do—and someone actually picks up.

And I know that it's Maverick.

"Tell me where?"

"What?"

Shocker, Maverick acting clueless.

I haven't got time for this.

"You've obviously done this to get my attention, so tell me where you are, so I can get this over and done with."

He sighs as if I'm ruining his fun, then gives me an address I haven't yet had the pleasure of visiting.

"Someone will escort you up."

I hang up.

This is going to be the first time I see Maverick after he screwed me over. I want to kill him, or lock him up in multiple cages to ensure he doesn't escape, but I can't risk Kassian's life. I have no doubt Maverick will do something to him if he hasn't already.

I don't sit down like he is, but he waits for me to. His gaze is borderline ravenous, it almost makes me feel uncomfortable and there's no sign of Kassian, though why would there be? Maverick is rich enough to have him shipped off to another country by now, or even hold him in the air until he's come up with a location he's satisfied with.

"Let's skip over the weird staring-patience competition, as well as the life updates and get straight to what you want, shall we?" I don't actually care for what he wants, because that is exactly what we are going to do.

"*Aros.*"

My eyes narrow. Not only is that the business I have no public connection to, but Medisa is currently there, sleeping.

I remind myself Aros is one of the things Kassian made Maverick aware of and not a threat.

"I like it. '*From the river's mouth.*' It's smart. I should've thought of that instead of '*Baronial.*' It would've had more of an impact."

I don't say anything, not when he's trying to get some sort of reaction out of me.

"But it wouldn't have worked out as well. Not when the whole idea in your head being 'one River takes away whilst another River provides.'" He dry chuckles. "What does the third River do?"

'*Don't do anything stupid. Don't do anything stupid.*'

"I'm kidding Kaden. Shit. Relax." He pours himself some water. "Kassian is fine. He's already agreed to be a responsible River, to take care of his side of things while also being a part of the family."

"That's what you want? For us to be a part of the family? Done." There are Rivers outside of us. I can survive only seeing Maverick at gatherings. Play pretend.

He lets out a prolonged hiss. "No, I'm afraid it's not that easy for you. You see, I'm not comfortable with Medisa knowing what she knows."

"She doesn't *know* anything."

"Well that's a lie. But don't worry, I can deal with her for you. That's what I'm here for, to take care of you."

My blood starts to boil. Soon I'll sweat from the anger and stress Maverick imposes.

"I won't let you kill her, or allow you to sign her life away."

Maverick distances his hands from one another then brings them together, creating a single clap. "Well, I'm not a monster Kaden. I am open to suggestions."

Fuck me, Medisa is going to hate this.

'But she'll understand.'

"I'll marry her." A jump, I admit. But it's needed.

Maverick freezes.

His eyes subtly express that I've said something to his advantage, which only furthers my growing regret. "She's quite plain compared to your normal type."

"She—We're—" My head wavers a shake. "It's not like that."

"Ah, don't piss on my legs and tell me it's raining."

My jaws clench. "I can't fault you for not knowing what a relationship with a friend is when you've never had one, but that is what Medisa is— a friend."

"A friend you want to marry?"

"A friend I'll marry to save." I counter.

The room becomes quiet while Maverick's face subtly

shows how much he's enjoying this.

"Convince me. How will marrying her make this all better?"

"There was an island we lived on." I say without pause.

He becomes serious, stiff looking. His body language screaming '*careful*' while also wanting to know where I'm going with this.

"I don't remember everything, but I know that it's ours and it's cut off from the world. I'll put Medisa there. She won't see anyone but me and the workers stationed there." My words aren't enough to convince him. I need to say more, something cruel, but not outrightly. "I might have disappeared these past few years, but everyone knows I'm alive. And since we have to get married and have kids to ensure our lineage continues, this would be me ticking those boxes. I'll be doing what is wanted from us…family duties." I mumble the last bit.

Maverick pours me a glass of water, before approaching.

I take a step back.

I may be desperate for him to agree, but I'm not stupid enough to allow him to get close.

"Okay." He semi-whispers as he nods in agreeance. "I'll get her for you."

What? "No—"

Before I can react, an injection is lodged into the side of my neck. He purposely stepped towards me knowing I would take a step back, closer to whoever is comfortable enough to drug me.

Chapter 71
Kassian
12/02/2022 (Saturday)

This is a joke.

It's not, but the fact that we are in this position is.

Medisa lies unconscious in bed (Maverick's put her in an induced coma), with a single IV drip connected to her, though from what I can see, she has multiple bags in line.

Why did they not puncture both arms to speed it up?

Kade—like me—is sitting on a chair on the other side of her bed. We've both been staring at her, thinking about what to do.

I can't stand the silence anymore.

"What the hell are we going to do now? How are we going to protect her here?" There's no one in the room with us, and we've already done a check for cameras and microphones.

"She's not going to stay here her whole life—"

"Yeah, because he's probably planning on killing her tomorrow."

Kade's eyes narrow to an extreme degree, I might as well say he's squinting.

"We've already agreed on what to do with Medisa."

Oh, no wonder why he's somewhat calm.

"Care to fill me in?"

He goes back to looking at her with soft eyes, but I notice him chew the side of his mouth and tense his jaw. "She's going to be my wife."

My eyes enlarge and I refuse to blink, causing them to sting from their outstretched positions. Kade doesn't pay attention to my reaction, so I'm stuck switching between looking at him and Medisa.

If Kade marries Medisa, me and Maverick won't be able to marry any South Asian.

"She's only here right now for him to dangle in our faces until things are finalised."

"She can't do that." I almost choke on the words. "It's haram."

Kade finally turns all his attention towards me. "Oh, look at you expanding your vocab."

The child in me wants to express that I knew certain words before him, hell, the adult in me wants to do the same.

"I didn't expect you to allow this to happen."

Kade chuckles with no amusement. "You're acting like pawns have a choice dear brother." He rubs his forehead, then stands up. "And what was I supposed to do? You were missing and her only other option is basically death."

"She'll hate you."

Correction, Medisa would understand why, but she won't agree with us continuing to be under Maverick. She'll want us to find a way out of it, but Kade won't do it when it's *her* life at stake.

"Yeah well, at least she'll be alive."

Chapter 72
Kade
13/02/2022 (Sunday)

Nothing says 'home' like a note summoning you to dine in the Garden Hall. Despite our years apart, this is one of the properties I know like it's the back of my hand.

Soon as I enter the Hall, I see Kassian. We haven't spoken since our time visiting Medisa and from the looks of things, he too is confused as to why Maverick wants us to eat together now. We only ever ate at a table when our grandparents showed up, but I suppose this is one of the things we have to do to prove we are a part of the family.

The entrance doors from the house open up and I expect to see Maverick. So when I see Medisa, Medisa who was supposed to be in bed, but is now dressed in some sort of couture, with no shoes and is also wearing… a bedsheet?

Butterflies swarm my stomach.

"Fuck me." I mutter.

She's divine.

Worry trickles over me as she's already rebelling against Maverick by making adjustments to her outfit.

"Shit." Kassian whispers, obviously coming to the same realisation.

Medisa is too busy taking in the hall to notice me and Kassian both admiring and internally panicking for her. When her eyes lower to view us, she walks over like she's on a mission.

"Where were you?" Her finger is directed towards Kassian as though she were about to scold him. Her brows then tense up some more as she moves her aim towards me. "Where were *you*?"

Her feet stop her from coming any closer and I know from the slight tilt of her head that she's put something together.

Just as I open my mouth to say something, but not really knowing what, the doors on the other end of the hall open. He's coming, and I don't have enough time to properly explain things to Medisa in a way she would understand or listen to.

"Medisa, please don't do anything rash. I'll explain everything later, I promise."

The waiters make their entrance, lining themselves on either side of this horizontal hall. Neither me or Medisa take our seat, while Kassian does, already looking as though the evening has played out in his head.

Medisa's eyes are glued to the open doors, waiting for my brother to make his entrance. I am 100% sure she will give him some lip, or some sort of expression he will find to be distasteful. But my worries, my worries stem from the unpredictability of the both of them.

"Move away from her Kaden, she won't run away." A shirtless Maverick walks towards his seat as he throws a blood-stained towel over his shoulder. Already he's given two things that are supposed to be taken as warnings.

I want to stay standing with Medisa, but I won't have him punish her because of my decisions, so I take a seat opposite Kassian.

A cruel thought circles my mind and I can't help but agree; Maybe Medisa needs to experience Maverick for herself for her to understand how to behave?

'Behave' I hate the word.

Nothing is said for what feels like an eternity. Will Maverick not start whatever this is until she sits down?

Hiding a knife in my sleeve, I prepare to strike in case he decides to go berserk on her.

"It's blood." Maverick talks to her. "Do take a seat, I don't want your legs to give out from what I'm about to say."

I slow my breaths.

What is he going to reveal?

"Is it worse than sending me a hand?"

And there it is; Medisa's attitude.

As alert as I am in this situation, I do make time to visually share my reaction. Kassian mirrors my poor attempt at suppressing a smile.

"Ha. I see what you mean." Maverick looks to Kassian before putting his ravenous eyes on Medisa. "I like her. Such *candour*." He spares me a glance, no doubt seeing my smile disappear.

Is he being serious? Is this a test to see how much I actually like Medisa? To test how far he can take this before getting a reaction out of me?

"You're not a child—"

"I am." She says too quickly, cutting him off. "So imagine how embarrassing it is for you to be that old and still act like one."

'God help us.'

Kassian uses his finger to continuously tap the table, loud enough to get my attention and my attention only. When I look at him, he slightly shakes his head as though he could sense that I am about to do something.

"Olivia, approach the table."

Kassian and I tense our jaws. We know this lesson all too

well, and as morally as incorrect as it is, Medisa needs to go through it.

"Wait-wait! I'll sit. I'm gonna sit." Medisa quickly gets to a seat, already putting together what Maverick plans to do.

"Don't be scared, don't worry, nothing's going to happen to you, come here." Maverick speaks to Olivia with his most approachable, comforting voice.

Kassian and I hold our head up high. We've been fooled by that gentle 'trusting' voice before. It's the type of voice that would make you feel okay with spilling your deepest darkest secrets, worries, actions.

"Maverick don't do this." Medisa's voice isn't as loud or as urgent as it was before, it's more of a '*hey, look at me, I'm doing what you want.*' "I'm sitting down!"

"Close your eyes for me Olivia." Maverick continues to ignore Medisa.

I haven't allowed myself to see who Olivia is, but we can all hear her fear. I feel as though I could feel her shaking too but that's most likely me struggling to contain my own emotions.

Medisa jumps out her seat—leaving behind her bed-sheet—which unintentionally calls me to get up as well. I stand to stop her from approaching him but I do not put effort into actually holding her back. If I did, I would have been the one to force her into watching whatever Maverick has planned for Olivia.

"I get it, I get it, just let go off her please!" Medisa gets closer to Maverick and I just watch.

"Do you?" Maverick asks as though he were genuinely curious. Then, without much time for either girl to prepare, he slams his steak knife into Olivia, again and again with no compassion.

Medisa who is a few steps away, jolts to a stop, bringing both her hands up to her ears as Olivia's shrieks are made louder by the hall.

Maverick quickly grows tired of Olivia's wailing, so he pulls out the knife once more. I keep my eyes on Medisa, slowly approaching her, knowing that her reaction will be explosive.

Maverick, of course, continues to worsen the situation, making it harder for Medisa to back down, but thankfully, I now stand besides her, ready to hold her or Maverick back.

She tries to move closer as Maverick whispers to Olivia, but I grab a hold of her arm. The betrayal and shock on her face stings, but I'd rather feel it than witness what Maverick will do to her if she gets to him.

"Someone take her away and clean this up." Maverick boredly moves on from his actions.

"You fucking pig!" She tries to charge at him but I continue to hold her back. "I sat down! You saw me sit down! You didn't need to do that!" Medisa tries to reach him with every point made.

"Oh, but I did. I did. How else was I going to get you to *know* to obey me. It's evident sending you a hand wasn't enough to show you how serious I am, how *genuine* this all is."

Medisa is no longer trying to keep herself calm. She is outraged and if her words weren't enough to show it, her breathing is.

I unintentionally divert my gaze to Kassian, who now has his eyes open and looks as though he just wants to be served his food.

Chapter 73
Kassian
13/02/2022 (Sunday)

I did debate with myself on whether or not I should help Kade hold Medisa back, but I came to the conclusion that she should only hate one of us at a time and I'm okay with Kade taking the fall this time.

The fork in my hand has become warm, that's how long I've been holding it for. I look towards Kade, Medisa and Maverick to see if we've made any progress and if we're any closer to actually having dinner.

Kade is currently channelling a wall and Medisa is trying to get past him. And since she can't, she uses her words against Maverick.

"Obey you? This isn't even my fight. I don't even know why I'm here! As far as I'm concerned, you're just fucking bored and need to get a grip!"

Oh shit. This is just too good.

Honestly, she is providing the right entertainment, I just need a meal to go with it.

Kade now holds Medisa back by her arm. I don't think he's realised that Medisa is probably the safest person in the room other than Maverick himself. I want to tell him to stop interfering, but I guess he adds to the drama as well.

"Get *off* me!" Medisa tries to free herself from one brother to go off to the next.

Drama, drama, drama.

Kade whispers something to her, but I don't hear it.

"Trust you?"

Luckily Mavericks ears are working.

"Are you sure she should do that?"

"Leave her out of this."

"Sit down and let Medisa say what she wants."

Kade ignores his demand, continuing to stand tall with his grip on Medisa's arm.

Things are getting intense.

"No?" Maverick raises a brow which can only mean he will find a way to ruin the relationship between Medisa and Kade tonight. "Did I just stab a girl's hand for fun?"

Just as I'm about to go back to playing with my fork, I blink and Medisa has thrown a drink all over Maverick.

My eyes grow as I summon the strength to hold back a laugh. They grow even larger as Maverick towers over Medisa, holding a knife to her side and her in place by clawing at her nape.

I stand as if I would be able to get there in time.

"Ah-ah, be a good boy and go back to your seat, we all want Medisa to spend at least one good night here…don't we?" He spoke to Kade.

Releasing her neck, he goes on to moving her hair out the way and conversating about God knows what in her ear. In the meantime, I notice the knife Kade has hidden from Maverick's view.

What's his plan? Killing Maverick right now is not wise. We don't know what the sly bastard has planned for us should things take a dark turn for him.

How do I communicate with Kade without getting Maverick's attention? Throw a grape? Clear my throat? Walk over to him?

All of a sudden Medisa raises her voice and I realise that

Maverick is no longer holding onto her.

"Why do they follow you if they know that you have no loyalties towards them, that you'll—"

"It's cute that you think they have a choice in the matter." He drinks some wine then goes back to standing in front of her. "Have you boys not told your new friend what we do? What we *like* to do?"

"Speak for yourself." Medisa continues to demonstrate how she does not care for her life.

My lunatic of a brother (Maverick not Kade) looks close to batshit crazy. "What was that you called me earlier?"

Uh no.

"A pig?"

Well, the good news is, we can all finally eat.

Maverick drags Medisa to a chair next to his, then forces her to sit down.

Both me and Kade, both protective and nosey (me), grab onto a chair closer to Medisa.

"Boys, if I wanted us to be seated this close, I would've seated us at a fucking picnic table."

We don't move.

"Oh, okay." He doesn't let another second pass without him aggressively angling Medisa's head back, holding the knife he used on Olivia, to her throat.

The moment he pushed it in, giving her a cut, me and Kade moved a few seats a way.

Ignoring her miniscule cut, and his constant threats, I am certain Maverick won't do any life changing damages to Medisa, not physically anyway, which is why I think I'm handling this better than Kade.

Chapter 74
Kade
13/02/2022 (Sunday)

"I'm not eating that."

"And why not?"

"You *know* why."

"Ah yes. I do remember Kassian telling me about how strict you are with certain things."

I look to Kassian. His plate is full, like everything going on is currently second on his mind after his empty stomach. His eyes switch between staring at Medisa and me. We know that he told Maverick information about Medisa, it's just not nice being reminded of it.

"You touch that tray and I'll assume you no longer need your fingers." Maverick's voice booms.

Medisa slowly moves her hand away from the tray that holds roast potatoes. Like Kassian, she must be hungry too, she must be starving.

I would end this now, I would have ended this at the start, but this is all a test. If I go against Maverick for Medisa, he would go on to assume that I would continue to do so, and this is for a friend, so how far against him would I go for my wife, for someone he suspects I would grow to be devoted to? I need him to see that I won't intervene, won't stand against him, even if he is taking the piss. If I fail, he will take things out on her, tonight.

"Listen, Maverick. I get it. You want me to know that you get whatever you want, I get it. So can we please stop whatever this is and talk about what we were supposed to before I *disobeyed* you." Medisa attempts to get back onto his good side.

Maverick's chuckles morph into some sort of cackle that spread across the hall, then like the psychopath he is, he comes to an abrupt stop.

"Drink." After giving her a glass, which I'm surprised Medisa took, he raises his own. "Let's all drink to Medisa finally getting it."

Nope. Not happening.

What he did to Olivia in front of Medisa is different to him trying to take down her personal boundaries. I won't let him force them down.

"She's not drinking or eating any of that."

"We can't be disrespectful to the cook or the pig that died for this. It would be a waste. Wouldn't it, Medisa? And isn't being wasteful a sin?"

"Give it to me then, I'll eat it and give compliments to the cook. Hell, give some to Kassian too, that fat bastard has been eating on the low anyway." Sorry Kassian, but I need to try and get some, if not all of the attention, off Medisa. And I'm not as worried about you carrying your own.

Kassian's shoulders slump as I out him and a part of me wants to laugh.

Maverick looks down at Medisa who hasn't picked up her knife and fork. "Honestly Medisa, after all I've done for you. The least you could do is finish your plate."

No one asked him to get involved. Oh wait...

"All that you've done for me? What the hell have you done for me?" Medisa spits back.

"Dealing with a dead body is not easy you know? There's the clean-up, the disposal, the—"

Excuse me?

First my mind travels to the thought of Maverick getting to Medisa's family before me, but I stop because he wouldn't do that. Not yet anyway. It's too early for that kind of lesson.

"What body?" Medisa asks.

"The body of the man you murdered of course." Maverick speaks so casually, rubbing it in us all.

My head swivels towards Kassian. This bloody idiot happened to leave out this piece of information. And from the way Maverick is towards him, treating it like this is some sort of inside joke, I would say Kassian revelled in this fact previously.

My mind makes connections before I seek answers elsewhere. This event obviously happened at the pub. One of the bodies—I say 'one' and not 'two' because Maverick said 'body'— was there because of Medisa, and judging by her reaction, she had no clue.

'Does she have no clue because she blocked it out, or because she really did not know what she'd done?'

I look to Kassian, burning into him as though he could hear my thoughts. He should bloody hear them, maybe then he wouldn't be such an idiot.

'Don't you open your mouth. Don't you confirm.' I push my thought across the table. We'll deal with this later, when Maverick isn't here to gloat, though I assume this is enough for him.

For now.

Maverick sighs when no one talks, when no one moves.

"Let's make this fun for us all." He places a hand on her shoulder and I feel it's weight.

I won't let this slide.

"The longer Medisa refuses to eat, the more I'll fill her

in on what you boys have clearly missed out. If any of you would like me to stop, Medisa must drink the whole cup."

I look to Kassian as he looks to me. I have more secrets than him, but there's no way in hell I'm forcing that drink down her throat. And I don't think he's desperate to tell her about his relationship with Amana anymore, so this is just a matter of which one of us breaks or gets bored first.

Maverick starts to walk around the table, moving towards Kassian first. "Let's start with family."

We all—minus Maverick—simultaneously take a deep breath as we keep our eyes on him. He stops when he's behind the chair opposite Medisa.

"What tradition so deeply engraved in our history, in our bloodline, so sacred to our name, did Kaden break?"

I don't think I've told Medisa about this, but it's okay, it's not something that would heavily impact her.

'Until Maverick wants nieces and nephews and she wants to cut their hair.'

Despite it being an easy question, none of us answered. It must've really rubbed him the wrong way for it to have even be on his list of questions. I now wish I sent him a picture of me with a buzzcut.

"C'mon boys, this one's easy. In fact, there are at least two things."

Two things?

"He cut his hair." Kassian's voice gives away how bored and unamused he is by all this. "Abandoning our signature look, our tradition, our rule. Cutting one's hair shorter than their ear is a good way to outwardly show no longer being a part of the family, or in his case, going against the family." His voice was as monotone as someone reading a dictionary.

Maverick is somehow on our end of the table now.

"This one's good." He rubbed his chin. "What did Kaden do that Kassian got the blame for?"

That is not a question that has one answer. Is he going to bring something up from when we were kids? Is he talking about the man I killed in my container? Is he talking about signing on Amana?

"Okay, fine I'll help." He stops at a chair near Medisa. "Kaden can be…territorial. Not just over his space, but over people too."

Is he going to say I was jealous of Kassian's relationship with Amana, which is why I signed her on? Or is he going to say how I killed every single man from the construction site for thinking that they could get away with touching her?

"He craves some sort of release. He tries to bottle himself up because his saint side—it's small, but it's there—doesn't always agree, and when that happens and a trigger is also present, he blacks out to stop himself from feeling guilt. Though I'm not quite sure if that part's true…The blacking out? We all know you enjoy it. All but Medisa."

Confession; I don't always black out or feel guilt. I simply move on.

I keep my eyes on the plate in front of me as I find a bit of comfort in stroking the handle of the knife assigned to me. I can see where he stands now in my peripheral, I can also see how the knife would travel in the air until it finally pierces into the side of his neck.

"Medisa, would you like to see the state of the men at the construction site after Kaden had left them?"

I stop playing with the knife and look to Kassian, thinking he might be able to keep me grounded. Medisa seeing how Maverick is; fine. Medisa seeing how Kassian is; fine. Medisa knowing about what I can do… I might as well kill him where he stands to show her myself.

Before I can do anything, the workers gasp and when I see why, I stand up.

Medisa tried to stab Maverick, and she did, he just stopped it from entering any deeper. He now holds her up by her hair, angling her so she has no choice but to look him in the eye. She wobbles as he practically holds her up enough for her to be struggling on her tip-toes. And I hate it, so without much thought I throw my knife at the hand that held her in place. Maverick, being the super being he is, is able to hit my rotating knife away, using the knife he pulled from his own body *while* holding Medisa in place.

I didn't realise myself that I had been following the moving knife until I see the details of Medisa's hair.

"You take one more step and I'll kill her now." Maverick angled the knife up to Medisa's throat, already pinching her skin. He didn't even bother to look at me. Everything that he's done, including swatting away my knife, has been done using his peripheral vision.

His expression turns from wild to somewhat calm as he continues to stare Medisa down.

"Dismissed."

Every worker lined up against the walls begin to approach. Intentional or not, they manage to surround me while clearing away the table. And I'm not blind, so I do see how Maverick uses this opportunity to throw Medisa over his shoulder to take her away. And there's nothing I can do without him hurting her first.

That thing that Maverick said about triggers…he's right. I feel it now, and I could clear this room of every living being in five minutes, ten if I make it difficult by banning the use of weapons.

Chapter 75
Kassian
13/02/2022 (Sunday)

Kade is breathing like he's *trying* to get his shit under control. A first. But, still scary. From experience I know that I am safe in these types of situations, but it's been a few years, so one can't be too confident.

"Kade." I haven't done this in a while, and even when we used to be around each other, I rarely dealt with him. Not because I didn't want to, but because he tried to deal with it away from me. "Kade, he's not going to hurt her. We just witnessed her try to seriously damage him after constantly going against his words and he did not kill her for it."

His breaths slow down, not completely, but at least I know I'm getting somewhere.

"You told him that she will be your wife, right? So, if Maverick truly wanted us brothers together, he knows that he can't do shit to her. Not unless he wants you *and* me to take things further and kill him."

His breaths are close to normal now and before I am able to close the distance between us, he walks away like he's on a mission.

"Where you going?" I ask, but it doesn't really matter because I'm going to be following him anyway.

Chapter 76
Kade
14/02/2022 (Monday)

Charles Brown.

He's been loyal to our family since before we were born, since before Maverick was born, which makes him one of the only people Maverick trusts. If there's something that Maverick has planned, he would know.

We've been waiting for him to come back to his quarters for some time now and it's gotten pretty late. When me and Kassian were younger, we used to think he never rested, not when he was what made the house run.

"Alright Charlie?" Kassian says soon after Charles turns on the light, revealing us in his space.

I stay leaning against his wardrobe as Kassian stays seated on his chest of drawers.

I'm taken aback for a moment. Since when did Kassian become comfortable enough to address him like that? There was a time we both called him '*Mr. Brown.*'

"I had my suspicions that I would find you two here." Charles walks over to his little table, placing the picnic basket he brought on top. "There's enough in there for two. Eat whilst it's hot."

Kassian does not have to be told twice. He seats himself on one of the two chairs. I, however, keep my eyes on Mr. Brown. He's always looked old to us, but now I can really see it. His skins not exactly slipping off his bones, in fact, he looks quite healthy, he's obviously been keeping up with his routine, staying in shape. But there are parts of him now that give away a sense of vulnerability. It's saddening when I know back in the day, he was one who could beat someone senseless and not break a sweat about it. Seeing him as he is now makes me regret not visiting.

"Charles." I sense my eyes give away my new thoughts of him. "What has he got planned for us?"

"The only thing I know young Kade, is that the girl will become a River."

I ignore Kassian's gaze as he momentarily stops chewing.

'*Charlie's*' words settle it.

No harm (at least the usual harm we usually inflict) will come to Medisa, so I may as well sit and force this food down my already tight feeling body so that I have enough energy to deal with the day.

"Forgive the boundaries I cross Charles, but aren't you planning on living your own life?" I say after I take the empty seat across Kassian.

His old eyes let me know that he's in his own head somewhere, kind of like what Medisa does sometimes. "I've got one or two things to do here yet."

"Anything we can help with?" Kassian asks.

"No. Not you boys."

He takes a seat on a single couch on the side, his own reading corner, but I find it hard to believe that he has any time to.

"So, I've been thinking." Kassian speaks while chewing and stuffing his mouth. "Maverick's attention is on Medisa, making this the perfect time to snoop." He turns to give Charles a cheeky thumbs up.

We aren't afraid of discussing in front of him because in

the past, he tried his best to divert both our brother and some workers attention for as long as possible, while Kassian and I were doing something against Maverick's wishes, or, just simply having fun.

Charles rolls his eyes before turning a page.

"I can check if I've slept with anyone here—" Kassian continues.

"What?" First, he chugs his drinks, parties, smokes (which I will put an end to) and owns a bunch of clubs, and now, he's revealed that he's even slept with the workers. Am I supposed to continue regretting hiring Amana?

"Don't even." He holds his palm up while rolling his eyes and stuffing his gob with the roast potatoes Medisa wanted. "Anyway, I'll see if anyone's here and if they know anything. Who knows, Maverick might be a pillow talker?"

Chapter 77
Kassian
14/02/2022 (Monday)

"Anna." I extend her name. Thankfully she is in this house because I cannot find anyone else. "Darling, you wouldn't happen to know of any suspicious activities, would you?" I snake my arm around her.

"Kassian River." She dramatically escapes my arm. "You don't see a girl for months and the first thing you do when you come back is talk business?" Her fake offence is borderline dramatic.

I dig into my pocket.

The last time I was here, I had a gift for her, a gold bracelet with a ruby that reminded me of an apple. I bought this gift because one, she reminds me of snow white and two, she's never tried to use me. I couldn't give it to her when I had intended because Maverick sent her away for a few days and my life continued to be the mess it is.

Anna holds out her hand as I slowly drop it onto her palm. "A group of people were seen earlier. Three men and two ladies. They looked like they were rushing to get whatever they're here for, over with."

"Has anyone ever seen them before?"

"No, at least not the girls I'm around." She touches the apple on her bracelet, restraining her gasp. "There was someone who mentioned something about a marriage."

Oh shit.

In a rush, I kiss her cheek and then run off to confirm

things before going to the room Kade designated as our meeting point.

"We could get Nene involved." I suggest. "She would stop it and Maverick would listen to her. He always listens to her."

"Maverick would put on an act for her, then show us creative ways of ridding someone without it having any connections to him." Kade opposes, again. He's not even stressed, he wants this. He wants to go ahead with the marriage

He's as sick as Maverick.

"Then what do we do?" My frustration starts to make an appearance. "Do you not understand? This isn't like before! He's not casting her to the side like he's done before. He's rushing things." Probably still has plans to give her an early death. "You fucked up and you *know* it."

The door I thought was locked swings open, revealing Medisa. She doesn't seem or look beaten, so that gets rid of any worries.

"Alright, that's the second time I've heard him say something like that. Kade what did you do?"

The second time?

Kade moves to shut the door behind her, though if Medisa heard our whispers, it won't be long before Maverick does.

"Yes, do tell her brother, do tell us what your plan was."

He holds a flat hand out to me, visually telling me to stop before he does something he regrets.

Medisa is guided to the stool and all I could think is '*yes, we don't want her to fall and hit her head, again.*'

"I made a deal with Maverick."

I shake my head, still opposed to what they agreed to and Medisa notices.

"He wants us to be a family. But he sees you as an obstacle preventing him from achieving that. Now obviously I wasn't going to let him '*take care of you*,' and we don't want to be back, not unless he's dead or close to it. So…to get what everyone wanted, including your safety, we… *I*, suggested marriage."

We wait for Medisa to respond, to react even. The only thing that give us some sort of indication to how she is feeling are the number of times she blinks.

"Marriage?" She chuckles, or rather, breathes heavy through her nose with an awkward smile on her face. The poor girl looks to me for some sort of…support? But I can't even bring myself to tease her. "*Marriage*?" She says a little louder, a little more like she's finally processed it. "Who?"

We don't intervene as we can see exactly how things are going crazy behind her eyes as she puts it together herself.

"Kade. Who is getting married?" She stands up when he doesn't respond fast enough.

"A marriage between me and you of course."

All of our heads turn to Maverick at the door and I quickly realise how this situation has gone from bad to worse. I am actually close to calling Nene and telling her everything. Medisa can stay in Turkey with her, I don't care.

"That wasn't the deal." Kade becomes a shield for Medisa.

"No, but I like the way it would go. What's yours would become mine. You all would be taught a lesson and, in a couple of years, when we have kids running around, I'll get to teach them some lessons too."

Ignoring Kade in between, Maverick approaches Medisa.

"She leaves *now* and we'll stay here. We won't leave again." Kade attempts to better things with his words instead of scratching an itch we all feel.

Maverick acts as if he is considering it. "I'm afraid I can't let her do that." His eyes move off Kade. "C'mon Medisa, has it not come back to you yet?"

Sitting up straight, I try not to react too harshly to avoid scaring Medisa. "It's too late."

Anna said the group were rushing, but when I tried to find them inside, I couldn't. The CCTV showed them leaving within the hour they arrived.

"He's already done it." Medisa's words temporarily immobilise her.

"What?" Kade looks to Maverick for some sort of explanation.

"12 am. You missed it. They all thought it was true love once I told them about her terminal illness and how we wanted to marry before she passed."

'*Terminal illness?*' He has no shame in telling us, Medisa included, that he's already covered her reason of death.

"The process was too quick for me to have even bothered with the invitations. But don't worry, you've already met my wife."

Kade punches Maverick with a lethal looking swing, calling me from my seat to hold him back.

"One's enough!" It's not. "Think about this!" I play the part of someone trying to stop this from progressing, but I don't put effort in keeping Kade away. He better get a few more hits on this prick.

To escape my already loosening grip—obviously Kade did not realise—he elbows my face, freeing himself and getting his shots in on Maverick. Anyone could see Maverick has no intention of fighting back. I'm even sure he will allow Kade to kill him as long as he does so in front of Medisa.

When I realise his sick plan of slowly turning Medisa away from Kade, I do everything in my power to hold Kade back. Even if it means hitting him myself.

After struggling to hold Kade away, I get a good grip on him, allowing Maverick to move away. My focus is on Kade, so when Medisa suddenly runs out the room and Maverick playfully goes after her, I freeze.

Chapter 78
Kade
14/02/2022 (Monday)

"Don't you fucking touch her!" I shout from the top of my lungs as I bash into the locked door.

My energy may be wasted on trying to open this apparently unbreakable door, but it's better for me to focus on trying to get it open than turning around and taking my anger out on Kassian. If he hadn't held me back, we would not be stuck in this room.

There are two reasons as to why Maverick has locked us in here. One: to stop us from going after Medisa and Two: for him to return to some sort of bloodbath.

Barging into the door is useless, I got that after trying and failing two times, then noticing how it is built to specifically be pushed in from the hallway. So now, instead of using my body, I plan to use the ugly metal lamp as a hammer on the door handle.

"Why would you suggest marriage, out of all things… marriage?" Kassian the useless being finally talks after staying in place, against the windowsill.

I stop hitting the handle.

"Marriage is the only thing that interested him enough to consider. And if she were married to me, she would have access to my money, my properties, anything that is mine would be hers and she would be protected—"

"Protected? Marrying you would put an even bigger sign on her back, practically begging Maverick to kill her and that's ignoring all the other people you've managed to piss off. And what about what she wants? Her—"

"It was supposed to be a contract marriage. To have Medisa on the side, ready like some sort of incubator that's only used when I'm bored and in the mood of carrying on the bloodline. *That's* how I sold it to him. And even that was just to get him to like the idea enough for him to agree. Then we could get close to him like he wants—"

"And we could kill him. Yes, you've said that." Kassian pushes himself off the windowsill, holding his hand out for the metal lamp.

"And she would've had the option to get a divorce after." It's a weak plan made with naivety, but it was the best option in the moment of slight panic, and a risk that had to be taken.

"Let's go find our sister-in-law before she gets pregnant." Kassian raises the lamp to bring it down on the door handle, but before he could, I punch his arm.

"I'm joking." He rubs where I made contact. "It's a joke… there's no way they'd be done this quick."

I'm about to hit him again, this time harder, but the door handle starts to turn.

The door is pushed open, revealing Mr Charles Brown who stops me from immediately leaving the room.

"If you want to help your friend, might I suggest you do some things behind the scene, like swapping out the meat to some halal options. Perhaps even acquiring items that bring her comfort?"

I think it over and he's right. Arguing with Maverick will not help anyone. He's already married her and he won't rape her, we know this. Despite his business venture, he will not personally cross that line. He even made sure that we did not abuse our power and cross it—not that we ever would.

Once Charles witnessed me physically calm down and think things over, he swiftly leaves as though he were being summoned elsewhere.

"I'm going to see if this marriage is even legit, or if it's just one of his tricks." Kassian actually has a bright idea which leaves me thinking, why am I not functioning properly? Why did I not think that it could be a trick? Why did I not think to swap the meat out or bring her something familiar?

Chapter 79
Kassian
14/02/2022 (Monday)

"What you doing?" Anna comes out of nowhere with a banana in hand.

"I'm lock picking, obviously. Can you keep watch?"

"Sure." She leans against the wall with her banana, clearly lacking experience in making use of her eyes, that, or she does not think the consequence of me trying to get into Maverick's office is serious.

The door unlocks and Anna follows me inside. I go straight to his desk despite the chances of me finding anything being low.

"Care to fill me in?" Anna is now near the end of her banana.

"There's a girl here. Medisa."

"Oh yes. I've yet to meet her."

I roll my eyes. "I need to see what he has on her, most importantly I need to see if I can find a marriage contract or anything—"

"Marriage contract? *He* married *her*?"

"Yes." I try not to roll my eyes again as I lock pick the lowest compartment drawer. When it opens, I make Anna search its contents while I go through all the potential hiding spots.

"Oh my God." She says, calling me to her side.

She hands me files she's already read and continues to go through other documents before me. The documents she passes over after skimming them raise a low level of concern.

How did Maverick get his hands on Medisa's birth certificate and passport?

"Oh shit." Anna says as she reaches the end of the file in her hand. I'm about to take it off her to read for myself but the door opens in an aggressive manner.

"Put everything back and get out." Charles speaks with a voice I haven't heard him use in a long time.

We do as we've been told, then Charles gives me a talking to by the door as Anna waits outside. "Young man, you are lucky it was me who was told about what you were doing."

He's right.

Charles sighs. "Do not have any more bright ideas. Maverick has already planned for people to deal with Medisa should anything happen to him."

Aw, how romantic, he wants them to be buried at the same time.

I thank Charles for giving me this insight. He's never really gone against Maverick and that includes telling us about what our brother has planned. He usually finds a way for us to prepare without giving anything away. It's all riddles with him, but I guess something is different now? Perhaps he doesn't agree with Medisa's involvement?

Anna rubs her hands as she approaches after Charles leaves. "You are going to love and hate what I saw."

She sounds sure.

"Tell me."

Chapter 80
Kade
15/02/2022 (Tuesday)

"Medisa?" Kassian randomly says as he looks out, grabbing my attention.

My breath hitches. I know that Kassian said her name like that because he did not expect to look out and see her, but my mind has a funny way of working these days because I automatically assumed Maverick had done something to change her appearance. Not that it would change the way I see her.

I watch as Kassian, without hesitation or delay, throws whatever was in his pocket in the direction of Medisa because apparently using his voice is not enough.

"I was trying to find you guys, but I gave up. I'll come up to you now." Medisa says shortly after being attacked by whatever junk lived inside my brothers pocket.

Her voice gives away her distance. I'd say she were just below us, not on the ground floor like I'd originally thought.

"No-no." Kassian waves his hand out towards her. "Don't worry, we'll come to you. Stay right there."

'*We'll.*' The idiot gave away that I'm with him. Medisa doesn't need more fuel to think that we purposefully leave her out, or with Maverick.

"You go ahead." I say, but only to use him as a test subject. Medisa may not be the same with me after the way I treated her at dinner and at the announcement of her being a wife, both failures in different ways.

"She's in the fitting room." Kassian runs ahead, but does not go in the direction I planned to go.

He must know a shortcut, some sort of hidden passageway. Either way, I know that I do not have to slow my steps for him to get there first.

Turning into the hallway that would lead me to her chosen room, I watch as Kassian is dragged in. She must be desperate for someone familiar on this large estate. Perhaps I should've gotten to her first?

Being outside the door, I hear them more clearly.

"I don't even remember that name being on the list of people on your course." Kassian sounds a little panicked, but I don't think Medisa will pick up on it since its masked with a '*I'm not dumb*' tone.

"She's not on my course. And if you didn't tell him, how does he know?"

I enter the room to save Kassian.

"How does he know what?" Almost immediately I notice how Kassian is against the wall by the door and how Medisa is barely two steps away from him…

"He said '*wifey*.' It's something me and Amana would say to each other sometimes. It can't be a coincidence. He knows and you guys need to get her to safety…please."

Maverick's subtly planting in Medisa's mind that he knows about Amana and has the power to do something, but is choosing not to act, yet. I look to Kassian to see how he's holding up before I even begin to let my mind humour the thought of Maverick holding back how I was the one who signed her on.

Kassian can't give away that he too is affected by this, but that doesn't mean I want him to be completely numb by it.

"*Hello*? Did you guys hear what I said? We need to get Amana away." Medisa continues to only react and care when others are involved.

I hope she has some of that empathy to spare. I'm relying on it.

"Leave this whole Amana thing to us. We don't know if he's made a strong link between the two of you yet. He could be testing the waters, testing how close you actually are before he makes a move. If we go after her and he finds out, he'll make it his life's mission to get her. So, we'll keep an eye on things from a distance." Kassian gives her a completely rational explanation. "Also, I told him that you have a habit of caring too much about strangers, like they're your friend or something. So do with that what you will." His nonchalant approach seems to be working and I'm honestly proud of how quick he is with his words.

"We have things that we know to be true to discuss, and you need to eat as much as you can because I don't know how long it'll be until you can have halal meat again." I've already arranged for the next delivery to be suited to her diet, so what I am saying is a lie. The option to burn all the meat we have to get the next delivery faster was discussed and so was the option to give it all away. In the end, I decided to do Medisa's food runs until the next drop-off, damn the consequences.

There are three chaise longue in this room, all giving attention towards the fireplace. Kassian sat on the one with its back to the door, Medisa (finally) sits on the one that faces the fireplace, and I claim the one that faces the door, the fireplace and Medisa.

"Are you allowed to come and go as you please?" She asks before taking a bite.

I shake my head. "We don't have that privilege anymore."

"He snuck out to get you some food." Kassian cuts in.

His words vex me.

I did not do this to rub it in her face, nor did I do it to be praised and thanked. Before I act on my initial thoughts, I try to see it from a different angle. An angle where Kassian is just trying to let Medisa know that she is constantly on my mind, even when she is not with me.

"I knew it'd been a long time since you last ate some proper food, and I wasn't going to sit around and watch you slowly wither away." I explain myself.

Medisa's eyes enlarge ever so slightly for a quick second. I assume it's because of my choice of words and I am not going to allow myself to see another angle with this one. Not when a possible angle is Maverick spoon feeding her, or holding up a cluster of grapes, giving her no choice but to angle her head up for him.

Suddenly, I've ruined my own mood.

"When are we leaving?" Her eyes jump from me to Kassian before staying on me. She doesn't ask with a *'I'm bored, I want to go home,'* tone or expression. She is composed, which makes me think she has an answer in her head and wants to compare/confirm with ours. "You do have a plan, right? To leave?"

I'm right, and if she is as good as I know she is, she's seen that we do not have a plan she would like.

I sit on her sofa, a seat away from her.

"Medisa, Love." We'll ease her into it. "That's what we need to talk about."

If she needs someone to hold onto, I'm here.

I give Kassian a gentle, single nod. She would want to hear it from him, since he was the one to find this all out.

"While he was away trying to find you some meat, I'd

done some research." He pauses for God knows what reason. His eyes flicker in my direction then go back to looking into Medisa's. "We think you have less than three months to live."

'For fucks sake. Why did I think we were on the same wavelength with how we go about this?'

"What he was meant to start with—" My tone lets Kassian know that I will punch him when she is not looking, then I soften my words. "—was that the marriage is legit. You *are* married to Maverick—" though I don't let myself think about it past a superficial level. "But after three months as the 'Heads' partner you will have a say and piece in everything. Making you a threat to everything that he, and everyone before him has done to give us our reputation and fortune. So, we think after three months he'll either file for a divorce—"

"Or kill you—or have you killed." Kassian cuts in.

'First of all that's the same thing you twat. Second of all, I was going to take it in a completely different direction.'

Medisa has no reaction. She doesn't even feed herself. Her eyes aren't on Kassian, nor are they on me.

"That's why he said that I'm terminally ill, to make my death less suspicious." She looks to us to confirm what we already knew.

"I won't let him do that, I swear it, you won't get hurt, you won't be murdered." I stay calm as I resist the urge to get down in front of her, to hold her hands in between mine.

Loud rustles interrupt mine and Medisa's eye contact. When we look to see where it's coming from, we see Kassian picking up one of the crisp packets I got her. "Should I tell her the next part, or are you?"

'Oh, I'm sorry. Is this too boring for you? Wanker.'

Medisa slowly moves her head back to face me. I can see that she wants to know more and is hoping for some good news.

"We're going to stay here for eleven weeks." I say weeks instead of months because weeks do not sound as long as months, even if the number is three when rounded up. "Up until then, we're going to do as Maverick says, but when there's an opening, we're going to make a run for it and keep you hidden until you have access to everything. Then if you want, you can free a lot of people, including yourself." Personally I couldn't give a shit about what Medisa does with what will be hers. I just know that bringing up her new ability to help others would give her the push she needs to get through this.

Medisa goes off somewhere in her head, but I don't push for her to come out before she's ready.

"Three more months."

"Three more months." I repeat after her. "I'll be with you through it all. I promise."

"Me too." Kassian joins in. "You won't be alone." He throws her empty crisp packet in the middle of our sofas as he puts his feet up.

You know what? Now is the perfect time to ruin Kassian's comfortability whilst also making things up to Medisa.

"After all this, I want a raise." Medisa stretches as I smile.

My mind's occupied with how I should get Kassian to do what I want without her knowing.

"After all this, you won't need a raise." She'll be richer than me.

I walk over to the door then call Kassian over. He gets up and approaches immediately, probably thinking I've spotted something or need help barricading the door.

"You reckon he's back?" I whisper.

Kassian's cheeks enlarge before he blows his gathered

breath out. "He's definitely on his way back."

"<u>Great. Then we have time. Pick an instrument and meet us in Tier Hall.</u>"

Kassian's shoulders drop. "<u>Seriously?</u>"

I don't use my words anymore, I just glare.

He leaves without prolonging his disapproval, so I turn to retrieve Medisa, who looks more interested in the minute conversation me and Kassian just had than anything we just informed her of.

"Follow me."

Adjusting the lights so that they are dimly lit instead of announcing our location to the world, I watch as Medisa takes in the beauty of the Hall as I become distracted by hers. Medisa embodies the word enchanting and all its meanings. To think she hasn't even begun to tap into the things she could get me to do, to feel. It's exhilarating. I might even salivate at the thought of it all.

Kassian quietly rushes in, shutting the door behind him. Medisa is about to question the meaning of all this, but pauses when she notices me waiting for her.

"You wanted to experience a ball. A *masquerade* ball. So I thought giving you a taste would help you look forward to the one I will throw you one day." I remember her list of things off by heart. I remember how she poorly crossed out 'maqurade' and 'masquerade' (the correct spelling) and settled with 'Masked ball.'

Kassian begins to make use of his violin.

I bow, holding my hand out.

The sin in me does not present her with her options,

wanting her to reach out and allow me to briefly indulge in what, up until this moment I could not bring myself to steal.

Medisa's hands hesitate towards mine and that's when I snap out of it. Something as 'simple' as this is a big thing for her and has turned out to be a big thing for me. I won't allow myself to be selfish with this.

"It's okay." I say, not wanting to ruin her mood. "Just hover."

And she does.

And I know I'm imagining it, but I can feel the layers that make up my hand buzz just from the presence of hers. If I give it enough attention, I would probably be able to see how the cells in my hand distort themselves in attempts to get a little closer.

Chapter 81
Kassian
15/02/2022 (Tuesday)

I play something Nene said dad composed for mum. Something she said our parents actually danced to. At first, it was for the comfort I know that it brings, but now I play it to the best of my ability for my brother Kade, and my friend Medisa.

Tier Hall helps make it sound like I'm not the only one playing, it also gave them enough space to move around. Medisa is filled with joy, giggling away and trying her best to be a good partner. And Kade, he looks at her like she's his life mission. I've never even seen him look at one of his own pieces like this. His eyes are filled with desire, his view obviously being his dream and I've heard him laugh before, but this is different. There's something about his laugh and smile now that radiates warmth. I also notice how careful he is to not touch her, even when she accidently comes too close, he doesn't use it as an opportunity to brush his hand against hers.

I'll help him with that in a bit.

Admittedly, I've been hopeful with how things may play out with Amana. I don't think I'm as delusional as before, but I would certainly fight for Amana, even if the odds were not in my favour. If she is open to it, I will fight for her, I will do everything I can. Which is why I was *upset*—to say the least— over Kade's proposal.

But now... I don't think I can pursue her, not after I've seen the way Kade looks at Medisa, and how he is willing to put himself in distress to make sure that she is comfortable. We've swapped places, him and I. He's confused, blurring the lines between what a friend and partner are, while I'm starting to see clearly.

By the time the song comes to an end, I made up my mind. I will apologise and make up for my faults with Amana, but for the sake of my brother, I will not court her. I won't even think of it.

Before they distance themselves, I quickly trip Medisa which then of course alerts Kade. The plan was for him to catch her, which is what happened, but now I think it's better if I just push them both to the ground.

Medisa lands on top of Kade, and Kade the opportunistic bastard has his hands over not just her head, but her waist.

You're welcome.

Chapter 82
Kade
15/02/2022 (Tuesday)

I held Medisa against me.
Medisa was against my chest.
Medisa.

I can't even be mad at Kassian right now because I'm too distracted by the fact that Medisa was on me. I hope she didn't hear or feel how fast my heart was, and still is.

"You guys just *summon* tears to my eyes." Kassian says in the background, but I'm too busy trying to slowly get air into me after realising I've been denying myself of that right.

"Kade, do you know how to play?" The moment Medisa looks down to me for an answer, I realise that I am still on the floor with my hand over my heart.

I sit up, putting most of my weight onto my hands as I lean back. My cheeks continue to rat me out, but slowly return to their normal colour…I hope.

"Yeah of course he does." Kassian answers for me, though I am surprised at his response as I rarely approached a musical instrument. "Whilst I played for them—"

'Who is he talking about?'

"—He was in another room using his fingers and instrument on an interactive audience."

'Oh.'

My head rotates in Kassian's direction.

Sinister thoughts pair with justification as Kassian's 'favour' (pushing us to the ground) does not mean he should get away with exposing teenage antics.

"I'm kidding. I'm kidding." He holds his hands up. "Kade practices art-art, not the musical form of it. He spent a lot of hours in his studio."

Medisa turns her attention towards me. "Is your work still here?"

I slowly nod. I don't see why Maverick would have my studio cleared out.

"Can you show me your studio one day?"

The thought of Medisa in there surprisingly does not agitate me. In fact, I want her to give her opinions and drown me in compliments (highly doubt it, she's already said in the past that she doesn't want my head to get too big). I would also like to draw her *with* her knowledge.

"Of course." I try my best not to smile so hard.

Chapter 83
Kassian
15/02/2022 (Tuesday)

Once we got back to the room, comfortable on our own sofa's, I thought '*yeah, that's a wrap,*' but no, it is not, because Medisa and her mind are still awake.

"What do you think happened to Maverick? For him to be the way he is? It's a thought that's been growing for a while now, I just haven't been able to give it any attention because of how fast things have been going. But now we have three months and he's been playing this weird grey character and I'd have to remind myself of what he's done."

She's falling for his traps already.

"Don't try to find reasons to justify his actions, Medisa." Kade gives her a polite warning.

"I'm not. I'm not trying to redeem him, I swear."

She's definitely trying to save him, or is thinking to. A waste of time really, but how can she know that?

"Medisa." I call out to her. "There are going to be times where you think Maverick is good... *Don't* trust that side of him." Not only is Maverick a good actor and a skilled manipulator, but he's also smart as hell *without* having knowledge on someone. But the thing is, I've told him almost everything there is to know about her, so if she falls for his bullshit, it's my fault. "I made the mistake of telling him that you have a certain soft spot or weakness towards good but broken people."

Kade mutely reacts to my words. I don't know if it's because he falls under that category, or if it's because he doesn't like to be reminded of my part in all this. Maybe it's both?

I may be able to make this easier for her. There's a way for Medisa to not find out for herself how shitty Maverick can be.

"What happened to Olivia may not have had a big impact on you because you didn't know her. You didn't spend time with her. But you've spent time with me. So hopefully what I'm about to tell you will help you remember what he's like whenever he puts on an act."

I almost don't want to do this. But out of all the things Maverick has done to me personally, this is the one that would get Medisa's head straight, especially since we have them on show. They can be a constant reminder to her.

"Kassian, you don't have to tell me anything, especially if this is to make up for telling Maverick things about me." She sits up.

"No. No, I want to tell you." I sit up as Medisa bobs her head, ready to listen to what I have to say. "Maverick taught us a lot, he did. We know several languages, how to defend ourselves, how to cook and clean, how to handle our businesses, people, many things, the list can go on." And almost all of them were taught using unorthodox methods. "Something else he did for us, is give unique goals or wishes. For example, for a time, mine was wanting clear skin, or skin that didn't itch or hurt when it was touched. Do you know why Maverick was responsible for that wish?"

Medisa's eyes lower onto my arms then quickly come back up to my eyes.

"Because he used my body as his canvas." Thankfully, I'm no longer bothered by it. I've come to love my scars. I just hate that a younger me had to go through it. "Not with the usual tools of course. With needles, blades, knifes, anything that would make a mark." Sometimes even heat. "He scratched away at my skin creating these beautiful patterns, again and again. Redoing them if they disappeared. At first it was my hands and arms, but then it moved to my neck, back and abdomen." Though this all happened, I don't recall it as something I physically remember going through. It almost feels as though I'm talking about a character I watched on tv. I guess that's how far I dissociated. "He made Kade watch. As punishment. None of us were allowed to move whilst he did it and Kade wasn't allowed to close his eyes. If he did, Maverick would cut or scratch a little deeper, or come up with something else to torture him with." Honestly, I can't remember why I was punished like this, or if it were even a lesson. The only thing I 'learnt' was the fear of sharp objects. "Eventually, with the number of times he etched onto me. My skin started to remember. To scar and lift a little from where he had touched. It started off pink, or deep red, then it turned to lighter shades, or white."

Medisa's eyes slightly enlarge as she slowly faces Kade. Kade who looks as if he's been transported back in time and is being forced to watch again. I recognise that face of helplessness with a smidge of anger anywhere.

Anyway, now to make things light-hearted whilst also doing Kade a solid. "I had a fear of needles, knifes and such, until eventually Kade got me off my ass and taught me how to handle one. To literally fight it away. And then there was a day he came to me, acting hurt and like he needed help undressing." I chuckle as I recall because why did I not question that, or the fact that he came straight to his studio and not to our doctor? "I should've seen it coming, he'd been covering for months. Anyway, when I helped remove this idiot's jacket and top, I saw he had gotten each and every scar I had, tattooed onto himself. Somehow, he had it memorised down to the smallest one." My lids glide a little easier over my eyes. I can't believe this idiot somehow managed to convince Maverick to brand him instead of me. I also can't believe how quick I was to forget it. "Soon after that and a speech or two from Kade," And Amana. "I wanted to own them, so, I got them tattooed. I darkened the colours, turned them all black so they're more visible and in doing so, I got rid of what was left of my fear whilst also rubbing it in that pigs face."

Medisa's eyes are filled with admiration I did not deserve. And I hate to make myself the victim of poor choices, but I really have screwed us all over, haven't I?

"Anyway, the point of stepping onto this little memory lane is to prove to you that Maverick does not care. If he could do that and so much worse to his kid brothers, he could and would do anything to you without losing sleep. So don't be fooled by any act of kindness, be wary of it."

"Be *offended* by it." Kade finally talks. "Because it just means he's trying to screw you over."

The room gets quiet. Medisa looks down at her hands while she bites at her lip to peel its skin off, and Kade is somewhere, distracted by his thoughts or memories.

Bloody hell, I feel awkward.

"Well shit. I thought I would at least get *some* tears." I laugh to hide my sudden embarrassment.

Medisa gives me a chuckle which summons Kade's polite smile.

"I just wanna hug and squeeze you." Medisa tenses her hands out in front of her. "Maverick is an idiot for treating you guys the way that he did. He's missing out on two of the most beautiful, amazing, somewhat funny—"

I am hilarious but she makes a point with Kade.

"—People that I'm so happy that I've met and become friends with. I genuinely trust you guys with my life."

This is getting too much for me, so I pretend to cry and hold out my arms like a child. Medisa copies me and for a few seconds we look like a couple of idiots who are too lazy to get up and hug each other.

"Ugh, can we get some rest now." Kade, the sudden diva speaks while me and Medisa continue to flap our arms in the air. He's obviously jealous but his words work because now we've both thrown in the towel and are getting comfortable.

"Kade?" Medisa calls out to him a few seconds after I close my eyes.

He hums '*yeah*?' in response. His eyes are closed, I don't know what for, I don't remember sleep coming to him easy.

"Thank you for going out of your way to get me food." She adjusts herself. "Kassian?"

"What?" I snap, but it's a joke.

"Tell me a bedtime story."

I can't tell if she actually wants one or is taking the piss. "I don't feel *that* bad for you."

Hearing her quietly snicker brings out a smile.

After nothing being said—I wait a few long seconds—I assume that everyone is now focussed on trying to get some rest.

"Medisa?" Kade calls out.

For flips sake.

She mimics his hum response.

"Shabba Khair."

I scrunch my brows and go over every language we know. Is there a language under my belt that I'm not actually fluent in? I've never heard him or anyone else say that before.

I try to close my eyes and leave it alone but fail.
"What the *fuck* does that mean?"

Chapter 84
Kade
16/02/2022 (Wednesday)

Light taps by some sort of cold, dense metal material are made on my head. I don't open my eyes straight away, but only because it takes a second for me to realise that I had fallen asleep. I open my eyes to see Maverick wearing an eerie smile as he holds a finger to his mouth, signalling for me to keep quiet as his gun now points to Medisa's head.

Soon as Kassian spots Medisa at the end of Maverick's gun, he stops struggling against someone three times his size.

The room becomes somewhat quiet, any noise made isn't enough to wake Medisa. Maverick gives a single nod to the man holding Kassian, directing him towards the door. He does the same to me and I do as I'm told, remembering that we have to be on his good side to make Medisa's experience here be somewhat enjoyable.

I look over my shoulder to see if she's waking up from somehow sensing us leaving.

She does not.

Maverick is the last to leave the room.

"I don't appreciate you sleeping in the same room as my wife." He says like he didn't just take Kassian out of the room with me. Taking a deep breath as though the matter truly bothered him, he speaks again. "It's okay. You can make it up to me."

I don't ask how. I already know.

Maverick turns to the man besides Kassian. "Take him

to my office."

Kassian moves his arm away before the man is able to hold him. "I know where that is."

"Shh. Did you forget that Medisa is still sleeping?" Says the brother who barely let us sleep at one point in our lives.

Another man approaches and I have the strongest feeling he is here for me.

I turn to Maverick.

"The Arena?"

He sneers. "Don't disappoint."

Chapter 85
Kassian
16/02/2022 (Wednesday)

I am moved from Maverick's office and led to the part of the house where the workers are given accommodation and their own version of the dining hall. It's about the size of Kade's kitchen, maybe a little bigger but I suppose they aren't expected to eat at the same time.

The man who was supervising me has been gone for about five minutes now. I could leave, but that would just be prolonging whatever Maverick wants to talk about, and since my sleep has already been ruined, I might as well stay to hear him out.

Speaking of the man who comes second to the devil, he walks in. "Do you remember the lesson I taught the two of you when you were kids?"

I suppress a laugh. I don't exactly have a catalogue on the topic.

"The one where I showed you what happens to workers who try to use us? You know, the ones who try to take initiative instead of sticking to what they are meant to be doing?"

I remember.

Not very clearly, but I recall parts of what happened. There was a woman who tried to take advantage of us. She was clever and perverted. And made a strong attempt to build a bond over time. However, Maverick took notice and dealt with it, but he also wanted us to learn our lesson, so one of us had to take her life. Kade was the one who did it—I think that was the first person he killed—and straight after the matter, Maverick told us if we didn't want to experience that again, we needed to stop feeling sorry for the workers. To get used to their jobs and to not let them take advantage of our emotions or positions. They're not our friends, they're not our lovers and they will do anything to get some sort of advantage. And if we were to go out of our way to give them some sort of ease, it would end badly for all parties involved.

"I thought you learnt it, but I guess not." He examines a banana before peeling it.

The giant who left me here comes back into the room, pushing Anna towards me.

"Anna, tell Kassian what you're allergic to." Maverick takes a bite of the banana.

She looks to me but cannot keep her eyes in one place. Her hair is damp looking, her skin is pale and dewy from sweat and she can barely stand straight.

"Peanuts." She barely manages out as I hold onto her.

Maverick takes a seat on a stool and pulls out an EpiPen. "Did you know, she's had a severe allergic reaction to peanuts before? It's on her medical history."

He takes another bite.

I'm stuck between holding her up and rushing over to grab the pen from his hand.

"Maverick, she needs that now."

Anna brings a hand to her throat, looking worse as the seconds go by.

"Did you or did you not go through my office with this woman?" Maverick plays with the tube, rotating it again and again.

"I did." There's no point in lying. "But it's not her fault you prick!"

Anna lowers herself to the floor, her breaths now hoarse, slow. Clawing at her throat, her eyes double in size, filled with panic and fear.

"So you *made* her help you?" Maverick's voice is so unbothered, borderline entertained, that you would not place him to be in the same room as me.

"*Yes*! Yes!" I hold out my hand for the pen, then look down to Anna. "It's okay, it's okay." I resist the urge to rock her as I pull her hands away from her bleeding neck.

"Hmm. I'll let you save one just this once." He gets up to leave, bins his banana peel, then throws two pens before the door is shut on us.

Immediately ripping into the packaging, I stab her thigh and hold it in place. "Come on, come on."

She's not reacting and it's been ten seconds. What do I do? *What do I do?* I look around for the second pen and as I'm about to use it on her, I try to think if this is going to have some sort of opposite effect. Should I wait five minutes or should I pump her with adrenaline and deal with the consequences once she's awake and can be flown to a hospital?

Fuck.

I collect her in my arms, clear her air passageway and hold her upright. Come *on*. Did I not do it right?

The door swings open, Charles comes in with two of our doctors who lift and carry her away.

"Charles! Charles, she's not breathing! I don't think I did it right!" My voice shakes with urgency. I try to go after her but I'm held back.

"Kassian, what are you talking about? You did it. She's going to be taken in and looked after." Charles holds me in place.

"I don't understand. I—she—"

"She's fine."

Chapter 86
Kade
16/02/2022 (Wednesday)

I sit away from the stage, as far back as possible. There are a mixture of people in here, some did not have one fighting bone in their body and look as though they had been dragged here straight from their office, others look as though today is just another Thursday.

Thick clothes or even layers that could serve as some sort of protection aren't allowed in these fights. But there are some people who take it too far and refuse to wear something other than shorts.

Big-headed idiots.

I turn to the direction of said desperation and lo and behold, there are people here that would like to make an example out of me. I wouldn't be surprised if they momentarily team up just to kill me. I kind of hope they do.

Maverick's staff begin to hand weapons out. Two metal poles, two wooden bats and two knives. Six weapons across what, twenty-five of us? The numbers bother me, he should have made it five weapons.

Once the body from the first fight is removed, we are all shoved onto the stage where things begin straight away. And like I thought, people do temporarily ignore the threats they are to each other to come for me. Usually, I ignore those who are at severe disadvantages and let other people deal with them, or I let them have a weapon. But these guys have come to me in a group and I would say that's close to levelling out the playing field.

I hold my fists up and go for the weakest link. Acting as though I'm about to go one way, I swerve and duck last minute, uppercutting his jaw, sending him to the ground.

While I deal with another, my back is attacked by someone with a metal pole. Frustrated, I pick up my second victim and throw him onto the person with the pole, instantly taking him to the ground. Snatching the pole off him, I struggle to keep myself and the way I deal with them sane. So, instead of repeatedly shoving one end of this pole into his face again and again and again, until I can't make out any features. I decide to connect his head with the smoother part to knock him out.

Same treatment for the man I threw on top of him.

Sensing someone behind me, I swing the pole as I turn, bashing their knuckles, knocking the knife from their grip.

He was going to kill me.

I mean all of them are trying to kill me, but *he* tried to kill me, took the steps towards me and everything. Now, if I handle this the way that I should, I'm going to be the villain, but if I don't, Maverick is going to come up with another shitty thing for me to do.

I pick up the knife. It doesn't take much more convincing for me to grab this person's throat, figure out that my arms are a lot longer and stronger than his, then stab him multiple times below his lungs. This way, there is a chance of survival.

'If the help comes quick enough.'

Someone whacks the back of my head and honestly, if it's with the metal pole I dropped, I kind of deserve it for leaving that weapon lying around.

As I'm on my knees, acting out the level of pain I *should* be feeling, but don't, the two people left feel comfortable enough to close in on me. And this is when I decide to make use of the knife. Slicing ones Achilles tendon, then stabbing into the others thigh and throat once they bend over in pain, I stand up and look around at who's left.

Four people.

I am one of the final five.

We all create some distance between us after I finish off the guy with the sliced ankle. I admit, I get carried away and a little messy, but at least I tried to make my attacks survivable at the start.

Four chests heave in and out as we all crave a break but are on high alert. The two at somewhat of a distance from me but not each other, begin to attack one another, which I guess leaves me with no choice but to handle the man near me.

He has no weapon and no clothes on his back, which means he is experienced and is cocky about it.

I smile as I drop the knife, not wanting to cut this opportunity short.

We barely complete a full circle around our space before he decides to attack. He dodges two of my punches, then gives them back which is impressive in itself, but he lets himself down as he gets carried away and tries to kick me at the wrong time. I instantly grab his leg, pull him forward then headbutt him. I could quickly grab his damaged head and break his jaw, or even squeeze his eyes, but I want to see what else he's got.

Allowing him to stumble back, I walk a few steps to the side, almost mocking his recovery time, but boredom finds me quickly. So, I move to attack him and at the same time he decides to swing at me.

Changing my mind at the last second on what to do to him, I dodge his punch by rotating my upper body to the side and latch onto his wrist before he pulls it back to him. He panics, of course, but I don't allow it to settle, instead I break his elbow. Before he drops to the ground to cry or goes onto having whatever suitable reaction to the crunch of his own bones, I let go of his limp arm and slingshot my elbow into his nose. Not allowing him to make sense of things this time, I swipe at his legs, knocking him to the floor, once again injuring his head.

I think we both know that this fight is over, so I move to pick up the knife to give him a quick end.

"Pussy."

He's managed to get onto his knees and instead of attempting some sort of attack, he spits at my feet and wears a mocking smile. I'm *almost* impressed.

I think things over and decide it's best to show him how I don't actually need a knife. So, without wasting anymore time, I boot his nose, knocking him onto his back again. But the thing is, knocking him out is no longer enough for me anymore, so I crouch by him and give him a few light smacks to get him to wake. When that doesn't get me the results I want in the two seconds I wait, I pull him to his knees and stand behind him, holding him up.

I won't use the knife as the final blow, I'll just use it to aid me.

As I grip onto his hair, forcing his head back, his lids flicker showing his consciousness arriving, but I don't care. If anything this is great, this is a lesson to not be so bold. It'll be his last lesson of course, but who's to say others would not learn from this?

I jam the knife into his mouth from his cheek, and slice through, extending his lips. It shouldn't be enough to kill him unless he's weaker than I thought.

Throwing the knife to the side, I have a quick debate on whether I should pull down from his bottom lip or if I should get a good grip of his lower jaw from the inside of his mouth. I decide on the latter, and am ready to pull him apart.

I put all my strength into it, hearing Medisa's voice alongside the sounds I create through the vessel in my hands.

Frantically looking around, holding the man up by gripping into the hole in his face like he's some bowling ball, I pray that she's just in my head.

Until I find her stunned eyes.

'Did she see everything?'

When I take in the rest of her, I see how Maverick holds her in place. Her body is pressed against his, not that it's her choice, his arms are snaked around her and one of his hands covers her mouth.

Blood or not, I'm going to make him regret bringing her here. The human body can survive without an ear, an eye, a spleen, hands, and he's going to add to the statistic that proves it.

As they walk towards me, Medisa tries to keep her eyes on anything but me. I also notice how she uses my brother for support and it pains me more than any of the hits taken in the match.

Maverick prattles on about the winner's streak but is overshadowed when someone starts to choke on their own blood.

Medisa removes herself from his side and rushes over to the man who gained consciousness.

Does she know him?

She lowers herself to check his pulse, a second later and he stops making a scene. I focus on his chest and notice how he attempts to slow his breathing, or is actually dying. Medisa must've told him to shut the fuck up, and like a good desperate man, he's trying.

Maverick holds his hand out, calling Medisa to his side and that's when I look away. I can't stand the sight of it, even if she doesn't like him.

About twenty-four hours ago this room had the three of us.

Twenty-four hours.

Now Medisa has seen what is wrong with me, and Kassian is missing. It's different for her to assume how I have dealt with certain things, but for her to actually see me, see what I'd done, what I can do… it's both freeing and mortifying.

A few light knocks happen at the door, so in the background and slurred that I almost think I am imagining things. But then the handle struggles to turn.

I get up, my thoughts painting a picture of how bad Kassian looks.

Swinging the door open, prepared to catch his body, I instead uncover a barely awake Medisa, who lets herself in.

She gets comfortable on the sofa I had slept on the night before.

My mind forces me to see glimpses of the expression she made back at the arena, but they disappear when Medisa gets up and moves like a drunk sailor. She doesn't go anywhere, she just stands in front of the sofa, almost like she's waiting for me to approach.

Baffled by her behaviour, I move closer, and with further use of my senses, I know that she is drunk. Question is, was she forced to drink? Or was it the sight of me with that man that made her pick up a bottle?

I don't say a word as I walk over to where I had been sitting—where Medisa had slept the night before—to pick up a water bottle. When I turn around to pass it to Medisa, I turn to her right next to me.

"My head feels light but heavy. My eyelids feel heavy but I feel a little awake and my vagina…my vagina is *throbbing*. In fact, that whole area is pulsing—pulsating?" She pulls her brows together whilst her eyes turn to slits, then looks to me for some sort of confirmation. "One of the two." She continues when I say nothing.

'She's in heat.'

A smile almost cracks through, but is put on hold as Medisa looking up to me gives an illusion of her eyes being bigger than what they were, and fuck me was it a better sight than the eyes I saw back at the arena.

I try to the best of my ability not to give too much attention to how her eyes morph from sweet innocent doe eyes to ones that mirror sirens when they look over my lips. It's made easier when my own eyes travel over her once more, putting together why she appears a little different.

She's not wearing her own clothes.

My mind runs through all the things Maverick could've done to her in the condition she's in, and it takes everything in me to stay with her instead of dealing with him. How did she even get here? Did she somehow escape or did he allow her to—

"You're not understanding. *I'm* horny." She lays her hand flat just below her collarbone, determined to clarify and find a solution.

Grabbing a hold of her arms, as if to keep myself grounded and in the room, instead of dealing with Maverick, I gently sit her down on the sofa with the water bottle in her hand.

Medisa purposely drops the bottle to the side, using the opportunity to use her free hands to pull on my hand—and then my forearm—to get me to sit beside her.

'Not a good idea.'

I give in to her somewhat weak pulls, not exactly expecting her usual behaviour, but still taken aback when she straddles me. Her knees barely reach the sofa and her '*pulsating*' bits are a bit too close to mine. Suddenly, I am all too aware of my heart and second brain.

Placing some weight into my hands to keep them to the side is a battle within myself. I do not want this this way even if my body says otherwise. And Medisa does not help as she unintentionally grinds herself against me, trying to sit as close as she can get as I lean back into the sofa.

Getting closer to my face is simultaneously getting closer to a part of me she would not move to sober, so I promptly put a stop to that, gripping onto her thighs to keep her in place despite my 'new-found' ache.

"*Drink*." My voice is against me as it soughs my demand. I keep my eyes on hers, my peripheral vision on the other hand, took in every bit of the scene. Since Medisa can't lean in to me like she wants, she leans back, one hand holding onto my knee whilst the other feeds her the water. Her head is held back as she chugs. Some water trickles down her face, her neck, down *Maverick's* top.

Once that reminder clicks, my hands grip her thighs a little harder, fighting to not be stupid by ripping the material to replace it with mine, but also deeply wanting to do so.

When she is done, she looks back down to me, gasping, her chest almost exaggeratedly heaving in and out.

'Take her off.'

Both her hands are now holding on to each of my knees, holding her body up as she tries to catch her breath.

"I'm horny." Her tone cannot be paired to her mild salacious actions, it's more '*I'm sick of it,*' than '*I'm yearning to cross over and do every single thing that we can together, and I don't have it in me to wait any more.*'

"You've said that." My voice remains low, soft, as I continue to hold her in place. I stroke her thigh with my thumb when all I want to do is feel her. Feel her with my fingers, feel her with my tongue, feel her body begging for—

'Stop.'

Massaging her thigh and keeping her at a distance is the best thing I can do for the both of us without taking it too far.

"Yeah, but what you gonna do 'bout it?" Medisa cocks her head to one side. Her brows now slope as her eyes question and plead.

My lips slightly part, allowing me to breathe out a breath I held in. This is wrong and I know it. Her seeing me that way in the arena does not mean I can now fall back into my old ways with her. I am her *friend* and I will not do this.

"You're drunk." I keep on a poker face.

"And you look so good right now." She leans in after stripping me with her eyes. "Will you let me do what I want?" She whispers into my ear, then moves to hover over my lips as her hands made their way over my body.

We're both noticeably breathing heavy now, no one making the first move.

"Don't make me sin Medisa." I whisper between us, my plead against my actions. One hand snakes itself round her neck, making its way up her nape, lightly tugging her hair, while the other made its way to her waist, begging to pull her closer. Shortening the distance between us, up from my casual lean stance, I'm a heartbeat away from doing something that cannot be taken back.

'*Something that cannot be taken back...*'

I pull away.

Not enough for there to be an actual distance between us, but enough for me to extract myself from this situation or get back into it.

Removing my hand from her hair, I move it to her waist, holding her away before she does something she regrets.

Medisa tries to gently caress and guide my head forward, making it harder for me to fight the urge.

"Do you want me to go to Maverick?" She whispers, her eyes glossing over mine and my lips.

I snap out of her trance, instantly standing and throwing Medisa over my shoulder. I carry her to the walk-in wardrobe and lock her in. She chose the right words to get me to touch her, just not in the ways she wanted.

Ignoring her words, I pick up some water bottles then open the wardrobe door so that there is only enough space to push them in.

"Wait! I want to give you something too." Her voice innocent, but laced with lust.

I don't say anything, but I do keep the door a little open, curious—but not stupid—as to what her 'gift' may be. Medisa holds out the clothes she was wearing and I grab onto them before my thoughts take over, then lock the door before she can even think to get it open.

Without wasting another second, I throw Maverick's clothes into the fireplace. I try to get comfortable on the sofa with my hands holding the back of my head, but comfort does not reach me. After several stimulating thoughts, and foot tapping, leg shaking, nose pinching (methods of trying to get rid of vivid passionate images and to calm myself down), I strip out of my top and throw it in to Medisa.

"Wear it. And drink as much as you can. If you do lay down, lay on your side."

"Do I just relieve myself here too? You won't give me a hand?"

Hitting my forehead against the door, I stay in place and sigh.

Medisa and her words.

Medisa. Right there. On the other side.

Scrunching my eyes then layering them with my fingers in attempts of ridding any images of Medisa pleasing herself (or me helping) fails. Stressfully hammering my forehead with the side of my curled-up hand, then rubbing my forehead, also fails.

I begin to pace as a last resort.

Maverick. He knows what he's doing. He probably planned all of our interactions from the start, waiting for one of us to screw up enough for him to do something outrageous. Even so, with the state she's in, I hope he bloody delivered her to this room himself. I don't even want to think about what could've happened to her on her way here.

Thoughts on Maverick and his plan end up turning into thoughts about Medisa. Her face and the way he held her pop up again. I was sure that she would never want to see or talk to me again, or at least for a while, but in reality, I am the first person she came to when she was most vulnerable. Well, that's what I'm telling myself anyways.

When things get too quiet in the wardrobe, I wait a minute before unlocking the door to check in on her, to make sure that she is covered (warm) and not choking on vomit. I peak in to make sure I'm not about to get jumped, then see her (wearing my top) laying down on the floor, hugging a thick jacket with both her arms and legs. I let out a dry chuckle, thinking back to the pillow I wanted to burn or hide back at Aros.

She's not wearing any pants so I take off my blood-stained jogging bottoms and put them on her without waking or looking at her more than I need to. Once we are both dressed, I pick her up like the bride she was supposed to be and put her on the sofa I slept on the night before.

I don't allow myself to get comfortable, I can't afford to fall asleep, not tonight, so I sit on the floor, leaning against the sofa she sleeps on. Watching how she peacefully sleeps, I question what ultimatum Maverick gave for her to drink as much as she did.

Chapter 87
Kade
17/02/2022 (Thursday)

I don't know how, but I wake up as soon as Medisa shoots up from her laying position. Her hand's over her mouth and her eyes grow as she spots me next to her.

"The fireplace." I point in its direction.

Medisa throws herself at the fireplace, I actually jolt because it looked as though she were about to throw herself in. While she empties herself out, I give her some space and grab some water and a handful of tissues.

When she's done, she puts her back against the wall, pressing her head with one hand and I don't know what to do. What more can I do but give her some water and some tissues? I can't offer to massage her back, her head, or her feet because sober Medisa is strict on the no-touching rule. That, and I don't know what sober Medisa thinks of me. Does she want me to stay in the room or does she want me to leave?

Cautiously moving around, I finally decide to sit on the floor opposite her. While she uses the wall to lean on, I use the sofa Kassian slept on.

We don't say anything for a while and it kills me, but I can't be the one who speaks first. There's nothing to say, not unless I want to manipulate her into liking me. And I don't want to put words in her mouth, or thoughts in her head to win her over to my side.

Medisa takes a deep breath. The one she does when she's about to say something to either get something off her chest, or to fill the silence.

"I don't see you as some sort of monster. If that's what you think." Her eyes travel over my face, to the ground then back up to my eyes. "Don't get me wrong, I don't really know why you did that to that man and it definitely showed me another side of you, one I had suspected but not to that extent, but I just can't see you as someone to hate, or blame. I don't think I ever will, so stop putting on a mask every time you're around me. Own it, and introduce me to your sides, your thoughts, your actions, so that I don't have to see you through Maverick's twisted lens. Because then, yeah, a part of me might actually hate you, or be wary of you. So, I'm just telling you now."

What the hell did I do to deserve her? There's not one thing I can think of, not one. I can't even bring myself to say *'I would love that.'*

I know what this is. This must be a dream. I somehow fell asleep watching over her... How low for my own mind to do this to me.

"Kovu used to scratch me all the time when he was a kitten." She says as her previous words circle my mind. "A lot of them healed as white lines and are taking forever to disappear, allowing me to see them but also make out how old they are. The cut on my thigh that was looked at by *your* doctors, is basically the same. The only differences is that its slightly raised and wouldn't fade as much, if at all."

My mind is still a little scrambled so I'm trying to figure out if this is leading to some sort of metaphor, or if it's another story that lets me learn a little more about Medisa.

She takes another deep breath, this one obvious and quick. "I know what you did for Kassian and I know that you don't plan on telling him—"

I stop inhaling, my thoughts are no longer on Medisa and her not seeing me as a monster.

"—I've seen your skin up close Kade. You took his punishments for him, covered for months then slapped on some tattoos to try and cover it up."

As weight is taken off my shoulders, some of it moves to my heart. It feels good to be acknowledged for something that's honourable and not lethal. But I didn't do it to prove that I have good in me. And I don't want something I did years ago, to be the reason Medisa refuses to be angry at me.

"You have a noble heart Kade. So just do me a favour and remember that. Don't be one of those people who don't allow themselves to be loved or forgiven… because they're annoying and—"

"Thank you." I barely get it out. There're many things Medisa has done for me that she is not aware of, and I will pay her back and then some. Not just because I owe it to her or because Amana had asked me to, but because I want to, as though it is my life's purpose. I will find different ways to make her smile. "Thank you, Medisa. For not telling Kassian."

Her lips barely turn upward before going back to normal.

"I've been thinking…"

I straighten myself out to hear what she has to say.

"What Maverick said about you craving some sort of release…"

I nod a few times, letting her know that I want her to continue, that it's okay to continue and say what she's been keeping to herself.

"I don't think it's the blood that calls you back. It's the lack of control. I think you're conditioned to think that you beating, or killing someone would make everything else around you okay. If you won, Maverick didn't punish you or Kassian, he would feed you, he would let you guys out and experience what you guys thought was freedom. And now when things fall apart, you think that violent acts is what would help keep things controlled, including your own emotions."

...

Serenity.

That's what Medisa brings. That's what she allows me to experience when I've been told I will always feel the opposite. It's like therapeutic rain, or calm open water mixed with a warm embrace. Where others see a lunatic, she sees more. She allows and encourages more as she's not given in to trap me in the same box others have. I am human in her eyes, not a puppet filled with anger or void. Human.

"Thank you for coming to my lecture." Medisa fills the silence when I did not.

"I agree." I finally manage out. "But I also just enjoy harming people—only the ones that deserve it." I quickly correct myself whilst also delivering the truth.

"O-kay." The extended word escapes through with her laugh. "That's cool. That's-that's—" She tries to find a word that both goes with what she's thinking and a word that won't scare me away. "Admirable?"

My sight is limited as my eyes squint with my smile.

Medisa pulls her knees to her chest and hugs them as her head rests back. I can't believe she's found a way to stay calm, or at least sane throughout what she is being dragged through. Despite wanting to hear more of her words, her thoughts or wanting to do something else on her list, I decide to use this time to give her some peace and quiet before things get loud again.

She raises her hand, which I thought was to start peeling the skin off her lips, but she uses it to press the side of her head. "What did I do?"

Her voice gives away how much she wants to get this particular conversation over and done with. She must be thinking she's done something embarrassing, or harmful.

"Nothing. You were just feeling a little hot so I gave you my shirt…and jogging bottoms."

"What happened to the ones I was wearing?"

"Your vomit is over their ashes."

Her head turns from me to the fireplace then back again. A chuckle of hers fill my ears and I join in because, well, it's funny, but also because I'm glad I haven't heard the last of her laugh.

"Did I stop you from cleaning yourself up last night—or er… early morning?"

"No, I actually had no plans to get cleaned up. I er…I was distracted. I thought I'd lost you after what I'd done and I didn't—still don't know where Kassian has been taken."

I continue to disappoint.

I should've looked for him, should've asked Charles to tell me where he is. I shouldn't have let myself focus on what I had done in front of Medisa, though I'm only saying this because I now know that she wouldn't have shut me out.

"We'll find Kassian today, don't worry, I'm sure he's still here…on the grounds…not dead." Medisa tries to save herself multiple times and I just chuckle. Her methods to comfort are…something.

"What you saw me do in the ring. What I did to that man, you might have to see me be like that again." I warn. It's okay for her to not be okay with it, but I will not be kind to those who have had a part in whatever Kassian has been put through. I'm also trying to figure out Medisa's boundaries with certain things, how far, is too far for her?

"You do what you have to do to survive and protect, I get it. Just don't hide things from me. I *hate* that. So, if there's anything that you're keeping from me, tell me now."

My heartbeat picks up its pace.

I'm going to be an idiot. I'm going to tell her.

Should I tell her? I should tell her.

"Perhaps I could shed some light on some things?" Maverick enters the room with a stack of papers in hand.

Photo prints.

"Perhaps not." Medisa counters.

As he comes close, he looks over my clothes, which was obviously taken from the wardrobe, and then looks over Medisa, who is wearing what I wore last night. He doesn't verbally say anything, though him dropping the printed photographs besides her is definitely his way of making a mess of things.

Medisa picks up the prints and since I'm not sitting or standing beside her, I can't see what my brother's decided to unravel today. Her expression does not change throughout viewing two of the images. It stays in between focused and confused, which I suppose is a good thing, unless I am the one that has to offer some sort of explanation. She hands over two of the images and I don't have to look at it for more than a second for me to understand what they showed.

I stay calm and avoid looking at Maverick.

The pictures show my container. The container Maverick sorted for me years ago so that I can deal with people without being disturbed. The man in the image is the one who'd assaulted Medisa at the pub. I'm in one of the images too, except my back is to the camera, but I have no doubt one of the next pictures will reveal my face.

"Medisa, maybe you shouldn't be looking at this right now." I try my best not to reveal any emotion that's not me caring for her.

She doesn't look at me like she usually does, her eyes stayed on the third photograph and I fight the urge to take it away from her. I don't even want to see what its captured myself.

She lets the third image fall to the ground instead of passing it over to me. I don't bother to go after it, I can imagine what it shows because I was actually there, in the room, doing those things.

Medisa quickly stands up with the fourth image in hand. I stand with her as not only does she have an unreadable expression, but she also isn't steady. Her eyes move from me to Maverick and back again until finally she keeps her eyes on me.

"Kade…" Her calling out to me is cautious. "We're going to talk about this later." Her head ever so slightly nods, as though she were needing to convince herself that she was making the right decision.

I mirror her.

"Maverick." She turns her head towards him. "Give up. I won't believe your words, your side, your anything. You can try as much as you want, but I won't see them differently."

"Even when boundaries are crossed?"

My heart skips a beat.

"Kade took advantage of you last night."

My breath is momentarily taken from me as I clock what Maverick is up to. I should have known. I should have bloody seen it coming but instead I let myself be naïve. Of course he's going to dump information that's a lot to take in now.

She's still recovering from what he'd done to her last night. And of course, she won't be able to think straight or trust me, not when she herself admits that there are sides to me that she does not know.

"You motherfuck—" I stop myself mid swing as Medisa steps in front. Her palms are raised to attempt to stop things from progressing while she tries to process what he accuses me of.

"He didn't assault me." She doesn't sound too convinced.

"Oh, so my *wife* willingly engaged."

I need his tongue.

I need it.

I need to put it on display.

I try to get past Medisa but she continues to block my path. I don't really relax until I see her whole body clenched as though I would lay aggressive hands on her. Slowly opening her eyes after realising that I haven't shoved her to the side, she allows her body to relax.

"We *didn't* sleep together." She looks me in the eyes and almost nods to get a confirmation out of me.

"Explain how you got to be in his clothes." Maverick refuses to give us a break.

Medisa half turns to face him. "I vomited over yours and needed a change of clothes." She spoke like it's the truth, there's no hint of fabrication. "And who swaps clothes after engaging in any sexual activity anyways? I would've been way too tired to even think of doing that." Her attitude sells it further.

Maverick's now narrowed eyes search hers, then like magic, it disappears as he takes steps towards me.

"Whatever relationship you two have, ends now." He speaks over Medisa, who continues to stand in between us, then turns around. And as though he sensed Medisa take a step towards him to argue, he aggressively turns back. "*Now*." He dared her to go against him as he lowered his head to hers. "If I see you so much as *breathe* the same air as Kaden, I'll break you." His eyes look into mine. "You want her to stay as she is? A breath of fresh air? Then you better treat my words as a law you will follow."

Medisa shakes her head and I can only imagine the face she has on. "No. No, I don't care about what you *think* we've done because *nothing* happened. We don't deserve this." She tries to argue against insanity with logic.

Maverick snorts at her words, then calls out to a worker who enters the room not a second too late. He orders her to show Medisa the phone in her hand, so she does, and this time I'm able to see what it is with Medisa. The phone gave away a moment of what transpired last night. It's the back of Medisa and it very clearly shows her straddling me, with only one of my hands on her thigh. You can't see my other hand, but it's easy to imagine where it could be.

How do I explain *that* to her? There's not enough time for me to even begin to process what's happening.

"*Lying* to your husband." Maverick grips onto her arm to take her away and I instinctively hold onto her.

Medisa's alarmed expression is given to the both of us as we pull her in different directions. Me and Maverick are given the *same* look, she doesn't see me any different. It makes me loosen my grip. A stupid mistake made in a moment of weakness. I *know* the truth and will tell it to her later. She doesn't have to understand now.

Instead of taking her elsewhere, Maverick drags her to a sofa.

"Stay back!" He warns. "Or I'll make you watch me go

the whole way!" He forces her over his knee in an instant.

I stop moving towards them as his forearm holds the top half of her body down. No matter what Medisa did to hurt him, he stayed unaffected, blinded by anger I can't imagine being real.

Maverick grips onto the waistband of the jogging bottoms she wears and is about to tear them off. His intended actions are to get rid of her lip, her confidence, her ability to fight back once and for all. He's going to humiliate her. She will become a shell of a person and will never heal when I'm around, not when my face would serve as a constant reminder.

"If you do this!" The amount of wrath and frustration I feel cannot be put into words and there's no one to blame but me. I want to do something to him, but I can't further his want to teach us a lesson when Medisa is going to get the worst of it. "Don't do this." I say as I try to calm the blood that's already been boiled without using its usual method of cooling down. "I'll do what you want, just please, don't do this to her." I almost choke on my own words as my throat swells.

"Kade don't—"

"Hush now wifey." He gently taps her back, his voice no longer filled with fury. "Kaden is talking."

'*Wifey*.' He *has* been taunting her with it. Trying to keep her from biting off the leash he's put on her.

I take a deep breath. I can't let it affect me now, not when she's still in a vulnerable position. Amana can wait, Kassian can wait, let me save Medisa first.

"Let her go and I'll pick up my duties as a River."

"That's not enough anymore." He plays with the waistband, slightly lifting and smoothing it out again and again.

"Then I'll fight. I'll go back in the ring as many times as you want."

Medisa is no longer struggling against him. I don't know if it was him tightening her leash, or if it's my words, but she is motionless. A frightening sight, but I push past it.

Maverick clicks his tongue. "Twelve matches and you are forbidden to speak or be around Medisa unless I am with her."

My eyes momentarily go out of focus, but my vision comes back as I slowly nod my head in agreeance. Maverick releases Medisa from his grip and as she sorts herself out, she looks out of it. I half expected her to attack him, but instead she quickly moves to be in front of me.

I don't look down. Her eyes would be too much for me, it'll add more weight than I've ever handled before and I don't need it. I'm doing this for her. She's taken over too much of my mind, rendering me weak and exposed to things that I would've seen coming from a mile away. Had I used my brain, we would not be in this situation.

"Kade, don't do this. Let him do whatever he wants to me, I can handle it. I'm strong remember? I'll handle it. Please, just *don't* do this." She tip-toes for a second to try to get me to look at her, but it doesn't add enough height for her to achieve her goal.

Maverick's deep laugh travels the room as he decides to make it abundantly clear on how amusing this is to him.

I stiffen my lip and tense my jaw.

"You promised." She says dejectedly, not making any of this easier. I did promise to not allow her to go through these weeks alone.

I have no choice but to convince myself that Medisa is someone under Baronial, someone who tried to screw me over, someone who used me, someone who was close to tricking me into exposing myself. It's the only way I'll get through these three months.

She drops her head millimetres away from resting it on my chest.

My thoughts of her have become infected by faux stories, I'm almost convinced enough to be disgusted by her presence alone.

Just as I think she will give up and be guided out the room, she turns and lunges towards Maverick, her elbow cocked back, ready to be punched forward. My brother doesn't move, he doesn't even flinch, he just raises one side of his lips when I grab onto her arm a second before she reaches him.

She whips her head around to see who held her back as though there were anyone else in the room fast enough to do so.

Her expression morphs from anger to dolour as her shoulder slump. And now that I got one look into Medisa's eyes, I don't let myself look away until she leaves the room.

Instead of taking steps away from me, she puts all her energy into pushing me back. I don't allow myself to reach out and comfort, but I do continue to stare into her eyes, to take it all in as I feed myself the delusion that it'll be enough to keep me going.

Medisa storms out the room with the lady who added to this mess. Soon as I hear the door lock in place, I launch myself at Maverick. We may be denied the satisfaction of killing him, but I will pay him back for laying his hands on Medisa.

We tussle—Maverick obviously letting me get some anger out—until I see enough blood on him.

"I'll live by your conditions, but if I find out that you've done something to harm Medisa, I'll kill you." I continue to grip onto his shirt.

Maverick wipes blood from his lips as he grins. "Are you threatening me?"

"I'm promising you."

"Right... because you keep your promises."

Chapter 88
Kassian
18/02/2022 (Friday)

The workers have been moving around me like I'm infected with something they've never seen. There is one or two that place a plate of fruit or some sort of meal next to me, but I can't bring myself to eat. I can barely get down the water in front of me.

No one has mentioned Anna, no one, and it's scary. She's been absent for two days, yet not one of them has batted an eye. It's like there's no bond between any of them. Some of them don't even know who she is. I've tried asking whenever someone new comes into the room but they just look at me like I'm crazy and have been hallucinating.

Have I?

"Kassian, what are you still doing here?" Charles approaches me in a rush as if I am needed elsewhere.

"Hey Charlie, any updates?" I stretch in my seat, barely sounding hopeful myself as I get off the stool to face him. If there's someone who knows something useful, it's him

He exhales. "She won't be coming back here. And there's no use in trying to hunt her down."

"But she's okay?" My shoulders slump.

"She's okay." His nods mimic a wobble.

I sit myself back down before I dramatically fall to the ground. I know there's no use in tracking her down because Maverick would've made it near impossible, but is Charlie also saying it because she herself doesn't want to see me?

Makes sense I suppose, she did almost die because of me.

"Kassian, you need to pull yourself together, now's not the time to get lost in your head. You need to be here, not only for yourself but for Kade and—"

"What happened to Kade?"

Charles looks done with everything, like all his hard work has been erased. "It's like he never left, except he's lost his lip."

Bloody hell.

"And Medisa?"

"They've all been told to report her actions, especially if she is seen with Kade."

Bloody hell.

Chapter 89
Kassian
18/02/2022 (Friday)

He will walk by here, I know it. He may not come in, but he will walk by. I'm just waiting for the perfect moment.

Someone opens the door I purposely shut on my way here, which means they are on their way to the studio, and unless 11pm is clean up time for this place, I put all my money on Kade… and maybe some on Medisa. Either way, whoever it is, I am grabbing them.

I have the studio door open so all they have to do is walk by, or be curious enough to step in.

The sound of their steps is almost non-existent.

It has to be Kade.

As soon as he approaches, I grab onto him and pull him into the room.

Does not happen.

I grab onto him and we both try the same move on each other and fail. When Kade realises who I am, he drops his deathly expression and let's go.

"What the heck is wrong with you?" He surprisingly talks first. The lack of English means that we're back to using all languages but, so that if anyone were spying on us, they could not understand, ergo, Maverick won't know shit.

"Me? *Me*? Seriously? What's this I'm hearing about you and Medisa? You need to '*fix up*'." I purposely use a phrase Medisa uses. "She won't last this week let alone three months if you keep up with this!" I whisper to the loudest whisper volume.

Kade pinches his nose and half twirls before looking back to me. "I know! I know."

Somehow, he looks fragile and ready to attack at the same time. He takes steps towards me and I don't know if I should be prepared for an attack or an aggressive hug.

"I'm doing this *for* her. You don't understand she's making me weak and blind. I didn't have enough time to physically train her, and I can't even bring myself to fight when she needs me to because I'm worried she'll get hurt when I look away. I need her out of sight and at the back of my mind. *Not* all over." He's using more of his hands to talk, he's more expressive and is actually using the space around us to take steps. She's really rubbing off on him.

Yikes.

I'm about to say something but he beats me to it.

"Kassian, what the hell is wrong with me?" His eyes flicker back and forth and for once, hold a mixture of confusion and fear. "It's only been what? A day? And I am already struggling. I can put on an act, I can do that, but on the inside, on the inside I'm *crumbling*."

Wow. I would not want to be the workers that get in his way these coming weeks. One tiny mistake and *bang*, you are now Kade's punching bag. Anyway, he is going down the wrong path, I need him to focus on the right things and not the colour of Medisa's eyes, or guessing the bloody face she would make when he behaves a certain way.

"I've had thoughts to kill her."

Errrrrr what now?

"Not now. I'm in too deep now. At least that's what I tell myself when the quiet thought does come about."

"Because of the way she makes you feel?"

Weak, pathetic, and only of use when you are doing something for her...

"Yeah."

His phone chimes and despite where he is mentally, he gives it his attention. Must be important.

"What is it?"

"It's a notification from her prayer app." His voice is calmer now. "I like to know when she should be praying so I can remind her, or know what she's up to." He answers the question I was about to ask, but something tells me it's more for him to talk about her than to inform me on what I am missing out on.

My head wobbles back and forth as I accept that my brother has *slightly* lost it.

"Give me the name of the app then delete it. Medisa does not have her phone so I can tell her when to pray. You focus on whatever the hell else and I'll keep her sane whilst doing whatever Maverick expects of me."

Kade actually does as he's told, reluctantly, but we get there in the end.

Over the next two-to-three months, while he gets dragged through his version of hell, I will do my best to make sure that she is doing okay. At least then he can focus on being a good puppet.

"Did he do anything?" He asks like his old brotherly self would. "After we got separated, what did he do to you?"

"To me?" I say as though I wasn't a part of a shared punishment. "Nothing."

Chapter 90
Kade
01/04/2022 (Friday)

A woman, Abigail, spends some time with Medisa throughout the days, and it is her who told Kassian about how Medisa is truly feeling. And it's those feelings that have pushed us to finally do something to give us all a break.

Kassian called Nene and begged her to cause some sort of commotion to take Maverick away. It took some sucking up, but it worked, she agreed, and now he is leaving to meet someone from our mums side of the family in London. He couldn't take Kassian with him, she specifically told him to go alone. He didn't take Medisa as there's no use in introducing her, and he can't take me, no one's heard from me for years, so I would only bring attention I know he does not want right now.

We have the afternoon, slash evening to ourselves. Kassian's plan is to take Medisa to his club, introduce her to new friendly faces as well as a change in scenery. I only agreed on the condition he stays by her side and makes sure no one gets too bold. I trust he would handle the situation accordingly—to my standards—should something like that happen. Or at least report back to me with who it is so that I could take my version of a break.

Before he takes her away for that breath of fresh air, I told him to bring her to my studio.

I wait here now, my stomach summersaulting at the thought of finally being able to look her way. My eyes and tongue have been fasting all this time, anticipating this moment. It's been so long that now, when she's going to be right in front of me, my throat feels dry, itchy, or closed up. I've been clearing my pipes again and again, but something tells me I won't use it straightaway. Not when I first see her.

I walk from one station to another, thinking this through. My mind becoming less about what I want and more on what I should do. And I shouldn't be doing this. We still have a month to go and if Maverick comes back and notices a change in the way she is towards me, he will give in to suspicions immediately. It's best for us to wait.

I hear them approaching and panic as there is no way of escaping this room without being seen. Kassian is not dumb, so I trust he hasn't sold Medisa too big of a dream—me waiting for her in the studio—so I hide behind a room divider that's been shoved in the corner and pray that he has enough sense to work out I've changed my mind.

They enter the studio together.

"Oh. My. God."

I rush to look in between the gaps of the divider. What is she looking at? What caught her attention so quickly?

"D'you like it?" Kassian asks a question that I would if I were beside her.

"Oh my God." Medisa says under her breath as she looks up and turns around to view the roof. "His studio is part dome. A dome. And not even a small claustrophobic dome roof, no, a huge one. Are you kidding me? And it's got a skylight in the middle."

I grin from ear to ear, half surprised she hasn't mentioned the balcony that wraps around, even more surprised she hasn't run to the ladder to get up to the narrow floor.

"Yes, I can see that." Kassian tries his best not to be so

obvious with his reaction to my lack of appearance.

When Medisa has her back to the divider I hide behind, I quickly lean out and wave my arm to get Kassian's attention. He spots me as soon as I half step out and I quickly do a '*cut it out*' gesture.

Medisa lowers her head and her body language looks as though she's about to face him, so I quickly go back to hiding.

"Seen any pieces you like yet?" Kassian starts a conversation so naturally I doubt she has any suspicions.

"I'm trying not to look at them properly because I want to go into detail with him—no offence."

"None taken."

"But I do like this one."

I fight to see which one she is talking about, but the divider and the position of where they stood did not allow it.

"I like this one too. I had to put it together because he had originally destroyed it's frame and part of the actual material."

There are *a lot* of paintings I've ruined and not one is coming to mind. I'm tempted to pick up the divider to move a little to the side and a step or two closer.

"Don't you think she kind of looks like me?"

"Oh yeah, I see what you mean." Kassian responds after angling his head.

Whilst I'm convincing myself that Medisa won't notice a six-foot-five divider move across the room, Kassian's phone receives a few messages.

"Alright, c'mon we should go."

Medisa continues to stare at the piece she likes, she may have even glazed her finger over a part of it as Kassian moves towards the door. When he does not feel her beside him, he turns around to wait. His gaze moves from me to her, giving me the chance to come out, but I won't do it. I'm not risking it, nor will I tease the both of us with this interaction.

"We can stay here if you want." Kassian suggests and my eyes quickly move to find him. It felt as though he were talking to me.

"No, let's go." Medisa half skips, half walks to him. "I want to see what you've built."

"Oh you mean these babies." Kassian lifts up his arm to show off his biceps (mine are better). "I was actually born with them." He says as they walk out the door.

Idiot.

I wait before coming out from behind the divider, then walk straight towards what they both claimed to like. It's a mixed media piece, it's main media being paint, both oil and acrylic. It's obviously something I've had some sort of episode on. The harsh strokes and aggressive layers on top of what looks as though it could be something decent had I finished it, give that away. They must be twisted if this is what they like and God, I do see what Medisa means about the girl resembling her a little, so now, naturally, I am conflicted. Do I burn it because I don't want to see Medisa that way, all restrained, forced to look up, tears mixing with blood that's been rained onto her, or do I keep it because Medisa likes it?

I throw a sheet over and move it to the back.

I do *not* have to deal with this right now.

Chapter 91
Kade
10/05/2022 (Tuesday)

I made sure to get all twelve matches done as soon as possible, though spreading them out would've been more useful—distracting. But I can't take Medisa away with a face that would bring about more attention than it usually does. It wouldn't be that hard to find someone with my build and a few cuts and bruises on his face.

The plan is risky.

From the moment we figured out we couldn't extract them both, we knew our chances of failing significantly increased. Medisa is easy to sneak out, she's small and can be hidden slash carried. Maverick on the other hand, he's big, and *actually* has loyal dogs in this place. I wouldn't make it to the door with the both of them, forget escaping the estate.

Kassian's job is probably the most important, but it is not the most difficult. I don't care how he does it, but he needs to knock-out and hide the delivery driver somewhere. Maverick restricts access to the estate after a certain time, so the past two months have been essential to our plan; switching the routine of deliveries being made to a much later time, so that Maverick gets used to the temporary routine.

The hard part of this entire thing is to get Maverick to accept the drink. I admit, I did pull it out of the blue. I did the dumbest thing and did not make it a part of his routine, but this is where I need Medisa to use her quick-thinking skills. I've done what I can on my end, now I'm just waiting for the right time to enter the room. If worse comes to worst, I can always knock him out myself. We'll be long gone before he wakes up or anyone notices anyways.

I take a deep breath.

I have *longed* for this moment and every moment after. When this is all done my time will be spent being lost in her pretty brown eyes and fulfilling every single one of her desires. If I am going to be under someone's thumb, I want it to be hers. I have been begging for it to be hers.

It's been some time since the drinks have been delivered and I don't care enough anymore to make sure that he has taken it, so I enter the room. No one is in the main part of the bedroom, but the bedsheets have been moved, so someone (looks like Medisa) was laying down.

"If you come out now, I'll forgive you. I promise."

I follow Maverick's voice until I see him leaning his head against the door, his hand in a ball of fist raised a little above his head as it leaks.

All the times he boasted about finding Medisa and taking her to his bed, all the times he forced her to watch me in arenas, all the other moments he got one up on us, help with how quickly I am able to deal with him.

Just as I'm about to make sure he stays down long enough for us to be at a safe distance, he turns and looks proud—too proud, which is alarming. Almost makes me feel the fear he invokes in others and want to stitch his hand up myself.

His body drops to the ground. I could have prevented him from hitting the floor but why would I do that? After hitting him again (and again) to make sure that he won't wake up early, I drag him to his bed. Not to put him on top of it—again, why would I do that?—but to tie him to it.

I rush over to the bathroom door but do not try to break

in. I drugged both glasses and if Medisa had the drink, she could be passed out on the floor in front of the door, making things just a *little* difficult.

"Medisa?" I call out to her and despite her and her name running through my mind every day, it feels unfamiliar to say out loud.

The door slowly unlocks a moment after I called out to her. The speed at which I open the door, teases the yearning I have to hold her, but I need to make sure I don't accidently hit her on my way in.

She's on the floor, barely able to be upright on her knees. Her hands go from holding the wall to holding my arms as I kneel down in front of her.

"Hey Trouble." My voice comes out low, soft. "Can you stand?"

'Stupid question.'

I lift her off the ground.

"Never mind."

I notice her body being limp and her eyes closing so I don't bother to hide what I had done to Maverick. If anything, she would be glad to see him like that, would probably want to get a few hits in herself.

This cottage has been booked under a pseudonym and neither me nor Kassian have visited this place before, we haven't even been to this part of Scotland. And just to be safe, we've booked several homes, all will be empty of course, but we needed to make this look less conspicuous and more like the area is thriving. We've paid a stranger with our build to take the van to London and to wear reflective clothing as well as sunglasses and a cap. The exchange was done at a service station where our new clothes had been stashed for a month (thank you Bellamy). Everything we have done thus far are steps made to minimise the chances of Maverick finding us, not eliminating them. My brother is not dumb, if he cannot be bothered to find us, he will light a fire and wait for us to run towards him. The hardest part of this whole plan is waiting it out.

There's only one bedroom in this place and it's been given to Medisa. Kassian is asleep in the room outside the bedroom and I am in a chair facing her bed. I'm not planning on sleeping, I am keeping my eyes on her and never taking it for granted again. If she begins to wake, I will be here to comfort, explain and apologise. Maybe not all at once, I don't want to overwhelm her, but I will make sure that she doesn't remain in the dark.

She begins to move and if the drugs are starting to wear off on her, they've definitely worn off Maverick. He must be rabid right now. I can't imagine how many people need to be replaced, or the mess Charles has to deal with.

Medisa slowly tries to lift herself up, but decides it's too much so she falls back onto her pillow.

"Kade?" She weakly calls out as though she were half asleep.

"I'm here."

As eager as I have been to interact with her, I don't move because from the sounds of it, she's going to pass out any second now.

"Get Amana."

'And so the fire is lit.'

Chapter 92
Kassian
11/05/2022 (Wednesday)

"I'm going to get Amana."

That's one way of making sure I'm awake.

"And what makes you think that she will just up and leave her family?" As much as I want to protect her, I am not letting it cloud logic or even my compass. We can't just save her knowing that her family is also at risk.

"I'd already arranged for her to be taken to a place, ready to be collected, and Bellamy should've sorted something out for her family. Right now, she has no choice but to come with me—"

"Because we can protect her? Or for Medisa?"

"Both." He stops moving around and peeking out the windows as if someone was already watching us. "What is wrong with you? Do you not care about her anymore?"

I don't reply straight away.

"Something about having her close to us doesn't exactly feel safe. It might actually be the worst thing."

"Well I can't exactly travel back in time or get her on a plane, so until we come up with something better, she is coming here. Or I might just stay with her until the 14th, I don't know yet."

He's right, as sad as it is, her safest option is being here with us. It doesn't even the odds but it's better than being left alone, in the dark.

"We should call Nene." I flippantly suggest, but I also

just want her to put an end to this.

"To what? Give her a heart attack?" Kade jokes, getting a gasp from me and a quieter one from himself. "Sorry, sorry." One hand is held out whilst the other rests on his heart. "God forbid. May she and our other grandparents live a long life."

"Amen." I look over my brother once more and decide that it's now or never. "She can't know your thoughts unless you offer them to her you know?"

Kade slightly scrunches his brows, which I suppose is fair given the change in conversation.

"Or should I say, *feelings*?"

He scoffs, shakes his head, then turns to walk away. I'm about to follow him when he turns around to face me. "I'll tell her when she's safe."

Would you look at that.

Thick-skinned Kade won't allow himself to prematurely be vulnerable. Not when Medisa's life could end soon, or even in the moment he tells her. Maverick would see to it I'm sure, in fact he's probably waiting for it. It's what we would wait for if it were someone else. We all love tragic compositions.

Some of the floorboards in the bedroom sound as if we've let a donkey in, but at least it gives me some time to mentally prepare for Medisa and her questions.

I know she's fully dressed, so I let myself in, just in case she starts to think that we've left her alone. "What d'you want for breakfast? We've got fresh eggs."

Please say no to the eggs

Medisa's eyes only travel over my outfit twice before she

responds. "I don't like eggs."

I gasp before recovering. "Well thank God because I didn't really have it in me to take them from her."

On cue, the chicken I've temporarily adopted walks in. I've named her Virile.

"The elderly couple letting us stay here said that we can have whatever eggs she provides, but after spending some time with her, I don't think that I can do that."

Medisa *slowly* nods her head. I could practically see her holding her words back, but I know, if she were in my position, she would be the same. "So, I've heard about the chicken, but when are you gonna tell me about what's going on?"

Picking Virile up, I signal for Medisa to follow me into the kitchen where I pull a chair out for her. I've already washed the dishes in this place so they're ready to use, and now that Medisa's awake, I can give her some water with dissolvable vitamin tablets. Then maybe a meal if she's up for it.

As I sit on the head chair of this dining table, I also place down her drink and her phone. Medisa's hand reach for the wrong thing so I cover her phone with my hand. I can already feel the whiny statements and questions that will take up the rest of the day, so I decide to summarise to get the majority of questions out the way.

"It's been a few hours since we've taken you. We're still in Scotland. Kade's on his way to London to get Amana, and Maverick—we assume—thinks that you have also pissed off back to London. Ergo, we stay here right up until the fourteenth, then we can safely take you to sort this all out." I think I've done a good job. Not too fast for her to still be processing and not too slow for her to be going back to sleep. I spoke at the right pace for the both of us to be happy. "Any questions?"

"When did he go?"

"Sunrise."

"Why can't I turn on my phone?"

Idiot.

"Do you want Maverick to know where you are?" Maverick's put his own password on her phone, the only reason we have it is because Kade insisted we take it for the 'memories' she's got on it. We haven't turned it back on since the house and we're not planning to until we are in a crowded area, not in the middle of bum-fuck nowhere.

"Do you think Kade's being followed?"

No doubt.

"Most likely."

"Can I add to the plan?"

For God's sake.

"No."

She chugs her vitamin drink like it's some powerup and I just *know*, I can just *sense* more words coming out of her mouth.

"We can make this easy for Kade."

"No." I just don't want to hear it. I'm managing to keep my own stress levels under control and that's only because I trust Kade to be able to do this.

"You stay here with my phone." Medisa says whatever spawns into her mind without giving it much thought. "You turn it on, instantly grabbing your brother's attention. Maverick would come here with his men and I will be far-far away, in London, at Aros, or somewhere out the way. You'd start running laps around, keeping them busy and away from Kade and me. Or at least taking away some heat off of Kade. Then on the fourteenth I'll go and sort this all out."

Yeah sure, I trust Medisa enough to be able to travel

unseen all the way to London—absolutely not—where she would be closer to Kade and Amana, making collecting us a fucking picnic. Not to mention, I will basically not be allowed to rest for days on end and if I get caught, Maverick would do some serious damage to me just for being an accomplice. Also, with the River name now being hers (along with *many* things) I won't be surprised if dad's dad pops out of nowhere just to handle Medisa (and us twins) himself.

I refrain from shivering.

"No."

She sighs. "It's a good plan."

"That's not enough."

"We—"

"Do you think Maverick opened the door for us to come in and waltz back out with you? No. We drugged him and when that didn't work like it was supposed to, Kade knocked him out then took you—Maverick's *wife*— and in three days you'll have joint ownership over everything. How d'you think he's going to be handling things now? A slap on the wrist? No. Do try and remember that he mutilated a girl's hand because you refused to sit."

I stand from my seat, needing some space before I make the days ahead difficult for the both of us.

Chapter 93
Kassian
11/05/2022 (Wednesday)

I've been keeping myself busy with Virile and any work the elderly couple needed doing, like the old fence. The whole point of these tasks is to distract, but the conversations I had with Kade and Medisa are pretty much the only things on my mind.

During the cutting of some firewood (and some to spare) I made a mental agreement to talk things through with Medisa when I'm done. I'm going to tell her everything, from the moment I saw Amana till now. It will keep her occupied and the three days in here will be better if we worked together than if we try to control the blind (Medisa and Amana). Also, I would much rather have sleepless nights because of Medisa's questions than have no rest because I'm too busy constantly moving, running from Maverick.

As I walk back into the cottage and into the cosy kitchen, the sun sets. I turn to call Medisa in here, to witness its colours with me and as soon as I do, I quickly notice a yellow sticky note lazily placed on Medisa's phone. I don't need to approach it to know what she's done, but I move to pick it up anyway.

'Sorry but we have to try. Turn it on tomorrow. Get to London on the 14th...Also I took ~~some~~ most of your money :p'

"Fuck." Frustrated, I throw the now scrunched paper across the kitchen. I pace, but that quickly ends as I sit down to try and gather my thoughts. She's already gone. I have no idea what route she's taken, or when she left for me to even catch up to her and drag her back.

I take a deep breath.

I might as well bloody do this. I get up and walk over to where the paper fell. Leaving it on the floor is rude, not to mention a fat clue to where Medisa is heading, so I burn it.

After clearing everything out and wiping the cottage of our prints, I grab Medisa's phone, pick up Virile and leave (after dropping the chicken back to its original owners) despite knowing that our chances of getting away with this had dropped considerably lower than before.

Chapter 94
Kassian
12/05/2022 (Thursday)

It's been a while since Maverick's put his hands on me himself and I have to say, I did not miss it. I used to think he was messed up for beating us with his full power when we were kids, but now, I know that it was not even close to it. At least now he's got my wrists tied and has me hanging like some sort of boxing bag, shows that he believes I have the power to fight back.

He stopped wailing in on me the moment someone came in to inform him about Medisa. I can't really hear because of the ringing in my ears, the numbness everywhere else and the slow increase in what feels like suffocation.

"Am I on speaker?"

Medisa's voice.

How the hell—what the hell? He hasn't got her yet, I know that for a fact. But how has she—he found a way to communicate with her?

What is she thinking?

"You are." Maverick says, his breath stable, like he hasn't been using his energy on me.

"Can he hear me?"

Maverick pulls my hair up, tilting his head to one side to try and catch my gaze. "He can."

"Kassian. I'm sorry. I'm so-so sorry. I should've listened to you, I should've stayed still, I'm sorry."

Don't say it. Don't you dare say it.

"I'm sorry that you have a piece of shit brother." She says with more anger than sadness. "And I'm sorry that I'm going to go against what you want again and come get you."

Before I could say anything, a bag is pulled over my head and tightened at my neck, restricting air from leaving or entering.

It might just be the worst move he's pulled yet.

Chapter 95
Kade
13/05/2022 (Friday)

Amana did not hesitate in leaving her family, but then again, I did not tell her the truth. I didn't exactly lie to her either, but having a way with words is what got us into this mess so it could be something that gets us out. Besides, I made sure to get Bellamy to sort something out for them, so my conscious remains clear, or a little murky.

We could've stayed in London and waited for the 14th to come and go, it would've been the safest option. But the coast was clear for our way back to Kassian and Medisa, so that is what I went with.

As we approach the cottage, I quickly become aware of its lack of life from afar. They should've noticed me and Amana coming up to the drive, yet not one of them has come out.

I slow down so that we move at a pace slower than a walk. Something is happening, or has happened. Amana notices the drastic change in speed and my observing eyes, so she begins to look around herself.

Her phone rings and I almost attack.

I don't question or give her the opportunity to explain. As soon as she brings her ringing phone into view and we both see the unsaved number, I answer.

"I've given your little friend and Kassian 24hrs to hide with the condition that if I find them, I'm going to do whatever I desire, no more privileges."

Kassian that fucking imbecile had *one* job. One job and he couldn't even do that. Keep Medisa here, keep Medisa protected. It's not that hard.

"Do you want to know where they are now?" A rhetorical question. "They're at Kassian's pub. I've found them and it hasn't even been close to two hours." He snickers. "In fact, I have people outside there right now, waiting for me to make the call to retrieve them."

"Why did you call?"

"To give you an opportunity to save them… bring yourself and Amana back to the estate, now."

I momentarily pause.

"She has a brother—"

"Ah, yes, Ayaan."

"Take him instead."

"Now *Kade*—"

He called me '*Kade.*'

"—we both know something happening to him wouldn't bring out desired results from her. Something happening to Amana however…"

I hang up before more is said.

He won't give the order to retrieve them, he will assume that I will do as he's said. Or he'll wait a little before the twenty-three hours are up before doing anything to make sure that it's a decision (me not going to the estate) I'm sticking with.

If I take Amana, there's a high chance she won't ever come back out those doors. But it's her, or Medisa and Kassian, two people who would be against giving her up.

'For fucks sake, none of us have time for this.'

I turn to her as I reverse the car away from the cottage. "Maverick wants us at his place or he will kill Kassian and

Medisa."

Her eyes enlarge as her brows are pulled closer together. "What? Me too? How does he even know—"

"He's made it clear that it's you or them."

"What are you going to do?" Her voice is a little panicked. One arm stretched, hovering over the door, the other hand near the gear stick as though she feels unbalanced.

'*No more privileges*' echoes throughout my mind and I have no doubt that he means it. Maverick has always been one to demonstrate how serious he takes his own words.

"I won't lie to you. I want to drag you there myself and I don't care for the consequences because right now my mind is on what will happen to my brother and Medisa, who are currently in danger and they don't even know it."

Her eyes continue to pierce the side of my head as her hand now grips onto the door and the back of my seat.

"I won't. But that doesn't mean that I know what I'm doing. I'm going to let you decide your own fate as well as theirs." I'm not a complete idiot. I'm going to find a way to communicate with Bellamy, see if he's gotten her family out the way, and if he can get those two to safety.

"Take me."

I look to her and not the road ahead.

"*Take me*." Amana reiterates.

"I can't guarantee that you'll walk back out those doors."

"I don't care. Take me. I'm tired of all of this and I'm not letting Medisa get hurt." She goes back to sitting like a person normally would, and I continue to drive in the direction I was always going to go.

Chapter 96
Kassian
13/05/2022 (Friday)

As soon as I am dumped on Medisa and she says that we need to run, my mind went straight to the pub. It's the most obvious place for us to go and hide, but it's mine, and I know it inside and out. If we do get surrounded, I know where to go and what to do. Besides, we need to take a break and figure out what to do next.

Once again, we are in the basement. I sit on the floor against the wall as Medisa decides to pace the space in front of me. She turns to walk the same steps again and again, almost accurately enough for someone to compare her to one of those hypnosis watches.

"Kade should be at Scotland by now, right? They're safe, right? When was the last time you heard from him?"

"Would you sit down. Your pacing is making me sick."

She plonks herself down beside me, her knees raised from the ground, one leg visibly shaking. Her behaviour is slightly concerning considering it not only reminds me of myself, but of someone wanting one last high.

"When did you last hear from him?"

"When I saw him back at the farm. He hasn't contacted me and I haven't had the chance to contact him since you ran off…Thanks for that by the way."

Medisa pulls her knees close to her chest and rests her head on her arms. Her face, though almost expressionless, gives away her regret.

"Hey." I nudge her, but not enough for her to topple over. "It's okay, we only have five hours till tomorrow."

"Tomorrows hours are still part of the game, and something doesn't feel right."

She uses my phone to call Kade.

"It wouldn't make sense if he had his phone on. We're all laying low remember?" We also couldn't risk turning his phone on just in case Maverick had somehow gotten into it before we did. If we were going to communicate, it would be Kade calling me, using another phone.

"If it *isn't* supposed to make sense, why is the call going through?" Medisa holds the phone that is now on speaker, between our ears.

She's right. Why is the call going through?

I try not to let my mind go down the path of Maverick already holding Kade captive somewhere, which is why he was so quick to play another game with Medisa. He knew that no matter what, Medisa will be in his hands. And if he has Kade, then he has Amana, unless he caught Kade before he had reached her?

Medisa ends the call after no one answers, and just as she's about to put it down, it begins to ring. She answers it immediately so I don't have a chance to interfere.

"Kade I—"

She stops talking and I can only imagine why. Kade is probably having a go at her or he's shouting down a bunch of information that's too much for her to process.

Or it's Maverick.

"Where is he?"

Maverick. It's Maverick on the other end.

I hold out my hand for her to pass me the phone and I almost snatch it from her when she holds a finger to her lips.

The only reason I don't follow through with desperate actions is because she puts the call on speaker again.

"Let's make things a little more fun. You can come to me— *your husband*, in Scotland. Come find out if I just have his phone, or if I have him. Or don't, stay at Kassian's pub—"

Our eyes burn into each other when our location is mentioned.

I'm right. One way or another he's going to have her.

"—and go through with your original plan, leaving me to have fun with whatever's in my possession. The ball's in your court darling—"

"It's not really though, is it? You prick."

There's something about the way she insults that's satisfying and it's not just me that thinks so, me and Kade have spoken about it.

"You have five hours." He ignores her words.

"Five hours? Five hours isn't enough!—"

The line goes dead.

Of course he's using his private jet to come and go as he pleases, but expects us to be there within five hours as if traffic doesn't exist.

"How the hell is he going from Scotland to London so fast?" She stood up as though she were about to damage my fine basement.

"You think he's driving? No. He's flying."

"A plane?"

I forgot that Medisa's never actually been on a plane.

"No, he has wings." I say seriously.

Her eyes turn to slits.

"We need to go. Now." She's begins to leave but notices me not move at her pace. "What is wrong with you? Kade's your brother!" She is triggered when I don't move a millisecond after she does.

Apparently, I have to spell this out for her.

"Maverick knows where we are. Why don't he just come get you himself? It has to be a trick."

"What if it's not? Are you willing to risk that?"

"Kade wouldn't want you to." And he sure as hell is going to kill me for letting her run away twice.

"I don't care! And how would you know what he wants, you guys didn't even speak or see each other for years. And why would Maverick risk leaving me here if he didn't have him back in Scotland? I'm going. I don't care." She forces me to stand and block her way to the door.

Arguing is pointless.

"Do you still have my money?"

Medisa scoffs as she tries to move past. "I'll pay you back after I've got your brother."

'*I've*,' now I really want to laugh. I pull her back by her arm so that she stood in front of me.

"No, we have five hours to get back. A car wouldn't be fast enough but a plane would be. Do we have enough money for a ride?"

"You couldn't have this conversation while dragging me to the airport because?" She drags out the '*cause*' and it's how I know she's calmed down.

I don't bother telling her that we won't be using a public plane and that we have to bribe someone I know. But I also can't let her have a point, so I flicked her forehead, to both temporarily take her mind of Kade and to have some sort of satisfaction myself.

Chapter 97
Kade
13/05/2022 (Friday)

No one collects us at the front door which only means we have to find him ourselves.

Amana stays as close as she allows, her eyes take in every room we enter. Just like Medisa, I can't tell if she's taking it all in and appreciating its beauty, or if she's scoping the place out, looking for something odd and the different ways of escape.

Eventually, we end up in Tier Hall where I see the highest balcony's doors open, as well as candle lights inside. He's in there.

"Do not test him. Do not lie. If you don't want him to know the truth, you're going to have to be smart with your words so that you're not exactly lying. If you think that there's an opportunity to escape, do not take it, it's a test." I try to get as many warnings as I can out to Amana as she looks as though she's mentally preparing herself to finally meet the man who controls us all.

The door opens before my hand reaches the handle. We both walk in and give some attention to the small group of people in the room with Maverick.

"*Oh*, you just keep bringing these girls to me Kaden." Amusement runs across his face. He raises a hand that swiftly dismisses Amana, who is taken out the room with no fuss. "Take a seat." Maverick's casual tone brings no comfort, but it also no longer brings fear.

I do as he says.

So far, Amana is okay. If he were to do something to her it would be in front of me. Perhaps he's saving her for when we are all here?

"We're almost at the end now so I might as well be out with it." He takes a seat in front of me, leaning back into his majestic wooden chair. "I knew about Kassian's obsession with Amana long before he spoke to you. I knew from the moment he set his eyes on her, just like I know about everything else you boys have done when you think I'm not paying attention."

"I know this. It's why you made me recruit her."

"I only did that because she started to change him. And I liked the changes, right up until he changed towards me, and this family."

"You're tapped." I try not to smile as I realise what's escaped my mouth. "It means—"

"I know what it means." He half snaps.

Now I am smirking. Medisa has definitely called him tapped in the past.

"All four of you will be punished tonight. Some will feel it more than others, but I can't exactly make everything fair."

If I wasn't staring intensely before, I sure am right now. We are going to be punished tonight. I don't question what the exact punishments will be, but he does see the change my face gives away.

"Kassian and Medisa will watch Amana die."

My breaths become slow and deep.

"This is punishment for Kassian stealing from Baronial

and giving to Amana, thinking that I would not notice. I did give him a chance to patch what he'd done, but it's been years now so." He shrugs as if there's nothing that he can do, as though he doesn't have money to give generations a lavish lifestyle. "I'm sure I don't need to explain why it's Medisa's punishment."

"What's mine?" My heart feels a little heavy, but I make sure not to show it. "My punishment, what is it?" I try to sound bored, nonchalant, even when I know that it's Medisa.

"Your first one is watching, hearing, experiencing Medisa—"

I almost zone out. The number of things he would make me watch be done to Medisa is terrifying and my mind does not spare me from vivid thoughts of any of them.

"—and Kassian witness Amana's demise. It'll be fake of course, her death, but only we will know that—"

I can't imagine Amana being on board with this.

"—And if you tell them before I decide they can know. I will actually kill her, and keep Medisa alive to give her the treatment she's been *begging* for."

"Where are they?" If he's planned these punishments for tonight, they must be here, or on their way.

Maverick pulls out a phone that looks identical to mine. "Well I made the call as soon as you were spotted at the gates, so they should be here in five hours."

Chapter 98
Kassian
14/05/2022 (Saturday)

Unless he changed his mind and wanted us at one of our other spots, I don't understand why the manor looks vacant.

"C'mon." I open one of the main doors, obviously no one is going to get us, it hasn't even been arranged for us to get jumped.

Inside, areas are marked with lit candles, strategically placed, guiding us to where he wants us to be. He's planned something, probably taken inspiration from one of Kade's twisted drawings. I wouldn't be surprised if Kade is strung up somewhere for us to find.

The candles lead us to Tier Hall. It's strange how this hall can go from being one I passed, to now being the hall I've spent/visited a considerable number of times. The chandeliers in here are on their lowest settings, the rest is barely lit by groups of candles. Makes me think Maverick does not give a shit if this place were to go up in flames. It would surprise me however, if he lets us burn to death, we've never taken things to the death before. I don't even think the Rivers before us have either.

We walk in with intentions of coming out the other end, but as soon as we reach the middle, the doors we entered in from slam shut. The emptiness of this Hall echoes the sound of the slam as well as the sound of the doors being locked, then all balconies minus one fill with Maverick's henchmen. It's like some sort of gladiatorial games were about to begin, me and Medisa being the gladiators. Food for the lions.

The doors to the last balcony open and Maverick walks into view.

"You all know my wife, Medisa. The girl you've been running after for days."

As his crowd go on to entertain him, I roll my eyes. I guess I'm going to be ignored here as well.

"If only you knew that all you had to do was set a trap." He continues, his lessons not just limited to his blood. Again the crowd reacts to his words and I just cannot be arsed for this. It's been a long day. A few long days.

"Maverick enough of this! Where is my brother?"

"Patience. You're ruining the surprise." He continues to disregard me as his eyes burn into Medisa like she is the one who interrupted him. Maverick turns his attention back to his followers. "Now we all know that she ran away, but does anyone know why?" He looks around for a few seconds as if he were actually scoping for someone to raise their hand. "No? Well let me fill you in." His gaze makes its way back to Medisa. I would move away to find a way to exit the room but I actually want to hear what he's going to say. "The boys and Medisa had it in their silly little heads that I would kill her before our anniversary, if not on the day... How daft is that?" Again, his question is rhetorical.

Maverick is petty, yes, but there's something in his behaviour that's inducing fear of the unknown. And that's saying something considering we barely managed to make accurate predictions on how far he would take things in the past.

Though I know he is pissed at the risk we took with our assets, Maverick's behaviour is like he's genuinely affected by Medisa's attitude towards him. If I were not here to witness, to experience the twinge of *something* different, I wouldn't be able to fathom it, hell, I'm barely fathoming it now.

"Anyway, she's back now and although she gave quite the scare running off like that, I got her a gift. It is our anniversary after all." He walks back into the connected room and all I can think about is what he's done.

It's been a mental agreement to not kill each other off, but that doesn't mean he can't strip Kade of his body parts. Maverick guides someone out onto the balcony with him, it's too dim to make any details other than their height out, but that's all I needed to know who it is.

My breaths become quick and heavy as I try to ignore thoughts about what's about to happen, and what could've happened to Kade, because he's still not made an appearance.

He takes her to the edge off the balcony, just about stopping before they are pressed up against the concrete railing. "Everyone, give it up for…"

I feel as though I'm having some sort of failed outer body experience, like I'm somewhere jammed in between.

Maverick rips the bag off and I half expect her head to go with it. "Amana!"

The sudden shot of conflict between anger and sadness spreads throughout and there's nothing I can do. I know what it means for Amana to be here with us, I know it, but that just adds to the burn of the shot, not make it any easier.

My eyes blur and whether it's supposed to shield me from seeing what he's about to do, or whether it's my body not being able to handle the intensity of it all, I don't care, because I will get a door open.

Chapter 99
Kade
14/05/2022 (Saturday)

The sounds that come from Kassian hit me harder than expected. I knew that it would be bad, but this is a form of torture. I've never heard him like this before, ever. I didn't expect it to affect him this deeply either, not when he himself said that he no longer harbours those feelings for her. I expected him to grieve, yes, but with this amount of potency? No.

The doors have been barred, practically welded shut, there's no way for him to break them. And yet he's rabid. I can tell from the sounds against the doors and the sounds he's releasing. His wasted energy is towards getting his hands on Maverick and he's never been one to think that.

I stopped standing around listening to the pleas of the doors within the minute they started. I don't care if Maverick notices that I'm no longer standing where he last saw me because I've already confined his followers to the rooms connected to their chosen balconies. It'll save me time in getting Medisa and Kassian out when I finally open the doors that keeps them in.

Wasting no time in grabbing what I can from the armoury, I rush to Tier Hall. Kassian is still hitting the doors, somehow more aggressive than before and that's how I know that it's done. Amana's passed out body is hanging inside.

My only other concern is Medisa. I can't hear her.

"Kassian move out the way!"

I don't really give him much time to move, but considering the doors are no longer being abused, I think it's safe to say that he listened. Without giving it much thought, I shoot at the hinges, the handle and everywhere in between and it works. The doors are destroyed and I am in Tier Hall.

Kassian yanks a gun away from me and goes straight to shooting each and every balcony. A lot of them drop like flies before they manage to get their doors open. They've obviously been given the rule not to shoot back, and those that do, are shot by who I assume is Maverick.

My eyes go straight to Medisa after confirming that Kassian is untouched by any bullets. She is in front of Amana's limp body, on her knees and continues to look up at her friend despite the commotion going on around her. I hurry to be by her side—ignoring the sprinkle of blood on her face—and gently shake her to pull her out of her self-sabotaging mind. It takes a few shakes to get her to finally lower her head, and when she does, I am able to see the red stinging the whites of her eyes.

"Medisa, we have to go. We haven't got time." I rub the top of her arms to both wake and soothe her.

Her head slowly shakes, almost convincing me that I'm imagining things.

"No." She finally manages to get out.

"<u>Come on! What happened to the cheers?</u>" Kassian shouts as he addresses the people who are no longer on the balconies, shooting anything and everything at this point. What he hasn't realised, or is simply ignoring, is the growth in light. Candles have fallen and things have started to catch fire. I wouldn't give a shit if it were just the bodies, but the fire has moved on to things that can very quickly light the whole place up as well as take it down.

We all need to leave *now*, while the attention and energy turns to putting the fire out.

I turn back to Medisa, at this point I am willing to say anything. "You're not leaving her. We're going to come back for her."

She tries to push me back, but I stay in place, my patience thinning as our time to escape quickly decreases.

"You don't have one scratch…" She stops talking as though her words are jammed, then she turns away, no longer wanting to deal with me.

I know what she's trying to say, I know it. She's accusing me but doesn't want to connect those dots. How is her friend hanging there, bleeding, while I'm here with no evidence on me that I fought for her?

"I'm sorry Medisa, but we haven't got time for this." Before her eyes look into mine, I hit her with the end of my gun.

'So much for protecting her head.'

The curtains are up in flames, Medisa's body is in my arms and Amana is still unconscious above. Am I an arsehole for what I'm about to do? Yes. But I don't care. I am choosing to believe Maverick won't let her die like this, that he will follow through on his side of things despite me leaving and taking Medisa and Kassian with me.

Before Kassian is able to use his brain, I push Medisa's body into his arms with a sense of emergency.

"Get her out of here! *Now*!"

Kassian finally seems to care about the fire and is given no choice but to do what I say.

As he runs out the broken windows with Medisa, I hear Maverick's little sheep scrambling around, but I'm not leaving until I do one thing. I'm not going to allow Maverick to 'accidently' let Amana burn to death and blame it on the fire we started, so I shoot at the rope that holds her. After placing her on the ground away from the fire, I leave before I am caught, forcing us into an endless cycle of escaping and returning.

Chapter 100
Kade
14/05/2022 (Saturday)

Kassian's infamous club, that's where we're resting. It's seems like the dumbest idea but by the time we drove away from the manor, we saw a huge part of it stone exterior up in flames. With trying to stop it from spreading, with dealing with the damages, the dead bodies and preventing certain details from making the news, I'd say Maverick has his hands full.

When Medisa finally woke up from what I had done to her, I made an attempt to clean Amana's blood off, but she wasn't having it. Other than her reaction to that, she seems to be in some sort of vegetative state. Kassian on the other hand, is bothered by everything and everyone around him. He hadn't really processed us leaving Amana behind until the Manor was at a distance. The only thing that had kept him in his seat instead of jumping out of a moving car was the sound of sirens, and Medisa's body.

Having enough of separating Kassian's fights, I kick everyone out. Kassian attempts to stop them from leaving, but even they are tired of his behaviour.

As I turn from seeing the last group out, Kassian launches a bottle at me, which I dodge with little effort and before I am able to grab and shake some sense into him, Medisa finally moves.

We both freeze as she gets up and walks towards the ladies room. I want to say she's avoiding both of our gazes, but it's just mine. She ignores my presence, but doesn't feel the same about Kassian, that much is clear. Though her expression remains the same, he is given the blessing of her gaze, even if it is for just a brief moment.

When she turns away from him, he grabs another bottle and heads in the opposite direction, past me and through the doors. Being displayed with two options; go after Medisa or go after my drunk brother who is exposing himself out in the open, I hesitate before following Kassian. Medisa needs some space, and I can't be the one who is at fault for Amana's 'death,' *and* the one who denies her some time to breathe and pull herself together. Not to mention, she's safe inside.

I don't know what I expected the street to look like, but it isn't it being close to empty. It's like those who left were sucked up somewhere and now only me, a hand full of scattered people, and Kassian are the only ones on this barely lit, misty road.

I can't handle two grievers.

And Kassian can act, I know that he can. He acted so well he convinced himself he was another version of me, so, I can tell him. He will not waste another minute in believing that she is dead and that it is his fault. And he'll act in front of Medisa and Maverick (when it comes to it) because it is necessary for Medisa and Amana's safety.

He walks away from his building and I follow, turning around at some point to see how far we are away from it. When it gets far enough, I put my hand on his shoulder to get his attention and instead of turning around or ignoring my presence like a normal human being, he turns around and his fist connects with my face.

I suppose I deserve that.

"She's alive." I say as I check for blood, then realise that it's coming from the inside of my mouth. Kassian doesn't respond, so I repeat. "Amana's alive. The sick fuck wanted you two to witness her death." I do the laziest, unserious, quotation marks when I say the word '*death*.' "Your punishments were the same and mine was to live with knowing the truth."

Kassian jolts forward and I prepare for another attack, but he turns at the last second to vomit. Honestly, I didn't realise how much he drank in such a short amount of time. The vomit just went on and on, until finally he stands somewhat straight.

"So you left her there *alive*? How does that make any sense? Was us leaving part of his plan too or did you decide—"

"He just said that you two had to see her die and I had to keep you from the truth. After his show, he will allow Amana to have a fresh start elsewhere, something you and I both know that she wanted to do anyways."

Kassian spits whatever collected in his mouth out.

"Charles swore that he will deal with Amana, that he won't let her die." I say to ease his mind. I'm not some heartless freak, I did leave her with someone I trust.

After trying to read if I were lying, he finally does something, he moves in the direction of his club. But there's a certain determination in his walk that tells me about his motive before his voice does.

"If you tell Medisa the truth, she might not be able to act if we're caught again."

"I don't care."

"You'll be ruining his fun and he'll kill her and Amana."

Kassian stops walking but from how he sways, I'm not sure if the drinks are starting to have more of an effect on him, or if he's understood the stakes.

He turns around to face me.

"I don't care. You don't know what it feels like. I barely knew—know Amana. I barely know Amana and it fucking hurt, it still lingers in the back even though you've told me that she's alive. And Medisa, she's known Amana for *years*. They're sisters." He points in the direction of the club, where Medisa is probably vomiting too. "I'm telling her everything."

For flips sake.

"Alright." I nod as I look to him then around. "We'll tell her everything. But we're not about to dump all these hidden pieces on her, we're going to take it easy. One step at a time and at her pace. I don't care if that takes a day, I don't care if it takes a week or a month or even a year, if she needs time to process, we're going to give it to her. Agreed?" I need to know if Kassian's head is the next one I'm hitting tonight.

"Agreed." He saves himself from pain, this time from me.

As we walk over to the club, I notice how we are the only ones out from how silent it is, and it's eerie. I almost get goosebumps from the lack of life.

Though Kassian seems to have sobered up, he gags and swallows whatever rose from his stomach. When we get inside, I seat him on the cushioned seat closest to the ladies room. If it were anyone else, I would expect to see them sleeping by the time I manage to get Medisa to come out, but because I know how stubborn we can be and how much he wants her to stop feeling what she is, I know that he will keep himself awake.

I knock on the door a few times like I would back at Aros. When she doesn't respond I push to let myself in, but the door does not budge. I try the one next to it and the same thing happens, nothing.

"Medisa? Medisa, have you locked the door?"

Kassian approaches, his face as perplexed as mine.

"It can't be locked. I didn't put a lock on these doors?" He mutters to himself as he mentally goes back to when he made decisions on this place.

"Talk to me Medisa." My voice isn't as calm as I want it to be perceived. I can't help but have thoughts of her hurting herself past a point of return.

"Let me try talking to her." Kassian moves forward with help from the wall, but struggles as he bumps into one of his pillar stands. Usually I would laugh and cuss him out but my mind is on Medisa.

"You idiot. I can't hear her."

"And I don't think you will anytime soon."

Nausea tries to kick in but I persevere. Maverick's in there with her, the doors locked, and she's not responding. I don't know how he got in, or how he's planning to get out, I don't even ask Kassian the damn layout of this place, I just barge into the door.

It barely moves.

I try again and again until finally I hear the wood begin to crack.

"Kade." Kassian calls out.

When I turn around, almost about to take my anger out on him, I see the red in his hands. Wasting no time, I snatch the axe and hammer it into the door. I want to swear at Kassian for using such thick wooden doors for a place like this. Why couldn't he just get something cheap?

The wood in the door cracks away, allowing me to look in to see Medisa about to walk away with Maverick. She's not on the ground bleeding out, or passed out in his arms, no, she's about to leave with him—willingly.

He's told her something.

She knows something.

"Medisa, wait, *wait*!" Everywhere a pulse could be found on my body, is felt in this moment, each beat was heavy and I'm struggling to think straight for the life of me. "I'll tell you everything! I *was* going to tell you everything! Just please, just listen to me and then if you want to leave after, you can, I won't be in your way. Medisa don't listen to him, he's *lying*! Don't go. Don't leave."

With every other heartbeat, my vision came and went, the silhouette of her walking away, walking beside Maverick—I can't, I can't breathe, I can't see. I lose my balance and maybe even my hearing because I can't hear what Kassian is saying. Something about the doors not opening? I don't—I don't know. Suddenly it's hot in here and despite my quick breaths not being able to pick up any oxygen, I can feel the heat inside me. My body trembles as Kassian tries to comfort. It's not helpful that I've never been like this before, it's probably scaring him more than its scaring me. It's different not having control over your own body, the betrayal, the deprivation, the oppression that you feel from something that's supposed to be in your control. I guess that's it isn't it? I've never really been in control.

A Little Letter From The Author:

Hi everyoneee I am thee person who came up with this story and wrote it. Thank you so much for supporting and giving it a read.

You could probably tell but I did not use an editor for this book lol. I started writing it when I was 18/19 when I had a bunch of stuff going on (you know..life) and wanted to see how far I could take it without any sort of guidance. What you read is the result of that decision.. well one of the results because silly me uploaded the wrong files (I was going through it and it was a now or never moment). So yes you got the main points of the story, but you also miss out because it's the version with less cool scenes/ interactions and what not. I was going to upload the right file when I had realised but then people had already purchased the wrong version and it would've been unfair for me to change it. (If I had the funds of course I would've changed it and given them the updated version for free but alas I do not *one tear on my face*)

I did however upload another version of the book (as I saw and corrected some stupid mistakes) and changed the cover a little to know who's got what version. If you are someone with the original failed version of In His Hands (the cover doesn't have the frame) please DM me on Instagram xx and if you are someone who's got the new version and still see some mistakes.. spare me

If you can be arsed, I beggeth you to please write a review of these books somewhere where others could see, or to DM me on instagram your opinions and how they think the books wouldve been better in terms of layout, pacing character opinions etc. (I will be using these reviews/words of advice to write my next book and yes if I can afford one I'll get an editor *another tear runs down my face*

If (through answered prayers) you did enjoy the book/s please recommend them, pass them around and let me know! I would love to see if the time I spent writing and not living life was well spent lol. Also I have a bunch of notes and things of where I purposely made mistakes, added parallels/mirroring, foreshadowing etc. so let me know if thats a discussion or something you would like to see xx

Stay blessed, take care of yourselves, enjoy some fresh air, interact with people and remember what you decide to not change, you are choosing and your life was not made to be wasted xx

The next page has a list of hotlines, please use them if you are in need of support and guidance.

General Crisis Helplines:
- International Helpline Directory (international): International Helpline Directory
- Samaritans (UK): call 116 123 or visit Samaritans.org for 24/7 confidential support
- Crisis text line (global): text HOME to 741741 (Canada & US) or visit crisis-textline.org for free support
- International Suicide Prevention Helplines: visit International Association for Suicide Prevention (IASP) for a list of helplines by country.

Domestic Abuse Support:
- National Domestic Violence Hotline (US): call 1-800-799-7233 or visit thehotline.org
- Woman's Aid (UK): visit womansaid.org.uk for support and resources
- Refuge (UK): call 0808 2000 247 or visit refuge.org.uk
- Hotline for Domestic Violence (Global) search local hotlines via UN Women's Global Database

Mental Health Support:
- World Health Organisation (WHO)- Mental Health Resources: visit WHO mental health for global mental health support
- NAMI (US): Visit nami.org for resources on mental health conditions, including local helplines
- Mental Health Foundation (UK): visit mentalhealth.org.uk for advice and support
- Beyond Blue (Australia): call 1300 22 4636 or visit beyondblue.org.au
- Mind (UK): call 0300 123 3393 or visit mind.org.uk for mental health support

LGBTQ+ Specific Helplines:
- The Trevor Project (US): call 1-866-488-7386 or visit thetrevorproject.org for LGBTQ+ crisis support.
- Stonewall (UK): visit stonewall.org.uk for resources an support for LGBTQ+ individuals
- LGBT Helpline (International): check out ILGA World for LGBTQ+ helplines in different countries.

Helplines for Children and Teens:
- Childline (UK): 0800 111 or visit childline.org.uk for support
- Crisis Text Line (US and Canada): text HOME to 741741 for support
- Kids Help Phone (Canada): call 1-800-668-6868 or visit kidshelpphone.ca

Emergency Services & Specialised Support:
- Emergency Services (Global): Always call your local emergency number (e.g. 911 in US, 999 in UK) for immediate help in situations that require urgent attention.
- Red Cross: visit redcross.org for resources on disaster and crisis relief.

IN SOMEONE'S HANDS

ROSE KAUSER

www.ingramcontent.com/pod-product-compliance
Lightning Source LLC
Chambersburg PA
CBHW030429010526
44118CB00011B/553